Trivia Quiz

THE BEST FAMILY QUIZ BOOK EVER!

Trivia Quiz

THE BEST FAMILY QUIZ BOOK EVER!

ARCTURUS

ARCTURUS

This edition published in 2015 by Arcturus Publishing Limited
26/27 Bickels Yard, 151–153 Bermondsey Street,
London SE1 3HA

ISBN:978-1-78404-298-1
AD004311NT

Printed in the US

INTRODUCTION

You may want to use this book to challenge yourself on a wide range of subjects, or to pit your wits against your friends and family by setting up an informal, enjoyable quiz at home. However it is also the perfect resource if you're holding a more formal event, whether in a pub or elsewhere. We've put together some tips gained from years of experience to help you organize the perfect quiz night.

WHY HOLD A QUIZ NIGHT?

Quiz nights are very popular and are a good way to raise money for a charity or local project, with relatively little outlay on the part of the organizers; people have fun, while at the same time donating to a good cause.

Moreover, people can, with very little persuasion, add to the funds raised by buying raffle tickets, or paying a nominal amount to enter supplementary competitions during the course of the main quiz, and these supplementary competitions are seen to add variety and amusement to the event.

PLANNING THE NIGHT

Think about the purpose of the quiz, and aim to involve the charity or project concerned by inviting representatives along to give a short speech of thanks at the end of the evening – after all, the participants have given of their time and money, and it is nice to be able to reward them with an acknowledgment of their donation.

WHO ARE THE PARTICIPANTS?

Are they adults, children, or a mixture of both? Is the venue suitable for the ages of the participants?

Most quiz nights are aimed at an adult audience, because of the nature of the questions, or the time of the evening at which the quiz finishes, or the location (a public house is a popular place for a quiz, but not suitable if children will be attending).

WHERE WILL THE QUIZ TAKE PLACE?

How many people are likely to attend and how many can the venue hold? Is the venue easy to reach by car, or public transport? Are there parking facilities?

WHEN WILL THE QUIZ TAKE PLACE?

Consider who will be attending the quiz: are they mainly young or old, working or not working, or will there be a combination of these? Starting too early in the evening may dissuade some people; and starting or finishing too late may dissuade others.

Generally, a quiz night will start at either 7.30pm or 8.00pm, with participants being asked to arrive half an hour before the start, in order to allow time for them to find a table, write their names onto answer sheets, provide themselves with food, drinks, raffle tickets, etc, take a comfort break, visit the bar, etc; and generally do what people do before the start of an event.

If you are selling raffle tickets, then you also need to allow time for the participants to view the prizes and buy tickets.

Think also about the day and date of the event. Many people will not attend if they are working the next day, so Friday or Saturday evening is generally best.

Try to find out if there are other events in the neighbourhood on that date, which might conflict with your quiz night. If a date near to Christmas, or one which clashes with a major sporting event is chosen, then this might also result in lower attendance numbers.

WILL HELP BE NEEDED?

It is very hard for just one person to run a quiz night, so it's a good idea to have a group of helpers lined up for the night.

Perhaps you have decided to sell tickets to the event, or perhaps an entrance fee will be charged at the door – who is going to collect the money?

Will there be a prize for the winning team or each member of the winning team? Will there be a grand raffle? If so, who is going to provide the prizes?

Many retailers (especially on learning that the quiz is being run in aid of a charity or local project) will donate a small prize or two, and individuals taking part in the quiz can be asked to bring along a small prize on the evening itself, particularly if you tell them that this could be something they received as an unwanted birthday or Christmas present!

If you are running the event for a charity, they may have a pool of prizes previously donated for raffles, from which they could draw a few things for your own raffle.

Of course, if you are lucky enough to attract too many prizes, you can also hold an auction at the end of the evening, or hold onto some of the prizes for your next quiz night.

HOW MUCH TO CHARGE

This can be a tricky one, because at the outset, if you have not run a quiz before, or there has not been one in the area, people may wonder what is involved.

Flyers (mini advertisements) given out before the event will give people an indication of what to expect to pay for entrance and participation, but if you are in doubt, charge a minimal amount for the entrance fee, and try to make a little more money on other games and raffles during the evening.

Once people are accustomed to your quiz nights, however, you will probably find that they are willing to pay a little more: after all, they are getting a whole evening's entertainment for a relatively small charge.

Another factor to consider is that people may want supper. If you intend to provide supper, you would be well advised to issue tickets for the event, so that you are sure of covering your costs with regard to food. A light buffet could be provided; a venue will sometimes offer basket meals for a small price; a local take-away could be persuaded to come and take orders: if you sell tickets, you could include a take-away supper in the price, and this gives the caterer advance notice of how many suppers are required.

DRINKS AND SNACKS

Unless your venue has catering facilities, you may need to think about providing a range of drinks and snacks, as people are likely to get thirsty or peckish as the evening wears on.

If you are providing drinks or snacks, make sure that you adhere to any laws (national or local) regarding the sale of food and drink (particularly alcohol).

CAN YOU BE HEARD?

When the room is full, and people are chatting, it is often difficult for those participants furthest away from the question-master to hear what is being said.

You may need to hire a microphone and amplifier for the evening; if this is the case, then be sure to try it out a few days before, to make sure it is working correctly.

INSURANCE AND PUBLIC LIABILITY

Another factor to take into consideration is insurance: is the venue's insurance cover up-to-date and will it cover such an event, including members of the public and all other people who will attend, plus helpers and yourself?

You have a duty of care to the public, and must make sure that the venue is safe.

If you are in any way unsure, speak to an insurance broker, who will be best placed to give you all the advice you need, and to answer your questions.

Do you need any public entertainment permissions, or any other permissions? If you intend to play any music, etc, make sure that the venue has the required permission(s): on balance, it may be a good idea to avoid music altogether, as it is often not worth it just for one evening.

PUBLICITY

Do remember to publicize your event, as well as informing people verbally.

Put posters on noticeboards, or ask shopkeepers if they would be willing to display one in a window: who knows, they may even sell a few tickets for you, too! Try to get a mention of the event in the media if you can, but bear in mind the limitations of the venue: if too many people turn up, you may not have room for them.

SUPPLIES CHECKLIST

Apart from raffle tickets, raffle prizes, tickets, flyers and advertisements, and a microphone and amplifier, there are a few other things to think about: answer sheets for the participants to fill in the answers to the quiz questions, scrap paper for the participants, supplementary competitions, etc.

It is a good idea to provide each table with several scraps of plain paper, on which people can write ideas and show them around, as team members will not want other people to hear a discussion they are having about a possible answer to a question. And it is surprising how many people will arrive at the quiz night without a pen, so it's a good idea to have some spares!

You will also need a float, that is some money that can be given as change to people who pay for entrance, raffle tickets, etc. Make sure that you have sufficient funds, as nothing is worse than having to write an IOU or trying to keep account of what is owed.

TIME YOURSELF

Try out a few quizzes, to see how long it takes to read each question, giving the participants sufficient time to fill in an answer (and allowing sufficient time at the end for anyone who didn't hear a particular question to have it read out again). Now add on five minutes, which allows for teams ask for questions to be repeated, to complete their forms, and to pass their answers to a another table for the scoring.

After each round, the question-master reads out the answers, and the teams score them: the usual number of points being two for a correct answer and one for an answer which is 'near enough correct'. A 'near enough correct' answer is, for example, one which is misspelled, or one where a name is requested, but the answer just gives the surname, as opposed to the full name required for two points. You can use your judgment on this, should any scorer raise the matter, or when checking the answer sheets after they are handed in for marking on the scoreboard.

Having decided how much time to allocate for each round, plus form passing, plus answers, multiply that time by the number of rounds you intend to have, and then add a few minutes.

It is better to allow too much time than too little, as any spare time can be filled with an interval (for comfort breaks, trips to the bar, etc), or for playing a game or holding a supplementary competition.

If supper is to be served, then time will need to be allowed for this, too.

You will also need time at the end of the evening for the presentation of prizes, the drawing of the raffle, a speech of thanks, and for people to get their coats on, prior to the close of the venue.

It is usual to have eight rounds of questions per quiz night, but if time is short, then this can be cut back to five or six rounds (just remember to alter the scoreboard to suit). Choose the subjects of your rounds carefully, making sure you pick rounds on a good variety of topics.

SCORING

Thinking of the scoreboard, it is a good idea to have a flip-chart, with a large piece of paper, on which the numbers of teams, as well as the individual quiz round numbers, have been written, so that teams can see how well they are doing compared to others. Here is an example:

Team	Round Number								Total Score
	1	2	3	4	5	6	7	8	
1									
2									
3									
4									
5									
6									
7									
8									
9									
10									
11									
12									

Do prepare this chart in advance of the night of the quiz, as it will save time. You won't necessarily know the teams' names before the night, of course, but remember to leave enough room to write in each name below the team number: some can be quite lengthy! Teams are encouraged to give themselves a name in addition to their number, as this adds to the fun: 'Universally Challenged' and 'Littlehaven Lounge Lizards' are a couple of names recently seen at quiz nights.

How many in a team? Between three and six is typical, but if individuals turn up on the night, then it is usual for the organizer to sit them at a particular table that has been set aside for the purpose of later matching them up with other individuals.

ON THE NIGHT

Aim to arrive about an hour before the quiz starts, in order to leave enough time to set up the tables and chairs, and to arrange the quiz-master's table and sound system, the entrance table (at which money or tickets for entry are taken), the scoreboard, the raffle table, etc, as well as put answer sheets, pens, and scrap paper onto the tables which will be used by the participants.

At the start of the quiz, explain that there are several rounds and then ask each round of questions in the way you practised when timing yourself.

While you are asking the first round of questions, the scorer will have time to mark up the scoreboard with the name of each team.

After each round, ask each team to pass their answer sheet to another team for scoring purposes, then to hand it to the scorer for marking on the scoreboard.

Half way through the rounds, you might choose to have a break, either for supper, or to allow people to fetch drinks perhaps: it is entirely up to you how many breaks you include in the evening, as this depends on the amount of time available.

After all of the quiz rounds are complete, it's time to total the scores and announce the winning team (presenting them with a small prize, if desired), draw the raffle, announce the winner(s) of any other competition(s), and thank the teams and the helpers for taking part in raising money.

By now you should have a rough idea of how much money has been raised by entrance fees, raffle, competitions, etc, and your audience will be keen to learn of the amount, even if you cannot give them a precise figure.

AND FINALLY...

Give everyone details of your next Quiz Night!

ROUNDS

History

1. Who drafted the American Declaration of Independence in 1776?

2. In which year did Queen Victoria succeed to the throne of the UK?

3. The 'War of Jenkins' Ear' was an 18th century conflict between Britain and which other European country?

4. Captain Matthew Flinders led the 1801-1810 expedition that saw the first circumnavigation of which island

5. Which year saw the start of the French Revolution?

6. The 1783 Treaty of Versailles ended which war?

7. In which country was the Battle of Vinegar Hill, in 1798?

8. What was the name of the WW1 German super-heavy Krupps howitzer?

9. In which year did the Berlin Wall come down?

10. The 1622 Indian massacre of English settlers in Virginia, took place at which settlement?

The Animal Kingdom

1 To which country is the burrowing parrot known as a kakapo native?

2 Which is the largest of all known animals?

3 Which state of dormancy in winter is experienced by many creatures to avoid death by heat loss or food scarcity?

4 The IFAW is an organization that cares for animals. What does IFAW stand for?

5 What sort of creature is a prairie dog?

6 What kind of creature is an affenpinscher?

7 A tigon is a hybrid resulting from the mating of which two animals?

8 Which breed of dog is noted for its blue-black tongue?

9 In January 1995, which animals were re-introduced into the U.S.A.'s Yellowstone National Park after an absence of 60 years?

10 What sort of creature is a krait?

Mythology

1   Who was the Roman god of agriculture and the father of the gods?

_____

2   In Greek mythology, who was the goddess of the underworld and the daughter of Zeus and Demeter?

_____

3   Which nymph, after falling hopelessly in love with Narcissus, faded away except for her voice?

_____

4   In Germanic legend which hero owned a sword named 'Nothung'?

_____

5   In Greek legend which Titan created man and endowed him with reason? He also stole fire from heaven to give to man.

_____

6   Leda was the mortal loved by Zeus in the form of what creature?

_____

7   Triton, the demigod of the sea, was the son of which god of the sea?

_____

8   Who was the Titan who held the world on his shoulders as a punishment for warring against Zeus?

_____

9   Which one of the following was not a Knight of the Round Table: Galahad, Gawain, Ivanhoe?

_____

10   In Greek and Roman mythology, what name is given to the river in the underworld, the water of which caused those who drank it to forget their former lives?

_____

General Knowledge

1. 'The Ambassadors' is considered to be the masterpiece of which American novelist?

2. By what name was the Swiss-born French architect Charles Edouard Jeanneret better known?

3. King Camp Gillette patented the safety razor in 1895; who in 1931 patented and marketed the first electric razor?

4. Which fungoid disease of trees was first described in the Netherlands?

5. What name is given to an extreme, irrational fear of a specific object or situation?

6. What name is given to a plant that retains its leaves all year round?

7. Which fungal infection of the feet is the commonest form of ringworm?

8. According to Jonathan Swift, "Promises and pie-crusts are made to be ..."

9. According to folklore, which bird can predict bad weather and if seen near a ship will bring a storm?

10. What is the standard monetary unit of Japan?

Literature

1 Which novel by Elizabeth Gaskell was left unfinished at her death?

_____

2 Who wrote 'I Sing the Body Electric'?

_____

3 What nationality is the novelist Margaret Atwood?

_____

4 Which Australian-born feminist author wrote 'The Female Eunuch'?

_____

5 Who's work on dreams was published in 1900 under the title 'The Interpretation Of Dreams'?

_____

6 What's the title of the novel written by Rumer Godden about nuns, passion and the Himalayas?

_____

7 What name was given to the literary movement in the U.S.A. in the 1950s of which William Burroughs and Jack Kerouac were prominent writers?

_____

8 What nationality is author Gabriel Garcia Marquez?

_____

9 Who wrote 'On the Origin of Species by Means of Natural Selection'?

_____

10 In the story of 'Peter Pan', Peter has to return to the Darling's house because on his first visit he left without what?

Geography

1 Usually formed by the top of a volcano that has subsided, what geographical term describes a crater flanked by steep cliffs?

2 What is the name of the principal Italian opera house which opened in Milan in 1876?

3 How are the states of Maine, New Hampshire, Vermont, Massachusetts, Rhode Island and Connecticut collectively known?

4 Which is the oldest national park in the United States of America?

5 Which long, narrow bay, an inlet of the Atlantic Ocean between Nova Scotia and New Brunswick, is famous for its high tides from which electricity is generated?

6 In which South American capital city would you find Palermo Park and the famous Teatro Colon opera house?

7 In which German city is the Brandenburg Gate?

8 In which European country are the ports of Narvik and Stavanger?

9 What is the name of the science that studies the occurrence and movement of water on and over the surface of the Earth?

10 Which natural phenomena is seismology primarily concerned with?

Sport

1 In which country did the Telemark skiing style originate?

2 Olympic tradition has it that the title 'World's Greatest Athlete' is awarded to the gold medal winner of which event?

3 At the 1988 Seoul Olympics, who was awarded Gold after the original winner of the men's 100 metres sprint final was disqualified?

4 What is the trophy awarded to the winner of the Superbowl?

5 In 2013, Tai Woffiden became the world champion in which sport?

6 At the 2014 Winter Olympics, Lizzy Yarnold won for Great Britain its only gold medal: in which event?

7 Which golf-course was the first to have an 18-hole circuit?

8 Which racehorse's grave is sited next to the winning post at Aintree racecourse, Liverpool?

9 Near which Brazilian city is the Interlagos motor-racing circuit?

10 The Heysel Stadium, scene of a football game serious riot in 1985, is in which European city?

General Knowledge

1. With which profession is Harley Street in London associated?

2. Opened in 1906, which famous hotel was the first important steel-framed building to be built in London?

3. What is your pollex?

4. Levodopa is a drug now commonly used in the treatment of which degenerative disease?

5. Which medical speciality deals with the problems and diseases of old age?

6. Mozart's 'Symphony No. 38 in D Major' was named after which European city to commemorate its first performance during his visit there in 1787?

7. Of which mineral is aquamarine a variety?

8. Nearly a third of the total population of Illinois live in which U.S. city?

9. Which British writer was born in Bombay in 1865, some of his best novels and short stories being set in India?

10. Which American novelist wrote: "If you pick up a starving dog and make him prosperous, he will not bite you. This is the principal difference between a dog and man."?

Movies

1   In the 1992 movie 'Aladdin', the vizier Jafar had a parrot who's name was that of which Shakespearean character?

2   Who duetted with Peabo Bryson on the Oscar-winning song 'Beauty And The Beast' from the movie of the same name?

3   Released worldwide in 2001, which movie features the characters Kusco, Pacha, Yzma and Kronk?

4   What is the title of the 1981 movie which features Tod and Copper, two childhood animal friends forced to become enemies?

5   Who appeared in the starring role in the movie 'Body Heat' opposite Kathleen Turner?

6   In which 1993 horror does Warwick Davis make his debut as a sinister pint-sized Irish fairy?

7   Who is the French director of the 1973 Oscar winning movie 'Day For Night', who appeared in the 1977 movie 'Close Encounters Of The Third Kind'?

8   Who played Carl Brashear, the first black salvage diver in the U.S. Navy, in the 2000 movie 'Men of Honor'?

9   In which 2001 Anglo-American movie did Alan Rickman and Natasha Richardson play a hairdressing ex-husband and wife?

10 Which 1962 movie was directed and written by Orson Welles from a novel by Franz Kafka?

Politics

1 Russian president Boris Yeltsin announced his surprise resignation on 31 December of which year?

2 Which former U.S. president once said: "It's true hard work never killed anybody, but I figure, why take the chance?"

3 What is the first name of former Russian leader Gorbachev?

4 Alfredo Stroessner was president of which country from 1954 to 1989?

5 Which U.S. president was rumoured to have carried on a 28-year affair with a black slave Sally Hemings?

6 What was the name of the Russian parliament from 1906 to 1917?

7 Which churchman was president of Cyprus from 1960 to 1974?

8 Who was the foremost U.S. military figure between the Revolution and the Civil War? He was the unsuccessful Whig candidate for president in 1852.

9 U.S. president James Garfield died from his injuries after being shot. At a railway station in which U.S. city was he shot?

10 Name the military leader who successfully defended Finland against greatly superior Soviet forces in 1939. He was president of Finland from 1944 to 1946.

Science

1. Which branch of physics is the study of heat and its relationship with other forms of energy?

2. What does the C stand for in the famous formula of Einstein's theory of relativity?

3. Which alloy of copper and zinc, formerly used to imitate gold in jewellery, is named after a watchmaker?

4. Which device for detecting and counting ionizing radiation and particles is named after a German physicist?

5. Which very hard grey dense metallic element is represented by the symbol Ta?

6. What unit of electric charge is defined as the quantity of electricity conveyed by one ampere in one second?

7. Which acid, used as an antiseptic, in food preparation and dyestuffs is the active constituent of aspirin?

8. Which element used in atomic bombs is represented by the symbol Pu?

9. Which silvery-white rare metal is represented by the symbol Te?

10. What can be measured in pascals, millimetres of mercury, or millibars?

General Knowledge

1. Which unit of weight for precious stones is equal to two milligrams?

2. Which was the first comet whose return was predicted?

3. Braidism, after James Braid who introduced it into medicine, is another name for what?

4. The five highest waterfalls in Europe are all to be found in which country?

5. Which British civil engineer is best known for his construction of the suspension bridge over the Menai Strait?

6. What is measured using the Beaufort Scale?

7. Of the 11 founder members of O.P.E.C., which was the only South American country?

8. Which U.S. city has an area known as Foggy Bottom, a nickname sometimes given to the city itself?

9. What name is given to rain that has absorbed sulphur dioxide and oxides of nitrogen from the atmosphere?

10. In the 'Jungle Book', what type of creature was Baloo?

Religion

1 Who is the patron saint of the U.S.A.?

_____

2 On which geographical feature, in present-day Israel, were the Carmelites founded in the 12th century?

_____

3 Who is the patron saint of animals and the environment?

_____

4 In which century was the execution of the last person to die under the Spanish Inquisition?

_____

5 The last Crusade, the Ninth, occurred during which century?

_____

6 Which pope instigated the First Crusade, in 1095-96?

_____

7 Which religion of Celtic Britain was wiped out by the Romans in the 1st century A.D.?

_____

8 Quetzalcoatl was a deity worshipped by the people of which civilization?

_____

9 What is the main indigenous religion of Japan?

_____

10 Which Muslim military leader defeated the Christian Crusaders and captured Jerusalem in 1187?

Pop Music

1   Which group first claimed to be 'Back For Good'?

_____

2   In 1992, Take That returned with the hit ___?

_____

3   In 1992, Jazzy Jeff and the Fresh Prince stirred things up with ___?

_____

4   In 1992, 'Never Ever' was a hit for ___?

_____

5   'Mmm Bop' was a 1997 hit for ___?

_____

6   In 1995, 'A Girl Like You' made it for ___?

_____

7   In 1995, 'Country House' was a hit for ___?

_____

8   In 1999, 'My Vida Loca' was a hit for ___?

_____

9   In 1999, soap opera star Martine McCutcheon sang ___?

_____

10   Who had a hit with 'Just My Imagination (Running Away With Me)'?

Geology

1   What term describes rock that has been formed through volcanic activity?

2   Which layer of our planet's composition lies directly under the crust?

3   Hornblende, schist and gabbro are all kinds of which material?

4   The K-Pg (or K-T) boundary event which resulted in a mass extinction of animal species, including the dinosaurs, occurred approximately how many million years ago?

5   What term applies to an underground water-bearing layer into which wells can be dug to extract the water?

6   In volcanic regions, what is a fumarole?

7   Lignite is commonly known by which other name?

8   What geological event caused the catastrophic tsunami of Boxing Day, 2004?

9   The Great Blue Hole, off the Caribbean Sea coast of Belize, was caused by what fairly common geological fault?

10   What kinds of rock are sandstone and limestone?

History

1 What is the name of the period of liberalization that Czechoslovakia tried to introduce in 1968?

2 At which Ohio university were student protesters shot dead by National Guardsmen in May 1970?

3 Who was the first president of the Fifth French Republic (from 1959 to 1969)?

4 Edward Whymper led the team that made the first ascent of which Alpine peak in 1865?

5 The death penalty in the UK was abolished in which year?

6 The Tet Offensive was a 1968 military campaign: during which conflict?

7 In which war did the naval Battle of Jutland take place?

8 Which African country gained independence from France in July 1962?

9 1901 saw the opening of a single track of which famous railway?

10 The successful expedition to conquer Mt Everest in 1953, was led by which man?

General Knowledge

1 What is the name for the layer of our planet that contains virtually all forms of living things?

2 The book 'Revolution in the Head' by Ian Macdonald concerned the recordings of which Sixties band?

3 Which country is the world's largest oil-producer?

4 What is the most common wildcat of South America?

5 Emperor, king and adelie are all species of which flightless bird?

6 The Parsec is a unit of distance used in which branch of science?

7 What is more common name for the mineral, kaolin?

8 Bauxite is the chief ore of which common metal?

9 Which animals belong to the Ursidae family of carnivores?

10 Titan is the largest moon of which planet?

Art

1. Which Paris-born Post-Impressionist painter moved to Tahiti in 1891?

2. In which Spanish city is the Prado Museum?

3. Who painted 'Woman with Crossed Arms', which sold for more than £38 million at auction in 2000?

4. What was artist John Callcott Horsley the first to design?

5. What name is given to the Japanese art of flower arranging?

6. Which Spanish surrealist artist painted 'The Persistence of Memory'?

7. Which arts prize was won by German photographer Wolfgang Tillmans in 2000?

8. Which U.S. artist achieved notoriety in the 1960s with his paintings of soup cans and portraits of Marilyn Monroe?

9. The Dutch artist Vincent Van Gogh died in which country?

10. 'Vision Of A Knight' and 'The Marriage Of The Virgin' are works by which Italian Renaissance painter?

Food and Drink

1 The town of Golden, Colorado is the home of which brand of beer?

2 Which beer is made in Wisconsin and is said to be "the beer that made Milwaukee famous."?

3 In which country did McDonalds open their first beef-free restaurant on 13 October 1996?

4 What is the main ingredient of a soubise sauce which provides its distinctive flavour?

5 Name the beef dish which gets its name from a Russian count.

6 Traditionally, which herb is used in the making of a pesto sauce?

7 Which salad dressing, made from mayonnaise with ketchup, chopped gherkins, etc, shares its name with a group of islands?

8 By what name is the plant Solanum tuberosum, supposedly introduced into England by Sir Walter Raleigh, better known?

9 What type of vegetable is an essential ingredient of moussaka?

10 What type of meat is used in coq au vin?

The Human Body

1 How is the contagious disease rubella commonly known?

2 What sort of condition is commonly treated with antihistamines?

3 The bacterial disease glanders can be passed on to humans from which animal?

4 In which part of the body can the cochlea be found?

5 In which organ of the human body can the pineal gland be found?

6 The disease pellagra is caused by deficiency of which acid in the diet?

7 Which common eye condition is also called strabismus?

8 What part of the human body is abnormally curved in a case of the medical condition, scoliosis?

9 In what part of the body is the fibula?

10 What name is given to tissue damage caused by exposure to extreme cold?

Entertainment

1 'Raging Bull: My Story' was the autobiography of which American boxer?

2 What is the name of the ginger tom known as the 'Napoleon of Crime' in T.S. Eliot's 'Old Possum's Book Of Practical Cats'?

3 Highly acclaimed Japanese movie director Akira Kurosowa's 1985 movie 'Ran' is a samurai version of which Shakespeare play?

4 Name the 19th century Italian composer who wrote the opera 'La Gioconda'.

5 Prince Aly Khan was the third husband of which Hollywood movie actress?

6 The Johann Wyss novel 'Swiss Family Robinson' was first published in which language?

7 Name the American champion of women's rights and dress reform who lived from 1818 to 1894 and gave her name to an item of clothing.

8 In the 'Arabian Nights', who relates one of the tales to her husband Scharier each night to keep him from killing her?

9 Who wrote the fairy tales 'Hansel and Gretel' and 'Snow White and the Seven Dwarfs'?

10 In 1996, which 80-year-old Hollywood actor became a father for the twelfth time when his former secretary Kathy Benvin gave birth to a boy named Ryan?

General Knowledge

1 Which Greek mathematician is famous for his book entitled Elements?

2 Which one of the following is not one of Canada's prairie provinces: Alberta, Ontario, Saskatchewan?

3 Which measure of the fineness of gold is equal to the number of parts of gold by weight in 24 parts of the alloy?

4 From what natural substance is lanolin extracted?

5 Which treatment for mental disorders is represented by the initials E.C.T.?

6 What was the surname of the uncle and nephew who discovered the North Magnetic Pole?

7 In geometry, how many minutes are in a degree?

8 In 1872, the Holtermann nugget, the largest gold-bearing nugget ever found, was mined in which country?

9 Which one of the following is not a prime number: 9, 11, 13?

10 Sloppy Joe's Bar in Key West, Florida has become famous for its association with which writer?

Geography

1   Of which French overseas region is Fort-de-France the capital?

2   What is the name of the largest inlet on the U.S.A.'s Atlantic coast?

3   Of which South American country is Mount Chimborazo the highest point?

4   Of which Caribbean country is Santo Domingo the capital?

5   Before the creation of the new northern territory of Nunavut in 1999, which was the largest province in Canada?

6   Of which state of the U.S.A. is Frankfort the capital?

7   Which English county contains Lizard Point, the most southerly point of mainland England?

8   The volcano Cotopaxi is situated in which South American country?

9   The region of Patagonia is located in which continent?

10 Which South American country runs some 2,700 miles north to south but is never more than 250 miles wide, east to west?

Statesmen

1 Which world leader died on 5th March 1953?

2 A former two-term prime minister, which Italian politician was kidnapped and later killed by Red Brigade terrorists in May 1978?

3 Between 1989 and 1993, Dan Quayle was the vice president to which U.S. head of state?

4 Who was the king of Libya when Colonel Gaddafi seized power in a 1969 coup d'etat?

5 Who was the Argentinian president at the time of the Falklands War in 1982?

6 Who succeeded Nikita Khrushchev as head of the Soviet Union in 1964?

7 Russian president Vladimir Putin was formerly a lieutenant colonel in which infamous organization?

8 Famous for his numerous gaffes, which U.S. vice president said "It isn't pollution that's harming the environment, it's the impurities in the air and water"?

9 Who did Angela Merkel succeed as the chancellor of Germany in 2005?

10 In which year did Nelson Mandela become president of South Africa?

The Wild West

1. 'Doc' Holliday, of OK Corral fame, was involved in which field of medicine?

2. What was General Custer's first name?

3. Which Nevadan city was named after a river which was named after a famous frontier guide?

4. Which explorer was the first man to find a viable route from the eastern U.S.A. across the central plains, deserts and mountains, and on to the Pacific?

5. In which state is the site of the Battle of the Little Bighorn, the location of Custer's Last Stand?

6. Which America adventurer, who died at the Battle of The Alamo, has a type of hunting knife named after him?

7. Which Tennessee politician, who campaigned for the rights of native Americans, was killed at the Battle of The Alamo?

8. 'The Town Too Tough to Die' is the bold slogan of which historic Arizona city of Wild West fame?

9. Which Indian chief was killed when policemen tried to arrest him at Grand River, South Dakota, in 1890?

10. Born Phoebe Ann Moses in 1860, who became a sharp-shooting attraction in Buffalo Bill's Wild West Show in 1885?

Literature

1. In which Jules Verne novel does Phileas Fogg appear?

2. Which novel by Charles Dickens features the character Wackford Squeers?

3. Which rap singer is the author of the book 'Angry Blonde'?

4. Which American author wrote 'Double Indemnity' and 'The Postman Always Rings Twice'?

5. Which U.S. children's author and illustrator created Huckle Cat and Lowly Worm?

6. Which Irish novelist wrote 'Finnegans Wake'?

7. Which famous secret agent was created by Ian Fleming?

8. Which novel by Dostoyevsky tells of a father murdered by one of his sons?

9. 'A Connecticut Yankee In King Arthur's Court' and 'The Prince And The Pauper' are novels written by which American author?

10. In Jack London's novel 'The Call Of The Wild', what's the name of the dog who became leader of the sled team and then ran away to join a wolf pack?

General Knowledge

1 First published in 1851, which U.S. newspaper is nicknamed 'The Gray Lady'?

2 Flight 370, which famously and mysteriously disappeared en-route to Beijing after leaving Kuala Lumpur on 8th March 2014, belonged to which airline?

3 Born Joseph Yule Jr. in 1920, which American entertainer and film star died in 2014? He married eight times.

4 Set to the tune of 'Eventide' which famous hymn's opening phrases are quoted in Gustav Mahler's last symphony, his ninth, completed shortly before his death in 1911?

5 The research station at Scott Base, Antarctica, is operated by which nation?

6 The Tupolev Tu-4 strategic bomber, in service with the Soviet air force from 1947 to 1965, was a virtual copy of which U.S. bomber-aircraft?

7 'Anything You Can Do' and 'You Can't Get a Man With a Gun' are numbers from which Wild West musical?

8 'Copenhagen' was the name of the horse belonging to which famous 18th-19th century British general and statesman?

9 Which religious order is often called the Black Friars or the Order of Preachers?

10 'The Angel of Death' was the nickname of which German doctor, notorious for his experiments on prisoners during World War II?

Classical Music

1. Which great tenor became ill with internal bleeding during a performance of "The Elixir of Love' in Brooklyn in 1920 and died a few months later, without having sung again?

2. Which other great Italian tenor was often referred to, to his annoyance, as the second Caruso?

3. Who composed the opera 'Russlan and Ludmilla'?

4. Two of whose operas were about the same character, Iphigenia, daughter of Agamemnon, King of Mycenae?

5. Where can you hear world-class performances of opera in the auditorium of an English private house?

6. Who was the 19th century French composer of several operas, the best-known being 'Faust' and 'Romeo and Juliet'?

7. The very beautiful largo 'Ombra mai fu' comes from which of Handel's operas?

8. Who composed the opera 'Hansel and Gretel'?

9. Complete the title of a Tchaikovsky opera: 'The Queen of __'.

10. Which one of the following operas was not written by Verdi: 'Tosca', 'Aida', 'Nabucco'?

Sport

1 How many events are there in an heptathlon?

2 The famous cycle race, the Tour de France, traditionally ends in which city?

3 What name is a city in Texas and is the surname of Tracy, winner of the women's singles at the 1979 and 1981 U.S. Open tennis championships?

4 Which Canadian achieved a hat-trick of men's world figure skating titles between 1989 and 1991?

5 Newton Heath was a forerunner of which present-day English football team?

6 With which sport is Jean-Claude Killy associated?

7 Who are the only father and son to both win a Formula One World Championship?

8 In which sport do women's teams compete for the Federation Cup?

9 At the 2012 Paralympic Games, which nation's medal total was the highest?

10 Muhammad Ali, then known as Cassius Clay, had his first professional fight on 29 October 1960. It was against Tunney Hunsakar and took place in the city where he was born. Which city?

Space

1. Of which constellation is Spica the brightest star?

2. Which unit of distance used in astronomy is approximately equal to 3.26 light-years?

3. On which planet is there a volcano called Olympus Mons?

4. On which asteroid did N.A.S.A. land an unmanned craft in 2001?

5. How is the Dog Star otherwise known?

6. The Galilean satellites are the four largest satellites of which planet?

7. Which is the second largest planet of the solar system?

8. In which year did the Gemini 6 and 7 spacecraft rendezvous in space?

9. In the 1960s the U.S. launched a series of meteorological satellites known as TIROS. What did TIROS stand for?

10. Of which planet is Deimos a satellite?

General Knowledge

1. What are the Palatine, Aventine, Capitoline, Quirinal, Viminal, Esquiline and Caelian?

2. Which 19th century American philosopher, poet and essayist wrote: 'Nothing great was ever achieved without enthusiasm'?

3. Name the German architect who was director of the Bauhaus school of design from 1919 to 1928.

4. Name the mongoose in Kipling's 'Jungle Book'.

5. Which Frenchman wrote: 'If God did not exist it would be necessary to invent him'?

6. The Imperial Hotel in Tokyo and the Guggenheim Museum in New York are two of the best known public buildings designed by which American architect?

7. What name was shared by a 19th century American physician and writer and his jurist son?

8. Which former American hero-turned-traitor conspired unsuccessfully to surrender the vital West Point position to the British in 1780 during the American War of Independence?

9. In J. M. Barrie's 'Peter Pan', what is the surname of the children Wendy, Michael and John?

10. And according to Peter Pan, what happens every time a child says: "I don't believe in fairies"?

The Answer's a Country

1 The farandole is a national dance of which country?

2 Which is the only European country without an army?

3 The Azores are part of which European country?

4 Of which European country is Valletta the capital?

5 The port of Ghent is in which country?

6 The Gobi Desert extends over China and which other country?

7 The site of the Biblical city of Troy is in which modern country?

8 Of which former Soviet state is Bishkek the capital?

9 In which country was the Nobel prize-winning nuclear physicist Ernest Rutherford born?

10 The River Rhine flows through which country before entering the North Sea?

History

1   The Statue of Liberty was given to the U.S.A. by which nation in 1884?

2   Said never to have lost a battle, which Federal general was ordered by Grant to make the Shenandoah valley 'a barren waste' during the American Civil War?

3   In 1898, which French novelist wrote an open letter entitled 'J'accuse' which attacked the French government over their persecution of the army officer Alfred Dreyfus?

4   Name the 18th century French philosopher who wrote: "Man is born free and everywhere he is in chains."

5   By what name were the Nazi police force the Geheime Staatspolizei known?

6   John the Perfect and John the Unfortunate were kings of which country?

7   French chemist Joseph Niepce took the first what in 1826?

8   From which country does the Uzi machine gun originate?

9   What sort of institution did London bookseller Thomas Guy found in the 1720s?

10 In which country was the first of the Pugwash Conferences held?

Book Characters

1 In which novel does Edmond Dantes appear as a prisoner?

2 Winston Smith is the protagonist in which dystopian novel?

3 Gustav von Aschenbach is the tragic central character of which Thomas Mann novel?

4 Ishmael is the narrator in which nineteenth century novel?

5 'Call for the Dead' and 'The Spy Who Came In From the Cold' by John Le Carre, both feature which spymaster?

6 George Milton and Lennie Small are characters in which novel by John Steinbeck?

7 'Slaughterhouse Five' by Kurt Vonnegut features which space-travelling protagonist?

8 The wizard, Rincewind, appears in which series of fantasy novels?

9 Tom and Ruth Pinch appear in which novel by Charles Dickens?

10 Humbert Humbert is the protagonist in which novel by Vladimir Nabokov?

General Knowledge

1. Which British pioneer of antiseptic surgery was the first to use carbolic solutions to sterilize surgical instruments?

2. In seawater, what percentage of an iceberg is visible above the water?

3. How many U.S. states are non-contiguous, i.e. they have no border with any other state?

4. As British home secretary (later to become prime minister), who founded the London Metropolitan Police in 1829?

5. How many feet are there in a mile?

6. The Japanese YKK Group is the world's largest manufacturer of which kind of product?

7. The term 'Cold War', as a description of the state of tension that existed between East and West during the years post-World War II, was coined by which British author?

8. In which month is Earth closest to the Sun?

9. 'Living in America' a song from 1985, was the only UK top ten hit for which famous American singer?

10. During the Cold War, what did the acronym MAD stand for?

Movies

1   Which movie icon made her last appearance in 'Sextette' in 1978, which was a movie based on her own play?

2   Which 1964 movie was based on Harold Robbins novel about a millionaire plane manufacturer, and was the last movie in which Alan Ladd appeared?

3   Which 1979 drama starring Anthony Franciosa and Carroll Baker was from a novel and screenplay by Jackie Collins?

4   Which Jerome Kern musical has been adapted to the screen three times; in 1929, 1936 and 1957?

5   Which 1953 Cole Porter musical starring Howard Keel and Kathryn Grayson was originally made in 3D?

6   Kurosowa's movie 'The Throne Of Blood' was his adaptation of which Shakespeare play?

7   What activity links the following movies - 'Blood And Sand', 'The Kid From Spain' and 'The Sun Also Rises'?

8   Who played opposite Marlon Brando in the erotic drama 'Last Tango in Paris'?

9   In which 1979 movie are the crew members of the spaceship Nostromo mercilessly killed off one by one?

10 In 'Gone With the Wind' what did Scarlett O'Hara say to Rhett Butler, which prompted the response of: "Frankly, my dear, I don't give a damn."?

The Bible

1 In Genesis, who are the two brothers who descend into conflict when one sells his birthright to the other?

_____

2 Which son of David died when his hair caught in a tree?

_____

3 What carried the prophet Elijah to heaven?

_____

4 Which prisoner was released by Pilate in exchange for Jesus, shortly before Jesus's execution?

_____

5 Who is said to have performed the 'dance of the seven veils' for her stepfather, King Herod?

_____

6 Two names are given for the place of Jesus's crucifixion; one is Calvary, what is the other?

_____

7 David interpreted the dreams of which Babylonian king?

_____

8 What were the most important items kept in the Ark of the Covenant?

_____

9 Who was the mother of John the Baptist and a relative of Mary, the mother of Jesus?

_____

10 What was it that barred the way of Balaam on his way to curse the Israelites, something he couldn't see yet his donkey could?

Nature

1 What name is given to a coral reef surrounding a lagoon?

2 Which festive shrub of the genus Ilex has spiny green leaves and female flowers which develop into red berries?

3 What are the khamsin and the simoom?

4 Which Australian tree is also called a gum tree?

5 Which songbird of the thrush family has an olive-brown plumage with an orange-red breast, throat and forehead?

6 What are the leaves of ferns and palm trees called?

7 Which word describes the periodic movement of animal populations between one region and another?

8 On a flower, what is another name for the petals?

9 Which one of the following birds is not a member of the falcon family: Merlin, Eagle, Hobby?

10 Which bird of the crow family has the Latin name Pica pica?

General Knowledge

1. In which limb would you find the humerus, ulna and radius?

2. Which term describes an integer greater than one that has no integral factors except itself and one?

3. Which character in 'Alice's Adventures in Wonderland' would often fade from sight until nothing but his grin remained?

4. What is both the surname of the president of South Africa from 1883 to 1902 and the name of a game reserve in north-east South Africa?

5. What is both the name of a German town which gave its name to a type of man's hat and the title of a hit record for the 1960s band Procol Harum?

6. The name of which breed of dog means butterfly in French?

7. What breed of domestic dog belonging to the hound family is also called the African barkless dog?

8. What would be the shape of a cupola roof?

9. What nationality was dancer Isadora Duncan?

10. What in Japan is a Samisen?

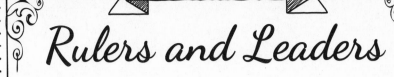

Rulers and Leaders

1 Which king and queen of Spain were the patrons of Christopher Columbus?

2 In which battle of 8 January 1815 did U.S. forces led by Andrew Jackson defeat the British?

3 The Ruriks and Romanovs were ruling dynasties in which country?

4 Of which country was Morarji Desai prime minister from 1977 to 1979?

5 Which Mongol leader was originally called Temujin?

6 Who was the first black officer to hold the highest military post in the United States?

7 Which French army officer was King of Naples from 1808 to 1815?

8 Who gained the Russian throne in a coup in which her unpopular husband Emperor Peter III was murdered?

9 Who was commander-in-chief of the U.S. forces which inflicted notable defeats on the British army at Trenton and Princeton in 1777?

10 One of the U.S. Navy's foremost strategists, who commanded the U.S. Pacific fleet from 1941 to 1945?

Geography

1. Which country in Europe is just over half the size of Scotland, has a coastline 4,500 miles long and is nowhere higher than 570 feet?

2. Which one of the following capital cities is not a seaport: Helsinki, Phnom Penh, Ankara?

3. Which U.S. state was founded by the English Quaker William Penn?

4. Which Turkish city used to be known as Constantinople?

5. In which ocean can the Marianas Trench be found?

6. Of which European country is Bergen the second largest city?

7. In which Scandinavian country is the port of Malmö situated?

8. Which modern day country was once home to the Aztecs?

9. What name is both the third largest city in Spain and the third largest city in Venezuela?

10. Which is the only one of the following that lies within the Tropics: Cairo, Karachi, Mexico City?

Pop Music

1 'Never Too Much' was a hit in the late 1980s for which American soul singer?

2 Long before it became the title of an album in 1993, 'What's Love Got To Do With It' was a hit single for ___?

3 For whom was 'Morning Has Broken' such a big, big hit?

4 Who, in 1976, complained that 'Breaking Up Is So Hard To Do'?

5 In 1986, 'The Lady in Red' was an outstanding success for ___?

6 In 1988, 'Sweet Child O' Mine' made it for ___?

7 Who released 'Call Me' in 1976?

8 Who released 'The Winner Takes It All' in 1980?

9 'A Town Called Malice' was a hit for which group?

10 'Golden Brown' was released in 1977 by ___?

Science

1. Which hard silvery metal is represented by the symbol Ni?

2. What name is given to all chemical compounds which contain carbon and hydrogen?

3. Which unit of pressure is represented by the symbol Pa?

4. Which radioactive metallic element is represented by the symbol Ra?

5. What machine tool shapes material by rapidly turning it against a stationary cutting device?

6. What calibrated calculating device was the standard tool for engineers and scientists prior to the invention of the hand-held calculator?

7. Charcoal is a form of which chemical?

8. Which metallic element is represented by the symbol Fe?

9. Which alloy of copper and nickel is used for coins?

10. With which branch of mathematics is Euclid chiefly associated?

General Knowledge

1 Which document of liberty and political rights was obtained from King John of England by his rebellious barons at Runnymede in 1215?

2 In TV's 'The Simpsons', what was the name of the man who owned and ran the Springfield nuclear power plant?

3 The dodo, a heavy flightless bird of Mauritius, became extinct towards the end of which century?

4 'The Thinker' (1880) and 'The Kiss' (1886) are the work of which French sculptor?

5 'La Bohème', 'Tosca' and 'Madam Butterfly' are notable operas composed by which Italian?

6 Private detective Philip Marlowe, who appeared in novels such as 'The Big Sleep', was the creation of which American author?

7 Which country lies between Romania and Ukraine?

8 Of the two capital cities Madrid and Lisbon, which is furthest north?

9 The Channel Tunnel, a railway tunnel under the English Channel, linking the coasts of England and France, opened in which year?

10 The Charge of the Light Brigade, a British cavalry charge in 1854 during the Battle of Balaclava in the Crimean War, was immortalized in verse by which English poet?

ROUND 45

Pen Names

1. A writer of suspense novels and science fiction, who sometimes used the pen names Deanna Dwyer, Aaron Wolfe and Richard Paige?

2. Which famous crime novel author occasionally used the pen name Mary Westmacott?

3. One of the Founding Fathers of the U.S.A., which writer and scientist sometimes signed himself 'Martha Careful'?

4. Which adventure-fantasy novel writer used the pen name Newt Scamander for her book 'Fantastic Beasts and Where to Find Them'?

5. Paul French was a pseudonym used by which science fiction writer?

6. Horror-fiction author Richard Bachman was better known by which name?

7. Which American poet, who committed suicide in England in 1963, sometimes used the pen name Victoria Lucas?

8. Who was the author of the 'Moomin' books for children, who sometimes used the pen name Vera Haij?

9. Samuel Langhorne Clemens wrote under which pseudonym?

10. Which British authoress uses the pen name Barbara Vine for some of her murder mystery novels?

Sport

1. Trampolining was introduced as an Olympic sport in which year?

2. Who became the youngest-ever snooker World Champion in 1990, aged 21?

3. Which U.S. tennis player was the first black person to win the Wimbledon Men's Singles title, in 1975?

4. Which Summer Olympic Games was the first to have female competitors in all sports types?

5. Who did Sonny Liston 'K.O.' to become World Heavyweight boxing champion in 1962?

6. Which game, similar to pelota, has recorded the fastest ball speeds of any sport (up to 217 mph)?

7. Which long-distance race is run over 26 miles 385 yards?

8. Which country is the only one to have competed in all football World Cup competitions since the first, in 1930?

9. At the 2012 Paralympics, Jacqueline Freney of Australia won eight gold medals in which sport?

10. The B.P.A. in the Americas, the B.E. in Europe, and the B.O. in Oceania, are governing bodies of which sport?

History

1. The Great Fire of London occurred in which year?

2. Explorer, Leif Ericsson is said to have discovered North America in which year?

3. Which English king was victorious at the Battle of Agincourt in 1415?

4. Which three European countries were united through the 1397 Union of Kalmar?

5. Which UN Secretary General died in a plane crash in 1961?

6. Which early modern humans, who existed at approximately the same time as the better-known Neanderthals, is the species from which most modern Europeans are descended?

7. In February 1971 which European country gave its women citizens the vote in national elections for the first time?

8. In which year of the twentieth century was the Great Tokyo Earthquake, that caused 143,000 deaths?

9. Which Russian city was besieged by German armies from September 1941 to January 1944, killing around one million people?

10. In what year was the first Russian Revolution, against Tsar Nicholas II?

Classical Music

1. The very first jazz opera ever was German! Composed by Ernst Krenek and performed in Leipzig in 1927, what was its name?

2. The fame of which Italian opera composer rests on just one work 'I Pagliacci'?

3. What was Beethoven's only opera 'Fidelio' originally entitled?

4. Benjamin Britten composed a 'musical play for children' in which the audience also participates. What is it called?

5. Giuseppe Verdi composed two operas based upon characters from Shakespearean plays. Who were they?

6. What is the actual name of Madame Butterfly, in Puccini's opera, 'Madame Butterfly'?

7. On 30th September, 1791, in a suburban theatre of Vienna, Mozart conducted the first night of which of his operas, only two months before his death?

8. In which of Mozart's operas is the role of the page-boy Cherubino, played by a girl?

9. Which one of the following ballets was not written by Tchaikovsky: 'Giselle', 'The Nutcracker', 'Swan Lake'?

10. If 'Opera' is a drama set to music, in which the dialogue is sung, what is the definition of 'Operetta'?

General Knowledge

1. In which city would you find the Petronas Towers?

2. Which ancient city, now occupied by the towns of Al-Karnak and Luxor was, for many centuries, the capital of Ancient Egypt?

3. In which city did Leon Czolgosz shoot and fatally wound U.S. president William McKinley?

4. Which year saw Willy Brandt elected Chancellor of West Germany, Samuel Beckett win the Nobel prize for Literature, and Golda Meir become Israeli Prime Minister?

5. Which year saw the resignation of the Canadian prime minister Pierre Trudeau, and the death of singer Marvin Gaye, who was shot by his father?

6. James F Fixx died of a heart attack in 1984 doing something which he pioneered as a method of keeping fit. What was he doing when he died?

7. Whose literary work 'The First Man on the Moon' was published in 1902?

8. Which U.S. state is known as the Heart of Dixie?

9. Which island was previously known as Formosa?

10. Which two Spanish cities have a population in excess of one million?

Around the Islands

1 To which country does the Atlantic island of Bermuda belong?

_____

2 What is the world's largest island country?

_____

3 New Guinea, the Solomon Islands and Fiji, are part of which Pacific Ocean region?

_____

4 Which island is located at the 'toe' of Italy?

_____

5 What is the largest of the Hawaiian Islands?

_____

6 Tierra del Fuego lies at the southern end of which continent?

_____

7 The Galapagos Islands are located to the west of which South American country?

_____

8 Which Mediterranean island is directly north of Sardinia?

_____

9 The Virgin Islands are divided into two territories; one British and the other belonging to which nation?

_____

10 What is the capital of the Philippines?

Inventions

1   Isaac Pitman invented what kind of writing system?

_____

2   Which ancient civilization is credited with the invention of concrete?

_____

3   Who invented the first sound-recording machine, the Phonograph?

_____

4   Which children's doll was 'invented' by Ruth Handler in 1959?

_____

5   The multi-plane camera, developed by Walt Disney from earlier ideas, is used in the production of which kind of movies?

_____

6   The production of what material was revolutionized by the Bessemer Process?

_____

7   Willis Haviland Carrier invented what system in 1902?

_____

8   In the 1670s, Hennig Brand's experiments discovered which chemical element?

_____

9   What was Thomas Twyford's aid to humanity by way of his 1885 invention?

_____

10   Kirkpatrick Macmillan is credited with the invention of which transport device?

ROUND 52

Religion

1 Of which religious movement is the Watch Tower Bible and Tract Society the legal publishing agency?

2 In what year did the First Crusade begin?

3 Which order of Roman Catholic monks was founded at Cîteaux, France in 1098?

4 What were found near Qumran, Palestine by an Arab shepherd in 1947?

5 In which city would you find the Blue Mosque and the Mosque of Suleyman?

6 In which city would you find the Potala Palace, a major pilgrimage site for Buddhists?

7 Which 4th century Roman Christian and martyr is the patron saint of virgins? Her emblem is a lamb and her feast day is 21 January.

8 According to Christian tradition, which saint, whose feast day is 26 July, was the mother of the Virgin Mary?

9 In the Hindu religion, who is the goddess of death?

10 Which supernatural beings rank immediately above angels in the celestial hierarchy?

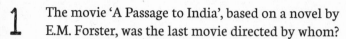

General Knowledge

1 The movie 'A Passage to India', based on a novel by E.M. Forster, was the last movie directed by whom?

2 A carioca is a native of which Brazilian city?

3 What was the pen-name of Charles Lutwidge Dodgson, whose works include 'Alice's Adventures in Wonderland' and 'Through the Looking Glass'?

4 Who was the 39th President of the U.S.A., 1977–81?

5 Which Russian jeweller of French descent is famous for the intricate Easter eggs made for royal households?

6 Which Flemish painter is best known for his portraits and mythological paintings featuring voluptuous female nudes, as in 'Venus and Adonis'?

7 Which ancient city in present-day Jordan is famous for its extensive ruins that include temples and tombs hewn from the rose-red sandstone cliffs?

8 Which English motor-racing driver won the Formula One world championship in 2009?

9 Who was the first person to set foot on the moon?

10 Which actress, originally an orange-seller, was a mistress of King Charles II?

Entertainment

1 Peter Wolf was lead singer of the rock group the J. Geils Band for 16 years. He was married for a short time to which Hollywood actress?

2 Which city in Indiana was the birthplace of Michael Jackson?

3 What word for a short, light piece of music also means something of little value and is also a game?

4 What is both the name of a U.S. daily newspaper and the title of a John Philip Sousa march?

5 Which movie director married Jane Fonda in 1965?

6 Why was the poet and author Edgar Allan Poe thrown out of West Point in 1831?

7 Which one of the following was not born in Russia: Irving Berlin, Al Jolson, George Gershwin?

8 Which American author writes the 'Goosebumps' series of novels?

9 What breed of dog was Nana, the dog featured in 'Peter Pan'?

10 In 1931, Zeppo Marx of the Marx Brothers and his wife acquired two dogs in England. The dogs, official names Asra of Ghazni and Westmill Omar, became the foundation dogs of which breed in America?

War

1. Name the American who was commander-in-chief of U.N. forces in the Korean War until relieved of his command in April 1951.

2. Some of the earliest war photographs were taken at the Battle of Antietam. During which war was this battle fought?

3. The S.S. were the elite Nazi military corps. In German, what did S.S. stand for?

4. What was the name for the line of demarcation between North and South Vietnam established by the Geneva Conference?

5. One of the code names of the five beachheads used for the D-Day landings was named after which U.S. state?

6. Name the American general who owned a white Bull Terrier named Willie who accompanied the troops during the Second World War.

7. Cape Trafalgar, where the famous naval battle of 1805 took place, is off the coast of which country?

8. What was the name of the powerful defoliant sprayed by American forces during the Vietnam War?

9. Which war involved a volunteer army known as the International Brigade?

10. Which Sioux Indian chief led the massacre of General Custer and his men at the Little Bighorn?

Literature

1. Who wrote the stories about Brer Rabbit and his friends which were narrated by Uncle Remus?

2. In Herman Melville's novel 'Moby Dick', what is the name of Captain Ahab's ship?

3. Which prolific American author wrote 'Riders of the Purple Sage'?

4. Which American author wrote 'The Sound and the Fury'?

5. Which British novelist wrote 'King Solomon's Mines'?

6. Which American author wrote 'The Beautiful and the Damned'?

7. Who wrote the play 'She Stoops to Conquer'?

8. What was the first name of Cervantes, author of 'Don Quixote'?

9. Which Anton Chekhov play tells of the destruction of a family estate for the construction of a new housing development?

10. Name the feminist, a constant companion of Jean-Paul Sartre, who wrote 'The Second Sex'.

Science

1. What name is given to the study of human improvement by genetic means?

2. What is the SI unit of radiation dose equivalent?

3. What is the second most abundant mineral in the Earth's crust after feldspar?

4. Which chemical element is represented by the symbol C?

5. Which acid is a solution in water of the pungent gas hydrogen chloride?

6. Which German physicist was the first to develop quantum theory?

7. Which word describes the rate of increasing change of a body's velocity?

8. Which brittle grey-white metalloid is represented by the symbol Ge?

9. Which chemical substance is produced by the Haber-Bosch process?

10. An acute, often fatal viral infection is sometimes called Marburg disease after the place in Germany where it was first described. By what other name is this disease known?

General Knowledge

1 Which US state lies between Minnesota and Missouri?

2 Of John o'Groats (at the north-eastern tip of mainland Scotland) and Stockholm (the capital of Sweden), which is furthest north?

3 What is the basic monetary unit in Kenya, Tanzania and Uganda?

4 Mary Ann Nichols was the first victim of which killer who stalked the streets of London in the late 19th century?

5 In 1966, the country of Bechuanaland changed its name to what?

6 The Russian spacecraft Venera 9 was the first lander to transmit colour images from the surface of which planet?

7 The House of Braganza ruled which country from 1640 until the end of the monarchy in 1910?

8 In 1938, who aired his realistic adaptation of 'The War of the Worlds', leading many radio listeners to believe that a Martian invasion was really happening?

9 Of which country is Ouagadougou the capital?

10 A wainwright was (historically) a builder of what?

Geography

1 Which sea lies between Vietnam and the Philippines?

2 To which country do Bhola Island, St Martin's Island, Manpura Island and Hatiya Island all belong?

3 Which country lies immediately to the north of Chad?

4 Mogadishu is the capital of which country?

5 In which state of Australia are Alice Springs and Uluru (which is also known as Ayers Rock)?

6 After Alaska, which US state has the longest coastline?

7 Which country was formerly known as Rhodesia before gaining independence from Great Britain in 1980?

8 The Taurus Mountains are in which country?

9 Tobermory is the capital and largest town of which Scottish island?

10 Which is the only sovereign state completely on the island of Borneo (the remainder of Borneo being divided between the nations of Indonesia and Malaysia)?

'The Simpsons'

1. Homer Simpson, Seymour Skinner, Clancy Wiggum and Apu Nahasapeemapetilon were members of which barbershop vocal group?

2. What are the names of Milhouse Van Houten's parents?

3. What is the common, popular name for the character called Jeff Albertson, who holds a masters degree in folklore and mythology?

4. Which department store is located in Downtown Springfield: their slogan is "Over A Century Without A Slogan"?

5. What is the name of the music store located next door to Moe's Tavern?

6. Which competitor of Duff beer is alleged by bartender Moe Szyslak to have made hillbillies go blind?

7. What is the name of the maritime-themed restaurant operated by Sea Captain Horatio MacAllister?

8. What is the name of the home for the elderly in which Grampa Simpson resides?

9. Marge had a schoolgirl crush on which member of the Beatles, to whom she wrote and sent a portrait?

10. Who co-wrote and produced 'Do the Bartman', a single from 'The Simpsons Sing the Blues' but did not receive credit due to his exclusive contract with Sony?

History

1 Which British surgeon is regarded as the founder of antiseptic surgery?

2 Cathay was the medieval European name for which Asian country?

3 Who was the famous daughter of the native American chief Powhatan?

4 What was the name of the deadly virus which struck in Zaire in 1995?

5 On 28 February 2001, which U.S. city suffered its worst earthquake in more than half a century?

6 In the 1830s, an American blacksmith, John Deere, was a pioneer in the development of which agricultural tool?

7 By what nickname is John Chapman (1774-1847), who is reputed to have spread seeds from which grew orchards in America's Midwest, better known?

8 In which country did light cavalrymen known as hussars originate?

9 Which Roman emperor was the stepson and successor of Augustus?

10 Who was the last king of Egypt?

Sport

1. In which year did Lance Armstrong last win the Tour de France race?

2. The Green Jacket is awarded to the winner of which golf tournament?

3. Zandvoort is a former Formula One racing circuit in which country?

4. Which country has its national football stadium at Hampden Park?

5. In athletics, what is the most common distance set for the steeplechase race?

6. In the early 1950s, three Italian constructors dominated Formula One racing: Ferrari, Alpha Romeo and which other?

7. Which British athlete won the decathlon Gold at both the 1980 and 1984 Olympics?

8. Any many players are there in a volleyball team?

9. Which teams competed in the 2014 Superbowl?

10. Which German boxer became the World Heavyweight champion in 1930?

General Knowledge

1 Joseph Priestley's chief work was on the chemistry of gases, in which his most significant discovery was of 'dephlogisticated air' in 1774. By what name do we know this gas today?

2 A tall coniferous tree related to the monkey puzzle, the bunya bunya is native to which country?

3 What is measured by a sphygmomanometer?

4 Known for hit songs such as 'Wannabe' (1996), how many Spice Girls were in the band?

5 The Arabian peninsula comprises the states of Saudi Arabia, Yemen, Oman, Bahrain, Qatar, the United Arab Emirates, and which other country?

6 In which ocean are the Galapagos Islands?

7 Servius Sulpicius Galba was successor to which Roman emperor?

8 Galena is the chief ore of which metallic element?

9 Which body, established in 1919 by the Treaty of Versailles, was superseded in 1945 by the United Nations?

10 Chris Bonington made the first British ascent of the north face of which mountain in 1962?

Entertainment

1   Which Oscar-winning actor married the daughter of playwright Arthur Miller?

2   Which lyricist collaborated with Richard Rodgers on 'Oklahoma', 'Carousel' and 'The King and I'?

3   At which movie festival are the Golden Lions awarded?

4   What name is given to a monologue in which a character in a play speaks his thoughts aloud?

5   With what style of music is Blind Lemon Jefferson associated?

6   Which British writer of children's books created the Famous Five and Secret Seven?

7   Which Greek dramatist wrote the plays 'Oedipus Rex' and 'Antigone'?

8   What name is given to the art of creating and arranging dances?

9   Which famous literary family is associated with Haworth Parsonage in West Yorkshire, England?

10 By what name was American rock-and-roll disc jockey Robert Weston Smith known?

Space

1. Which British astronomer was the first to realize that comets do not appear randomly but have periodic orbits?

2. Which is the nearest planet to the Sun?

3. Which Soviet cosmonaut was the first person to orbit the Earth?

4. Which year saw Russian spacecraft 'Lunik III' photograph the far side of the Moon?

5. In astronomy, what name is given to the apparent brightness of a celestial body?

6. Which constellation contains the Coalsack Nebula?

7. To what did Cape Kennedy Space Center change its name in 1973?

8. Who was the second man to walk on the Moon?

9. Which German astronomer discovered the three principles of planetary motion?

10. Which planet is known as the Red Planet?

Movies

1. Who plays brothel proprietor Mona Strangley in 'The Best Little Whorehouse in Texas'?

2. In 'The Exorcist', who plays the 12-year-old whose body is possessed by the Devil?

3. In the movie 'Star Wars', which character reassures Luke Skywalker: "The force will be with you – always."?

4. 'Happy Talk' and 'Some Enchanted Evening' are songs from which 1958 musical?

5. In which 1953 musical does Howard Keel star as Wild Bill Hickok opposite Doris Day?

6. In the 1978 'Superman' movie, which cinema icon plays Superman's father Jor-El?

7. Frank Langella is best known for playing the title role in which 1979 horror movie?

8. In the 1954 movie 'The Naked Jungle', what caused the jungle to be naked?

9. Who played a character called Pedro Jiminez in the movie 'The Dirty Dozen' and had a hit with the song 'If I Had A Hammer'?

10. Bob Hope and Bing Crosby appeared in seven 'Road' movies. Singapore, Zanzibar, Morocco, Rio, Bali and Hong Kong were the destinations in six of them, what was the title of the fourth in the series, released in 1946?

General Knowledge

1 What unit of weight equals 1000 kilograms?

2 Which London square contained London's principal fruit, flower and vegetable market for over 300 years?

3 What does an oleometer measure the density of?

4 In which year did Princess Grace of Monaco die after a car crash, Iran invade Iraq, and Italy win the Fifa World Cup?

5 In 1913, Which psychiatrist wrote: "conscience is the internal perception of a particular wish operating within us."?

6 Which unit was defined in 1791 as one ten-millionth of the length of the quadrant of the Earth's meridian through Paris?

7 What sort of plant is a saguaro?

8 In which country is the city of Tijuana?

9 Which snake shares its name with that of a short-range air-to-air missile?

10 What does CD-ROM stand for?

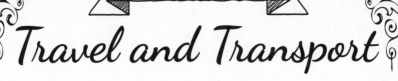

Travel and Transport

1 Avianca is the national airline of which country?

2 Real name Elizabeth Cochrane, which U.S. newspaper reporter became famous for her round the world trip which took 72 days in 1889/1890?

3 Which Portuguese navigator is frequently credited with having discovered Brazil?

4 In which year did the Soviet version of the Concorde airplane crash at the Paris air show, the Miami Dolphins win the Superbowl, and Edward G Robinson die?

5 What type of vessel to explore ocean depths was invented in 1947 by Auguste Piccard?

6 What, in mechanics, is the reaction force produced by the rotation of a shaft about its axis?

7 Which famous motor car did Ferdinand Porsche design in 1937?

8 What was the name of the ship that carried the Pilgrim Fathers to America in 1620?

9 Where, in Europe, did Charles Lindbergh land after flying the Atlantic solo in 1927?

10 How many nautical miles are there in a league?

History

1. Which famous event of 1773 gives its name to a present-day right-wing U.S. political organization?

2. Wellington defeated the French at Vitoria in 1813. In which country is Vitoria?

3. Which European city was devastated by an earthquake and tsunami in 1755?

4. From which island did Napoleon Bonaparte escape captivity in 1815?

5. In which year did the second Boer War begin?

6. Which civilization was subjugated by the Spanish conquistador, Cortes?

7. In which city was John Lennon shot dead in 1980?

8. Which northerly sea route was sought after by many explorers between the 15th and early 20th centuries?

9. Reigning since 1818, Bernadotte is the royal house of which country?

10. Which English war was fought between the Houses of Lancaster and York?

The Bible

1. Which friend of Jesus was the sister of Mary and Lazarus of Bethany?

2. What collective name is given to the Gospels of Matthew, Mark and Luke?

3. In the Old Testament, who interpreted the writing on the wall at Belshazzar's feast?

4. Who was the first person to see the resurrected Christ?

5. In the New Testament, what is the name of the site of the conclusive battle between the forces of good and evil?

6. In the Old Testament, who was the father of Ishmael and Isaac?

7. Who is the traditional author of the Second Gospel?

8. According to the Old Testament, who received the Ten Commandments on Mount Sinai?

9. Which ancient city of Sumer is mentioned in Genesis as Abraham's homeland?

10. According to the New Testament, which Apostle had a vision while travelling to Damascus, which led to his conversion to Christianity?

Food and Drink

1. What name is given to a whipped cream dessert, typically flavoured with white wine or sherry?

2. What spice is used to flavour the sauce that coats the dish called 'steak au poivre'?

3. Snøfrisk, Gamalost and Jarlsberg are cheeses from which country?

4. A Harvey Wallbanger is a cocktail made of vodka or gin, Galliano, and the juice of which fruit?

5. First produced as a drivers' manual, and now regarded as the bible for gastronomes, in which year was the first Michelin guide published?

6. Chorizo is a dry, highly-seasoned sausage made from pork. From which country did it originate?

7. From which country is carpaccio, an hors d'oeuvre of thin slices of raw beef or fish served with a sauce?

8. What marine creature is used to make the Mediterranean dish calamari?

9. What is the name of the tomato-based Spanish soup that is generally served cold?

10. Which liqueur of brandy and aromatic herbs was originally made by the monks of a Carthusian monastery near Grenoble in France?

General Knowledge

1. Of Ghana and Nigeria, which country is furthest west?

2. Which vitamin complex includes thiamine, niacin and riboflavin?

3. How many pieces in total are placed on a board with 64 squares at the start of a game of draughts (or checkers)?

4. The Pentateuch comprises the first five books of the Old Testament: Genesis, Exodus, Leviticus, Numbers, and which other?

5. Giovanni Cassini, an Italian-born French astronomer, discovered the gap, now known as Cassini's division, in the rings of which planet?

6. A magnum bottle for wine, champagne, etc, contains how many litres?

7. Which international agreement (first made in 1864 and later revised), governs the status and treatment of captured and wounded military personnel and civilians in wartime?

8. Which nuts are traditionally found on top of a Genoa cake?

9. Which US state lies to the north of New Mexico?

10. Someone who is an anthropophagist is more commonly known as what?

Classical Music

1 Who composed the opera 'If I Were King'?

_____

2 Who composed the opera 'L'Africaine' (The African Girl)?

_____

3 'They call me Mimi ___' sings the heroine of 'La Boheme'. But what is her real name?

_____

4 Which German composer wrote the 'Four Last Songs'?

_____

5 Which friend of Mussorgsky carried out a 'technical revision' of the opera 'Boris Godunov' after his death, and some say saved it from oblivion?

_____

6 Alexander Borodin wrote only one opera. Its name ___?

_____

7 Who composed the music for the opera 'Cavalleria Rusticana'?

_____

8 Who composed the music for the opera 'Lakme'?

_____

9 What were the famous composer J.S. Bach's first names?

_____

10 The opera 'The Snow Maiden' was written in the early 1880s by which Russian composer?

Who Said That?

1 Who said: "Marriage is a great institution, but I'm not ready for an institution yet."

2 Who said: "Power is the ultimate aphrodisiac."

3 Who said: "A successful man is one who makes more money than his wife can spend. A successful woman is one who can find such a man."

4 Who said: "A bank is a place that will lend you money, if you can prove that you don't need it."

5 Who said: "I don't want to achieve immortality through my work. I want to achieve it by not dying."

6 Who said: "There is nothing so annoying as to have two people go right on talking when you're interrupting."

7 Who said: "A woman drove me to drink and I didn't even have the decency to thank her."

8 Who said: "An archaeologist is the best husband a woman can have; the older she gets the more interested he is in her."

9 Who said: "I refuse to join any club that would have me as a member."

10 Who said: "The best argument against democracy is a five-minute conversation with the average voter."

The Animal Kingdom

1 Which breed of dog was developed from the fox terrier by the Reverend John Russell in the 19th century?

_____

2 What is the world's smallest bird?

_____

3 What is the fastest animal over short distances?

_____

4 What sort of creature is a kuvasz?

_____

5 Which is the largest living bird?

_____

6 What is the general name for any hoofed mammal?

_____

7 What sort of bird is a lammergeier?

_____

8 What sort of creature is a dragonet?

_____

9 What kind of arboreal primate is an indri?

_____

10 What sort of creature is a pratincole?

General Knowledge

1. Annual jumping competitions for which amphibians are held in Calaveras, California?

2. Architect Frank Gehry, who designed the Disney Concert Hall in Los Angeles and the Guggenheim Museum in Bilbao, was born in which country?

3. On a traditional typewriter or computer keyboard, how many vowels appear on the middle letter row?

4. Of what is arachnophobia an extreme or irrational fear?

5. Executed by guillotine in 1793, who was the wife of King Louis XVI of France?

6. Whose was "the face that launched a thousand ships"?

7. What is the colour of the circle on the national flag of Bangladesh?

8. The Chinese Zodiac, known as Sheng Xiao, is based on a cycle, each year in that cycle related to an animal sign. How many animals are represented in the Chinese zodiac?

9. Which US President was nicknamed 'Old Hickory'?

10. According to the creation story in the Bible, on which day did God create man?

Geography

1 Which one of the following is not both the name of a country and a river: Hungary, Jordan, Paraguay?

2 The rivers Ruhr, Main, Moselle and Neckar are tributaries of which river?

3 Which state of the U.S.A. is home to the Valley of Ten Thousand Smokes?

4 What is the smallest and easternmost of the Great Lakes of North America?

5 Which Russian city was formerly called Leningrad?

6 Of which Canadian province is St. John's the capital?

7 Which was the first of the Great Lakes to be seen by Europeans?

8 What name is given to a long narrow sea inlet resulting from marine inundation of a glacial valley?

9 In Hawaii, what is Mauna Loa?

10 Table Mountain overlooks which city in South Africa?

Politics

1. After agreeing to retire from politics, which Mexican revolutionary was killed in 1923?

2. Which president had held office for only six months when the U.S. stock market crashed in 1929?

3. In which country was revolutionary leader Che Guevara shot dead in 1967?

4. The American heiress Jennie Jerome, who died in 1921, was the mother of which leading 20th-century political figure?

5. Which Russian leader was associated with the policies of glasnost and perestroika?

6. Which former prime minister of Canada died in 2000 at the age of 80?

7. Which billionaire stood as a candidate in the U.S. presidential elections in 1992 and 1996?

8. In 1939, which two leaders signed a 'Pact of Steel' committing their nations to support each other in times of war?

9. Who was ousted as president of Yugoslavia in 2000 and was later tried for war crimes?

10. Which Indian stateswoman was prime minister of her country from 1966 to 1977 and 1980 to 1984?

Music

1 Who sang 'Hello Mary Lou' in 1972?

2 The court musician to the Duke of Mantua, which Italian composer of around 50 operas lived from 1671 to 1750 and was an influence on J.S. Bach? His 'Adagio in G Minor' is very famous.

3 The orchestral rhapsody 'Espana' is the best known work of which 19th century French composer?

4 Which member of the Rolling Stones broke both his legs in a car accident in November 1990?

5 Which alpine flower is the title of a song featured in the movie 'The Sound Of Music'?

6 What was the first solo single by ex-Spice Girl Geri Halliwell, which was a hit in 1999?

7 Which Barry Manilow song title is the name of a famous beach in Rio de Janeiro?

8 What is both the name given to a type of West Indian ballad and the name of Jacques Cousteau's famous boat?

9 Who played rock 'n' roll icon Tina Turner in the 1993 movie 'What's Love Got to Do With It?'?

10 The music for the nursery rhyme 'Twinkle Twinkle Little Star' comes from an adaptation of an early French tune by which famous composer?

Sport

1. Canadian, James Naismith is credited with inventing which sport in the 1890s?

2. Beating Australia 20-17, in which year did England win the Rugby World Cup?

3. What were the forenames of the Spinks brothers, who both won boxing gold medals at the 1976 Montreal Olympics?

4. Who, in 1998, equalled Björn Borg's record for the greatest number of consecutive Wimbledon Men's Singles wins (five)?

5. After the 1952 Olympics, China did not compete for several years. In which year did China next partake in the Games?

6. A statue of which pop star once stood outside the Fulham F.C. football stadium in London?

7. In 1985, who was the first-ever player to be sent off the pitch in an F.A. football cup final?

8. Having been awarded the 1976 Winter Olympic Games, which U.S. city decided to withdraw?

9. Which British cyclist won the 2013 Tour de France?

10. Giacomo Agostini and Barry Sheene were world champions in which sport?

General Knowledge

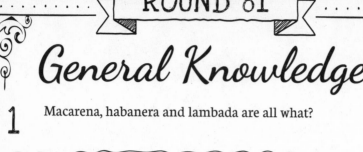

1 Macarena, habanera and lambada are all what?

2 Which English artist is best known for painting 'The Monarch of the Glen' and, as a sculptor, for the bronze lions in Trafalgar Square?

3 Which American abolitionist was executed in 1859 after raiding a government arsenal at Harpers Ferry in Virginia, intending to arm black slaves and start a revolt?

4 Which U.S. state is also known as the Buckeye State?

5 Which African country borders both Tanzania and Angola?

6 What was invented by Sir James Dewar in 1892?

7 Whose equation states that E equals MC squared?

8 A native to South America, which fruit is commonly eaten as a vegetable, and was once called the love apple?

9 Which singer, whose hits include "I Wanna Dance With Somebody" and "I'm Every Woman", was found dead in her hotel bathtub in February 2012?

10 Of which country is Asunción the capital city?

The Human Body

1 What is the technical name for weakening of the bones?

2 Which nerve connects the brain with the heart, lungs, stomach and gut?

3 In which gland can the islets of Langerhans be found?

4 By what name is the fungal infection tinea pedis more commonly known?

5 By what more familiar term is the habit, bruxism (often done whilst asleep) more commonly known?

6 The 'Kenny method', named after Australian nurse Elizabeth Kenny, was used as a treatment for which medical condition?

7 Which acute viral disease particularly associated with children is also called rubeola?

8 What form of laryngitis occurs most commonly in children under five years of age?

9 In which part of the body can one find the metacarpals and the phalanges?

10 Which part of the eye varies in size to regulate the amount of light passing to the retina?

Poetry

1. Which British poet and scholar of Greek and Latin wrote a cycle of poems under the collective title of 'A Shropshire Lad'?

2. Which Italian poet wrote the libretti for Mozart's 'Don Giovanni' and 'Cosi Fan Tutte'?

3. What is the title of the Clement Moore poem that begins "'Twas the night before Christmas"?

4. Which American poet wrote 'Hugh Selwyn' and 'Homage to Sextus Propertius'?

5. Which English poet wrote 'V' and 'The Gaze of the Gorgon'?

6. Which nonsense poem by Lewis Carroll is subtitled 'An Agony in Eight Fits'?

7. The superstition about a bird which brings bad luck forms the theme of the 'Rime of The Ancient Mariner' by Samuel Taylor Coleridge. What is the name of the bird?

8. Which British poet wrote the volume of poems entitled 'Look, Stranger!'?

9. Which Italian poet wrote 'The Divine Comedy'?

10. Which novelist and poet did Ezra Pound compare to "vile scum on a pond"?

Entertainment

1 Which novelist was a deputy inspector in the New York customs office in the middle to late 19th century?

2 In 1964, which French writer was awarded, but declined to accept the Nobel Prize for Literature?

3 In 1943, American playwright Eugene O'Neill became the father-in-law of a man who was only six months his junior and a lot more famous worldwide. Who was that man?

4 Name the American author who wrote the trilogy of novels – 'Rabbit Run', 'Rabbit Redux' and 'Rabbit Is Rich'.

5 That 'Rabbit' trilogy spans 30 years in the life of a salesman. What type of salesman?

6 Which reclusive American actor published his autobiography 'Songs My Mother Taught Me' in 1994?

7 Created by American writer Rex Stout, who was the phenomenally fat private eye who was assisted by a character called Archie Godwin?

8 In October 1996, which Oscar-winning duo were lost for 48 hours in the back of a New York taxi?

9 Name the New York newspaper first published on 10 April 1841.

10 In 1997, who won a Grammy award in the Best Spoken Word or Non-Musical Category for her recorded version of the best selling book about child rearing, 'It Takes A Village'?

General Knowledge

1. Which explorer discovered Newfoundland in 1497?

2. Which one of the following is not a satellite of Jupiter: Callisto, Hyperion, Europa?

3. To which family of plants does the cyclamen genus belong?

4. Which part of the body is inflamed if one suffers from encephalitis?

5. Which British physicist discovered the electron and invented the mass spectrometer?

6. Which great circle lies around the Earth at a latitude of zero degrees?

7. Which unit of measurement is equivalent to an explosion of one million tons of T.N.T.?

8. What memorial to Hans Andersen stands in Copenhagen harbour?

9. Which region of Spain is known as the 'land of Don Quixote and Sancho Panza'?

10. Who was the car manufacturer arrested on cocaine smuggling charges in 1982?

Rivers and Mountains

1. In which South American country can the River Xingu be found?

2. In which country is the mountain range known as the Apennines?

3. Mount Columbia, Mount Assiniboine and North Twin Peak are all mountains located in which country?

4. Which is the longest river in Russia?

5. Which river did George Washington cross on Christmas night in 1776?

6. The Texas city of El Paso lies on which major river?

7. Which U.S. city is bisected by the Santa Monica mountains?

8. What is the highest mountain in the continent of North America?

9. What is the longest river in Italy?

10. The Dolomites are a section of which major mountain range?

Religion

1 In which year did the Reverend Jim Jones lead the mass suicide of over 900 of his followers in Guyana?

2 What name is given to the Hindu custom of self-immolation of widows on their husbands' funeral pyres?

3 Who is the spiritual leader (currently in exile) of the Tibetan people?

4 What name is given to the act of depriving a person of membership of a church?

5 Which Jewish festival celebrates the flight of the Israelites from Egyptian slavery?

6 What name is given to the religious dramas usually performed on Good Friday?

7 What colour are the flat broad-brimmed hats worn by cardinals?

8 Which Indian religion and philosophy was founded by Vardhamana?

9 What name is given to the marks which appear on the body of a living person, that resemble the five wounds that Christ received at the crucifixion?

10 Which religious sect believes that Haile Selassie will arrange for the deliverance of the black races of the world?

Mythology

1. Name the rock in the River Rhine noted for its echo and association with a legend concerning a water nymph whose singing lured sailors to destruction.

2. The sorceress Circe turned the followers of Odysseus into what kind of animals?

3. Vulcan was the Roman god of fire. Also the god of crafts, who was the Greek god of fire?

4. In Greek mythology, the Pleiades were the seven daughters of which Titan?

5. The ancient Egyptian goddess Hathor, the goddess of fertility and love, was usually portrayed as which creature?

6. In the mythology of native Americans, what did they call their 'Great Spirit'?

7. Who was the ancient Egyptian god of the dead, renewal and rebirth?

8. In Germanic legend, who was the queen of Issland who had superhuman strength and vowed to marry only he who would prove himself stronger?

9. In Norse mythology, what was the name of the mischief-making god who had the ability to change his shape and sex? He was imprisoned in a cave for the murder of Balder.

10. In medieval Jewish folklore, what name was given to an image or automaton brought to life by a charm? They were supposed to have been used as servants by rabbis.

Food and Drink

1. What are the three main ingredients of rumbledethumps, a traditional dish from the Scottish borders?

2. In January 2009, which British prime minister submitted a recipe for rumbledethumps to a cookbook for Donaldson's School for the Deaf, describing it as his favourite food?

3. Generally created from a Curaçao liqueur base, of what colour is the liqueur Parfait Amour?

4. Now primarily associated with coffee, which company was established in 1753 in Joure, Holland?

5. Skyr is a dairy product similar to yogurt, and unique to which country, where it has been made for hundreds of years?

6. Originating in eastern Europe, what is the main ingredient of borscht soup?

7. The cherry-flavoured beer, Kriek Lambic originated in which European country?

8. The South American tree 'Bertholletia excelsa' yields which popular nuts?

9. What type of foodstuff are linguini, orecchiette and strangozzi?

10. What dish was invented in the 1890s by Auguste Escoffier at the Savoy Hotel in London, in honour of the Australian soprano after whom it is named?

General Knowledge

1. In the 2003 invasion of Iraq, the U.S. military developed a pack of playing cards to help troops identify wanted Iraqis. On which card was Saddam Hussein's picture?

2. Killed in an accident at the 1994 San Marino Grand Prix, what was the nationality of former motor racing driver Ayrton Senna?

3. What do sumo wrestlers throw into the ring prior to a match?

4. Typically, how many strings has a ukulele?

5. What is the capital of Tasmania?

6. Named after four Renaissance artists, the Teenage Mutant Ninja Turtles are: Leonardo, Michelangelo, Raphael, and which other?

7. The word 'lupine' relates to which animals?

8. In the stories by Carlo Collodi, which character was carved by a woodcarver named Geppetto in a small Italian village?

9. How many plane faces has a dodecahedron?

10. In which river was Jesus baptized?

Movies

1   In which 1938 movie did Bette Davis win her second Oscar playing a tempestuous Southern belle opposite Henry Fonda?

2   In which 1992 movie do Tom Cruise and Nicole Kidman sail for America and seek their destiny in the 1893 Oklahoma gold rush?

3   Which 1964 Stanley Kubrick movie starring Peter Sellers had the alternative title, 'How I Learned to Stop Worrying and Love the Bomb'?

4   In which 1972 movie does a crewman say to the Captain (Leslie Neilson): "I never saw anything like it – an enormous wall of water coming towards us"?

5   Which actress slaps Lee Marvin repeatedly in the 1967 cult movie 'Point Blank'?

6   Which actress starred in the movie 'Barbarella'?

7   What kind of imaginary creature is Jodie in the movie 'The Amityville Horror'?

8   Who plays the title role in the 2000 movie 'Shaft', a re-working of the 1970's classic starring Richard Roundtree?

9   Who directed the movies 'M*A*S*H', 'The Long Goodbye', 'Nashville' and 'Pret-A-Porter'?

10 Based on Marvel comic characters, can you name the movie released in 2000 starring Patrick Stewart?

Language

1. The word for which form of physical exercise is derived from the Greek words for air and life?

2. What is the meaning of the word 'rugose'?

3. What is the meaning of the prefix 'kara' in Japanese words such as karate and karaoke?

4. What does the Latin phrase 'exempli gratia' mean in English?

5. What are you if you are referred to as 'sinistral'?

6. What word meaning a person who suffers death rather than denounce their belief in a cause or religion, comes from the Latin for 'witness'?

7. What word means 'related to the culture, language and peoples of Spain and other areas influenced by Spain'?

8. What would a Maori be doing if he performed a 'haka'?

9. What, in a North African town, is the Kasbah?

10. Which soft, fine net material, used for making veils and dresses, takes its name from the town in the Correze department of France where it was first made?

Science

1. Which electrical component consists of two conductor or semi-conductor plates separated by a dielectric?

2. How are fluorine, chlorine, bromine, iodine and astatine collectively known?

3. Which English agriculturalist is best known for his invention of the seed drill in 1701?

4. Which precious metal is represented by the symbol Pt?

5. Who reputedly showed that the rate of fall of a body is independent of its mass by dropping weights from the Leaning Tower of Pisa?

6. Which Polish-born chemist discovered radium and polonium?

7. Hydrolysis is the reaction of a chemical compound with which liquid?

8. Which English inventor devised the spinning jenny, a machine which was named after his daughter?

9. A dilute solution of which kind of acid is used to make vinegar?

10. Which mathematical term describes a quantity larger than any that can be specified?

History

1 Which black American singer and actor had his passport withdrawn by the U.S. government in 1950?

2 Which American social scientist coined the term 'conspicuous consumption' in 'The Theory of the Leisure Class'?

3 Which French leader called the English a "nation of shopkeepers"?

4 Who was the director of the F.B.I. from 1924 to 1972?

5 Which Greek philosopher was appointed by Philip of Macedon to tutor his 13-year-old son Alexander?

6 What was the name of the imperial Roman bodyguard created by Augustus in 27 B.C.?

7 Which rare genetic disorder is believed to have been the cause of the madness of George III of Britain?

8 Which American general's famous last words were: 'They couldn't hit an elephant at this dist....'?

9 From which of the Marshall Islands were the population relocated on the island of Rongerik in 1946 due to U.S. nuclear testing?

10 Which year saw the death of former U.S. president Lyndon Johnson, and the kidnapping of Paul Getty's grandson?

General Knowledge

1 What number is denoted by the Roman numeral 'D'?

2 Which country hosted the 2014 Winter Olympics?

3 Which prime numbers comes between 283 and 307?

4 In which year did Elvis Presley die?

5 What name is given to a device used by musicians that marks time at a selected rate by giving a regular tick?

6 Which African country is closest to Spain?

7 Which gas is most abundant in the air we breathe?

8 Which country has the international licence plate country code AUS?

9 What sort of glassware has a name meaning 'a thousand flowers' in Italian?

10 In Greek mythology, who was the beautiful youth who rejected the nymph Echo and fell in love with his own reflection in a pool?

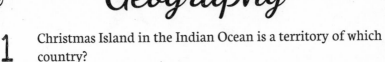

Geography

1. Christmas Island in the Indian Ocean is a territory of which country?

2. Which four countries share borders with Pakistan?

3. Of which country is Astana the capital?

4. Which river forms much of the border between China's Heilongjiang province and south-eastern Siberia?

5. Which sea lies between the Barents Sea (to the west) and the Laptev Sea (to the east)?

6. Hokkaido is the second largest island of which country?

7. Which capital city has the volcano Pichincha looming over it, to the west?

8. Which is the easternmost country of Africa traversed by the equator?

9. In which city is Sugarloaf Mountain and the giant statue 'Christ the Redeemer'?

10. Completed in November 2010, 'Christ the King' is a statue of Jesus Christ in Świebodzin, a town in the west of which country?

Jazz

1 Who was called the 'Queen of Soul' and 'Lady Soul'?

2 Which American jazz singer was born Ruth Lee Jones?

3 Who composed 'Body and Soul'?

4 Who composed 'Twelfth Street Rag'?

5 Who composed 'St. Louis Blues'?

6 Who sang the blues before anyone else? And received the homely nickname of 'Ma'?

7 Who was called the 'Empress of the Blues'?

8 Who was called the 'Queen of the Blues'?

9 Which English-born saxophonist and clarinettist of Jamaican background formed two bands: The Jazz Warriors and World's First Saxophone Posse?

10 Who is the English electric guitarist and bandleader with impressive speed and rhythm technique, whose music developed into a synthesis of Afro-American and Indian music?

Literature

1. Which Greek comic dramatist wrote 'Lysistrata' and 'The Frogs'?

2. Which Italian author wrote 'The Triumph of Death'?

3. Which Russian dramatist wrote 'Uncle Vanya' and 'The Cherry Orchard'?

4. Which British novelist wrote 'The Spy Who Came in from the Cold'?

5. Who wrote 'Silas Marner' and 'The Mill on the Floss'?

6. Who wrote 'My Cousin Rachel' and 'Rebecca'?

7. Which Russian writer wrote the novel 'Anna Karenina'?

8. Who wrote 'The Golden Notebook' and 'The Good Terrorist'?

9. Which American novelist wrote 'Moby Dick'?

10. Who wrote the novel 'English Passengers'?

Sport and Games

1 How many events are there in a decathlon?

2 In the 1930s, the American company Bally were forerunners in the development of which games machine?

3 On which American city was the first Monopoly game based?

4 Which popular toy is based on a weapon from the Philippines whose name means 'come come'?

5 Which horse race run annually at Aintree, England is the most famous steeplechase in the world?

6 Jai alai is a version of which game?

7 What nationality is the former skier Franz Klammer?

8 What name is given to a score of two under par for a hole in golf?

9 From which card game did bridge evolve?

10 What name is given to the declarer's partner in a hand of bridge?

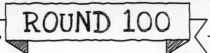
General Knowledge

1   In which London church is the Tomb of the Unknown Warrior?

2   Which of the signs of the Zodiac is the only one represented by an inanimate object?

3   What pigment substance makes plants green?

4   Carolyn Davidson created which ubiquitous brand logo in 1971?

5   What romantic and unrealistic state translates as Wolkenkuckucksheim in German?

6   What is the name of the nuclear power-plant rendered unsafe in the Japanese tsunami of 2011?

7   Who played the role of James Bond in 'Die Another Day'?

8   On a laundry label, what does a circle contained in a square indicate?

9   Batavia is a former name of which Asian capital city?

10 The name of which North African city comes from the Spanish for 'white house'?

History

1 Which era of geological time comprises the Cambrian, Ordovician, Silurian, Devonian, Carboniferous and Permian periods?

2 Which Carthaginian general provoked the Second Punic War with Rome?

3 Of which war was the Battle of Inkerman a decisive battle?

4 Which country was ruled by Casimir the Great from 1333 to 1370?

5 Which Serbian secret society was responsible for the assassination of the archduke Francis Ferdinand in 1914?

6 Which 15th-16th century Portuguese explorer led the first sea-borne expedition to India?

7 In which country did the Red Brigade kill Aldo Moro in 1978?

8 Which American poet and critic broadcast fascist propaganda during World War II?

9 Which Venetian traveller dictated an account of his travels to the Far East in the 13th century?

10 By what name is Roman scholar Gaius Plinius Secundus, author of the encyclopedia 'Natural History', better known?

Science Fiction

1 'From the Earth to the Moon' was a very early SF novel by which author?

2 Which early SF novel tells of a future Earth where humans have evolved into two species, the Eloi and the Morlocks?

3 Which Russian-born American author wrote the 'Foundation' series of novels?

4 "Keep watching the skies" were the words uttered at the end of which SF film of 1951? The film was remade in 1982, with many graphic scenes that shocked audiences.

5 "The drought had lasted now for ten million years, and the reign of the terrible lizards had long since ended" is the opening sentence of which famous SF novel of 1968?

6 Based on the novel by Walter Tevis, which film of 1976, starring David Bowie, tells of an alien visitor's attempts to find a way to save his own planet from catastrophic drought?

7 Who wrote the best-selling novels 'The Moon is a Harsh Mistress' and 'Starship Troopers'?

8 'The Gods of Mars' is a SF novel published in 1918. More famous for his 'Tarzan' novels, who wrote it?

9 Who wrote the short story collection, 'The Martian Chronicles'?

10 Which Canadian author received the first Arthur C. Clarke award, in 1987, for her novel 'The Handmaid's Tale'?

Around the Islands

1. Of which European country is the island of Lesbos a part?

_____

2. To which European country do the Cyclades islands belong?

_____

3. Of which Caribbean island is Castries the capital?

_____

4. In which group of islands is Rarotonga?

_____

5. On which island is Pico de Teide, the highest mountain in Spain, situated?

_____

6. Which state of the U.S.A. occupies a chain of over 20 volcanic islands in the Pacific Ocean?

_____

7. Which Canadian island is known as 'the graveyard of the Atlantic'?

_____

8. In which ocean are the Marshall Islands situated?

_____

9. On which Italian island was the movie 'Cinema Paradiso' set?

_____

10. The island of Bali is part of which Asian country?

Pop Music

1 Who released 'Brass in Pocket' in 1979?

_____

2 In 1982 Simple Minds had a hit single with ___?

_____

3 Which group released 'Everybody Wants To Rule The World' in 1983?

_____

4 Who had a winner with 'Teardrops' in 1988?

_____

5 Which group brought out 'Hangin' Tough' in 1989?

_____

6 In 1982 Paul McCartney and Stevie Wonder collaborated on ___?

_____

7 Which group first released 'Don't Dream It's Over'?

_____

8 In 1981 'Stand and Deliver' was a hit for ___?

_____

9 'Ghost Town' was a British number one hit single for ___?

_____

10 'Tha Carter III' was one of the biggest albums of 2008, by which rap artist?

General Knowledge

1. The Gulf of Venice lies at the northern part of which sea?

2. If you travel east from Cheyenne in Wyoming which is the next state you would enter?

3. The remains of which ancient city near Naples was rediscovered in 1748?

4. What, in Spanish-speaking countries, is a bodega?

5. Montgomery Ward was an American pioneer of what form of retailing?

6. From 1930 until 1971 what was the world's tallest building?

7. How many degrees are there in a right angle?

8. Which solid provides the biggest volume for its surface area?

9. What is the only number that cannot be represented by a Roman numeral?

10. Which U.S. air strategist advocated a separate air force ranking equally with the army and navy? On the creation of the United States Air Force as an independent service in 1947 he was the first to hold the rank of general of the air force.

ROUND 106

Nature

1 Magnetite or lodestone is a form of which metal's oxide?

_____

2 What is a honey locust?

_____

3 What is an instrument for measuring atmospheric pressure called?

_____

4 Which British environmental pressure group was formed in 1971?

_____

5 What sort of creature is a burbot?

_____

6 How many pairs of limbs does a crab have?

_____

7 What sort of creature is a crake?

_____

8 What name is given to the scientific study of plants?

_____

9 By what name do we know the spider Latrodectus mactans?

_____

10 Which green pigment present in organisms is capable of photosynthesis?

Religion

1. Which Italian town was the birthplace of Saint Francis, the founder of the Franciscan Order?

2. Which Korean businessman founded the Unification Church in 1954?

3. Which town in central southern Turkey was the birthplace of St. Paul?

4. Which nun founded the Order of the Missionaries of Charity in Calcutta, and received the 1979 Nobel Peace Prize?

5. Who is the patron saint of travellers?

6. Who is the patron saint of hunters?

7. What date is Saint Patrick's Day?

8. Which religious movement was founded in New York in 1848 by John Thomas?

9. In Tibetan Buddhism, which title is held by the chief abbot who ranks second to the Dalai Lama?

10. Which three-leaved plant was Saint Patrick said to have used to explain the Holy Trinity?

Crime

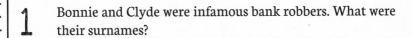

1 Bonnie and Clyde were infamous bank robbers. What were their surnames?

_____

2 Which Latin phrase means in the very act of committing a crime; red-handed?

_____

3 What S is a writ requiring a person to appear and give evidence in court?

_____

4 What name is given to the duplication of banknotes with the intention to defraud?

_____

5 Which word describes criminal damage committed by fire?

_____

6 By what first name was American gangster Benjamin Siegel known?

_____

7 What nationality was Abdul Baset Ali al-Megrahi who was convicted of the Lockerbie bombing?

_____

8 What was the name of the doctor who worked in Cheshire, England, jailed for life in 2000, and known to have killed more than 200 of his patients?

_____

9 What nickname was given to the unknown killer of prostitutes in London during the late 19th century?

_____

10 What remedy against unlawful imprisonment is in the form of a writ requiring a detained person to be brought before a court?

History

1. In which type of plane was U.S. pilot Gary Powers shot down over Russia in 1960?

2. Which Russian was the first woman to fly in space, in 1963?

3. Which island was invaded by Turkish troops in 1974, leading to the division of the island into north and south zones?

4. Who was the first U.S. president to be elected in the 20th century?

5. A German U-boat sank which passenger ship on 7th May 1915, killing 1,200?

6. Engelbert Dollfuss, assassinated by the Nazis in 1934, was the Chancellor of which country?

7. In 1525, which famous religious figure married Katharina von Bora, defying the Roman Catholic Church's decree for celibacy amongst the priesthood?

8. Which Italian explorer's name was derived to name 'America'?

9. The 1811 Massacre of the Mamelukes took place in which North African city?

10. What was the year of President Abraham Lincoln's assassination?

General Knowledge

1   Which play by Arthur Miller is based on the Salem witch trials of 1692-63?

2   The events on board the British naval vessel HMS 'Compass Rose' is the basis of the plot in which novel by Nicholas Monsarrat?

3   The juice of which fruit is mixed with an equal amount of gin or vodka to make a gimlet cocktail?

4   Mombasa is the main seaport of which African country?

5   What general name is given to trees that produce their seeds in cones?

6   In which Italian city is the famous La Scala opera house?

7   Published in 1755, who compiled a 'Dictionary of the English Language'?

8   Mistakenly bombed by American planes on April Fool's Day 1944, the city of Schaffhausen is in which neutral country?

9   Ornithology is the study of which group of animals?

10 What middle name is shared by ex U.S. president Bill Clinton and British politician William Hague?

Classical Music

1. How many overtures to 'Leonora', the original title of his opera 'Fidelio', did Beethoven write?

2. Who was the composer of the operas 'Manon' and 'Le Cid'?

3. Richard Wagner only composed one comic opera. What is its name?

4. What is the name of the beautiful and famous intermezzo from Act II of the opera 'Thais' by Massenet?

5. The overture is the best known piece from the light opera 'Donna Diana'. Who composed it?

6. Who composed the operetta 'The Beautiful Galatea' based on the Greek Myth of Pygmalion and Galatea?

7. Who composed the operettas 'Die Fledermaus' (The Bat) and 'The Gypsy Baron'?

8. Who composed the operettas 'Frederica', 'The Merry Widow', 'The Land of Smiles' and many more?

9. The 'Egmont' overture is the prelude to the incidental music to Goethe's tragedy of the same name. Who was the composer?

10. Who was the composer of the 'Festival Overture 1812'?

Geography

1 Which Canadian province's name means 'New Scotland'?

_____

2 Which Russian lake is the largest lake in Europe?

_____

3 Which South African province was formerly known as Natal?

_____

4 What is the smaller of the two main islands of New Zealand?

_____

5 Which two Asian countries are connected by the Khyber Pass?

_____

6 In which mountain range is the Matterhorn?

_____

7 On what river does Rome stand?

_____

8 Of which Canadian province is Edmonton the capital?

_____

9 Saint Thomas, Saint John and Saint Croix are the three islands of which U.S. island group in the Lesser Antilles?

_____

10 Which is the world's northernmost capital city?

Literature

1. Who wrote 'The Portrait of a Lady' and 'Washington Square'?

2. Which children's author created the characters Peter Rabbit, Jemima Puddle-Duck and Mrs Tittlemouse?

3. Which German novelist wrote 'Buddenbrooks' and 'Doctor Faustus'?

4. Which American author wrote 'The Fall of the House of Usher' and 'The Murders in the Rue Morgue'?

5. Which British novelist won the Booker Prize for 'The Sea, The Sea'?

6. Which French dramatist wrote 'Andromaque' and 'Britannicus'?

7. Who wrote the Booker Prize-winning novel upon which the movie 'The English Patient' is based?

8. Which American author wrote the novels 'Exodus' and 'QB VII'?

9. Who wrote the novel series 'A Dance to the Music of Time'?

10. Can you name the South African author of the novels 'Elephant Song' and 'A Time To Die'?

Sport

1 What name is given to a grade of proficiency in martial arts such as judo and karate?

2 What name is given to the knocking down of all ten pins with the first ball in tenpin bowling?

3 On which British river does the annual boat race between Oxford and Cambridge Universities take place?

4 Which ancient Chinese martial art was popularized in the West by movie-star Bruce Lee?

5 Which equestrian discipline is the first part of a three-day event?

6 Who headed the syndicate that owned the first non-American yacht to win the America's Cup?

7 What name is given to a score of one under par for a hole in golf?

8 What name is given to a score of one over par for a hole in golf?

9 Which German driver crashed out of his home Grand Prix at the first bend in 2000?

10 Which sport involves the snatch and the clean and jerk?

General Knowledge

1. In which city would you find the Cathedral of St. Basil, and the Rossiya Hotel?

2. In which American city would you find the Seagram Building?

3. In which Eastern European city would you find the cathedral of St. Vitus and the Bedrich Smetana Museum?

4. Which year saw the development of the first H-bomb, the death of American writer Sinclair Lewis, and Greta Garbo become a U.S. citizen?

5. The trumpeter, which breeds in North America, is the largest kind of which water bird?

6. The name of which gas is derived from a Greek word meaning 'sun'?

7. What method of photocopying was developed in the 1930s by Chester F Carlson?

8. Which oriental philosopher said: "A man who has committed a mistake and doesn't correct it is committing another mistake"?

9. Danny Kaye, who died in 1987, worked tirelessly as an ambassador for which organization?

10. With whom did George Burns form a comedy team in 1923, and marry in 1926?

Computing

1   Which numbering system, used in the operation of computers, uses only two digits, 0 and 1?

2   What W is the name given to an unauthorized independent program that penetrates computers and replicates itself?

3   What does the acronym ROM stand for?

4   What term describes a permanent record of work done on a computer in the form of a paper printout?

5   What term is used for exploring the Internet?

6   On the Internet, what does the acronym HTTP stand for?

7   What word, meaning the fifth element, is applied to Intel's fifth generation of sophisticated high-speed microprocessor?

8   What S is the name given to a computer that shares its resources and information with other computers on a network?

9   Which computer peripheral was first conceived and designed by Douglas Engelbart?

10 What C is a tiny wafer of silicon containing miniature electric circuits which can store millions of bits of information?

Movies

1. Which Milcho Manchevski movie about a war photographer won the Golden Lion Award at Venice in 1994?

2. Which 1995 Kevin Costner movie was rumoured to have cost £133m, making it the most expensive movie yet made at that time?

3. Which 1995 horror movie starred Ben Kingsley as a scientist and Natasha Henstridge as an alien desperate to mate?

4. Which 1995 Disney blockbuster was loosely based on the life of a 17th century native American princess?

5. Who won a Best Actor Oscar in 1971 for his role as Popeye Doyle in 'The French Connection'?

6. In the 1995 movie 'Waterworld', who played Deacon, the villainous leader of the Smokers?

7. Which 1994 Australian movie based on Chekhov's 'Uncle Vanya' starred Greta Scacchi and Sam Neill?

8. Which Hollywood star said "Young actors love me. They think that if big slob can make it, there's a chance for us."?

9. In which 1990 movie does Jeremy Irons play the aristocratic Claus von Bülow, accused of attempting to murder his wife, played by Glenn Close?

10. Which actress/dancer (born Johnnie Lucille Collier in 1919) frequently stole the show with her tap dancing routines in several musicals, including 'On the Town'?

History

1. Name the king of Macedonia, father of Alexander the Great, who was assassinated in 336 B.C.

2. Which U.S. lawman killed Billy the Kid?

3. What is the oldest university in the United States of America?

4. In which war did American forces battle at Pork Chop Hill?

5. Which Norse explorer is regarded by some to be the first European to reach the shores of North America?

6. Which American general directed the recapture of the S.W. Pacific as Allied Commander in World War II?

7. Which Italian dictator formed an alliance with Hitler in 1936?

8. Which two Middle Eastern countries fought each other in a war that began in 1980?

9. Which region of Canada near the Alaskan border became famous when gold was discovered there in 1896?

10. Can you give the surname of two explorers - one an American with the first names Frederick Albert and the other British with the first name James?

The Answer's a Number

1 What telephone number is associated with a 1940 swing jazz song recorded by Glenn Miller and His Orchestra?

2 What is the only number that equals twice the sum of its digits?

3 What number is represented by the Roman numerals XCIV?

4 What is the total number of spots (or pips) on a standard cubical die?

5 How many white keys are on a standard upright piano?

6 At the start of a game of chess, how many pawns are placed onto the board?

7 A typical violin has how many strings?

8 In 'The Hitchhiker's Guide to the Galaxy' by Douglas Adams, what number is "The Answer to the Ultimate Question of Life, the Universe, and Everything"?

9 Triskaidekaphobia is the unreasoned fear of which number?

10 If a couple are celebrating their pearl wedding anniversary, for how many years have they been married?

General Knowledge

1. What surname is shared by the rock star whose real name is Vincent Furnier and the author of 'The Last Of The Mohicans'?

2. The chrysanthemum is the national symbol for which country?

3. Which U.S. state has the lowest population?

4. In which American city would you find the John Hancock Center?

5. Which Swiss psychiatrist gave his name to a personality test involving inkblots?

6. In which Swiss city are the International Red Cross and the World Health Organization based?

7. What nationality was the pioneering psychoanalyst Sigmund Freud?

8. Which large Central and South American birds were greatly admired by pre-Colombian cultures and are found in their art and mythology?

9. In the metric system, what word/prefix stands for one-millionth?

10. Which scale of wind velocity was named after a 19th century English admiral?

Lakes

1. Which lake is the largest of the Great Lakes in North America?

2. Which three countries share Lake Constance?

3. Which lake is sited at the lowest point on the planet?

4. Near to which Russian city is Lake Ladoga?

5. What is the world's largest lake?

6. In which country is Lake Eyre? Its salt flats were the scene of several land-speed world record attempts.

7. Lake Van is the largest lake of which Middle East country?

8. Named after a former leader of the country, which lake was created by the building of Egypt's High Aswan Dam?

9. Located in Siberia, what is the world's deepest lake?

10. The Great Bear Lake and Great Slave Lake are located in which country?

Art

1. Which painter is famous for his nightmarish depictions of religious concepts, such as 'The Garden of Earthly Delights'?

2. Which Dutch artist, who, with his manipulations of perspective created celebrated works such as 'The Waterfall' and 'House of Stairs'?

3. Who painted 'The Night Watch', one of the art world's most famous works?

4. In which European city is the Rijksmuseum, an art gallery which houses the 'Night Watch'?

5. What is the name by which Italian painter Jacopo Robusti is better known?

6. Which family of Flemish painters included Jan, Pieter the Elder and Pieter the Younger?

7. Which Florentine painter created 'Mars and Venus' and 'The Birth of Venus'?

8. What was the adopted name of painter Domenico Theotocopoulos, who was born on Crete in 1541 and died in Spain in 1614?

9. Which American architect designed the Guggenheim Museum in New York City?

10. Which famous Paris art gallery houses Leonardo da Vinci's 'Mona Lisa'?

Television

1 In the 1970s TV series Harry O starring David Janssen, what did the O stand for?

2 In July 1992, which of Puccini's operas was broadcast live on worldwide TV, being performed at the exact times and in the locations specified in the opera?

3 Which actress played Mindy opposite Robin Williams' Mork in the TV series 'Mork And Mindy'?

4 Who played Steve Keller in the TV series 'The Streets Of San Francisco' before becoming a Hollywood star?

5 Name the character played by Doug McClure in the TV western series 'The Virginian'.

6 In the 1970s TV western series 'Alias Smith And Jones', was Hannibal Heyes known as Smith or Jones?

7 In the vintage TV show 'The Munsters', what type of creature was Grandpa's pet, Igor?

8 What was the name of the racing car driven by Dick Dastardly in the TV cartoon series 'The Wacky Races'?

9 Which American astronomer presented the television series 'Cosmos' and wrote the novel 'Contact'?

10 Who played Roseanne's husband in the American TV series?

The Animal Kingdom

1 Which breed of hunting dog, for which records date from 3600 B.C., is known to have been used to hunt the gazelle and is, therefore, sometimes called the gazelle hound?

2 What sort of creature is a Russian Blue?

3 The Great Gray owl is the provincial bird of which Canadian province?

4 The name of which common American nocturnal bird, which spends its day resting on fallen leaves, describes its distinctive call?

5 The rhea of South America closely resembles which bird native to Africa?

6 Which nocturnal and flightless bird is only found in New Zealand and adjacent small islands?

7 What sort of creature is a klipspringer?

8 Which order of mammals includes kangaroos, wallabies, bandicoots and opossums?

9 The peregrine is a type of which bird of prey?

10 Which dog, thought to have originated in Germany about the middle of the 16th century, is the result of interbreeding between the Irish Wolfhound and the Old-English Mastiff?

General Knowledge

1. During which years did the Korean War take place?

_____

2. Cryptography is the study of what?

_____

3. Known in Britain as a courgette, by what name is this vegetable known in North America and Australia?

_____

4. What is the name for the skull-cap worn by some Jewish men?

_____

5. Which is number one of the Seven Deadly Sins?

_____

6. The Andean and the California vultures are better known by what name?

_____

7. Which Francis Ford Coppola film is based on the novel 'Heart of Darkness' by Joseph Conrad?

_____

8. Connecting the west and east coasts of Scotland, which canal runs via the lochs of the Great Glen?

_____

9. The Japanese drink, sake is made from the fermentation of which staple food crop?

_____

10. Which Swiss-born French architect wrote 'Towards a New Architecture'?

War

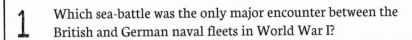

1 Which sea-battle was the only major encounter between the British and German naval fleets in World War I?

2 Which ship launched in 1906 became the basis of battleship design for more than 50 years?

3 What nickname was given to any one of four large German guns produced by the Krupp works in World War I?

4 Which weapon is represented by the initials S.L.C.M.?

5 At which naval battle in the Napoleonic wars was Admiral Nelson killed in the hour of victory?

6 The Hindenburg Line was a defensive barrier built by the Germans in which war?

7 By what name was the day in 1944 on which the Allied invasion of Normandy was launched from Britain known?

8 What name was given to the Nazi regime that succeeded the Weimar Republic and ended with Germany's defeat in World War II?

9 By what nickname was World War I German air ace Manfred von Richthofen usually known?

10 Which U.S. soldier commanded II Corps in Tunisia and Sicily in 1943, in 1944 he commanded U.S. troops at the Normandy invasion and later led the U.S. 12th Army through France?

Cooking and Food

1. Which type of Indian cooking involves baking food in a clay oven?

2. From which American state does the traditional dish, Gumbo originate?

3. Emmental and Gruyère cheeses come from which country?

4. Certain parts of which flower are used to make the spice, saffron?

5. The traditional dish, couscous, originated from the northern part of which continent?

6. Laying strips of bacon across meat or poultry during roasting to moisten the meat, is known as what?

7. What is the name for the breakfast dish of rice, hard-boiled eggs and flaked cooked fish?

8. With ingredients including apples, celery and walnuts, which salad gets its name from a New York hotel?

9. Which traditional Spanish dish is made from rice, chicken, seafood and vegetables?

10. What kind of nut is coated with sugar or syrup to make marron glacé?

Mythology

1 According to Greek mythology, which woman had a box which, when opened, released all the varieties of evil and retained only Hope?

2 In antiquity, which Greek town was the principal sanctuary and oracle of Apollo?

3 Which son of Percival in Arthurian legend is the title of a Wagner opera?

4 Who was the Greek goddess of agriculture?

5 Which mythical nation of female warriors were believed by the ancient Greeks to have invaded Attica?

6 According to Greek mythology, which daughter of King Agenor of Tyre was carried to Crete by Zeus in the form of a bull?

7 Which mythical monster is also called a yeti?

8 Who was the Norse god of thunder, after whom Thursday is named?

9 Which one of the following days of the week is not named after an ancient god: Monday, Tuesday, Wednesday?

10 What horse was ridden by Bellerophon when he slew the Chimera?

Entertainment

1. What is the name of the cartoon strip created by Chic Young and which by the 1960s was syndicated in more than 1500 newspapers throughout the world?

2. Which animated character made his debut in the 1928 cartoon 'Steamboat Willie'?

3. In broadcasting, recording etc., what device is used to transform sound energy into electrical energy?

4. In which New York City street are the majority of the leading commercial theatres situated?

5. By what name was Charles Stratton known when he was publicly exhibited by P.T. Barnum?

6. Which member of a famous family of actors once said: "Hollywood is tied hand and foot to the demands for artificiality of the masses all over the world."?

7. Who, in 1924, composed 'Rhapsody in Blue'?

8. Which rock guitarist had hits with 'Purple Haze' and 'The Wind Cries Mary' in the 1960s?

9. Which pop music idol in 1957 said "Don't Knock the Rock"?

10. Which Hollywood actress and her fiancé Tom Green were saved by the barking of their dog Flossie when fire destroyed their home in February 2001?

General Knowledge

1   Which arm of the Mediterranean Sea lies between Italy, and the Balkan peninsula to the east?

2   Anthony Schaffer's play 'Sleuth' was made into two films: in 1972 and 2007. Which actor starred in both?

3   Which sea was called Pontus Euxinus by the Romans?

4   Who was the manager of The Beatles from 1961 to 1967?

5   In 'Gulliver's Travels', what is the name of the flying island governed by deranged scientists?

6   Mount St. Helens, which erupted spectacularly in 1980, is located in which U.S. state?

7   The Irrawaddy is the principal river of which Asian country?

8   From the Greek for 'fire' and 'measure' which instrument is used to measure very high temperatures?

9   Which king of England was deposed in 1399 and starved to death in Pontefract Castle the following year?

10 Which female lyric poet was born on the Greek island of Lesbos in the 7th century B.C.?

Geography

1. Which is the largest lake in Canada?

2. Which island in Southeast Massachusetts is separated from Cape Cod by Vineyard Sound?

3. Cape Horn is the southern extremity of which South American archipelago?

4. In which U.S. state is Amarillo?

5. The river Niagara flows from Lake Erie to which other of North America's Great Lakes?

6. What is the name of the whirlpool in the Lofoten Islands off Norway?

7. What is the name of the self-governing community belonging to Denmark lying between Scotland and Ireland?

8. Jaffa is a part of which city in Israel which now incorporates its name?

9. In which U.S. state is Daytona Beach?

10. Which is the largest province in Canada?

Literature

1 Which American novelist wrote 'Gentlemen Prefer Blondes'?

_____

2 From which planet do the invaders come in 'The War of the Worlds' by H.G. Wells?

_____

3 Which novel by Thomas Hardy tells the story of Michael Henchard?

_____

4 Which character in 'David Copperfield' by Charles Dickens is famous for his false humility?

_____

5 What was the pen name of Samuel Langhorne Clemens?

_____

6 On whose book was the movie 'Fahrenheit 451' based?

_____

7 What was the name of the lion cub raised by George and Joy Adamson, as recounted in 'Born Free'?

_____

8 Which British zoologist wrote 'The Naked Ape' and 'Manwatching'?

_____

9 Which Japanese novelist and playwright, who committed suicide in 1970, wrote 'Confessions of a Mask'?

_____

10 Which American science-fiction author wrote the novels 'The Martian Chronicles' and 'Something Wicked This Way Comes'?

History

1 What nationality was the explorer, Jedediah Smith?

2 Which Aztec ruler was killed by Spanish conquistadors in 1520?

3 In 1879, which two European countries took control of Egypt?

4 1930 saw the end of British interest in airships after the crash of which craft, on its maiden flight?

5 In which year did the Wall Street Crash occur?

6 After independence in 1957, what did the Gold Coast rename itself?

7 On 21st December 1913, The New York World was the first newspaper to print what kind of puzzle?

8 What feat was claimed by both Robert Peary (1909) and Frederick Cook (1908)?

9 Which queen was the first woman and last monarch of the Habsburg line?

10 Which war began in July 1936 and ended in April 1939?

General Knowledge

1   The summit of the volcano, Chimborazo, located on the Equator, is considered to be the farthest point from the centre of the Earth. In which country is Chimborazo?

2   Meaning 'self-boiling', what is the name of the traditional Russian tea-urn?

3   In Japan, what kind of musical instrument is the samisen?

4   Albert Einstein once said that "If I were not a physicist I would probably have been…" what?

5   In 1610, Galileo discovered the four major moons of which planet?

6   Napoleon Bonaparte's favourite horse was named after which battle of 1800 in northern Italy?

7   Oloroso and Fino are types of which fortified wine?

8   On which island of the Inner Hebrides is Fingal's Cave?

9   Dedicated by President William Taft's widow, Helen, in 1931, in which U.S. city is the Women's Titanic Memorial?

10   Which Arabic-derived word is given to a dried up river bed which floods in each rainy season?

Pop Music

1. 'Boom Boom Pow' was a 2009 big hit for which Los Angeles hip-hop band?

_____

2. In 1987 'Livin' On A Prayer' was a hit single for ___?

_____

3. In 1987, U2 had a big hit called ___?

_____

4. Who declared to the world 'I Want Your Sex' in 1987?

_____

5. 'Don't You Want Me' was a hit for whom?

_____

6. 1983 saw a massive hit with 'Every Breath You Take' for whom?

_____

7. 'Relax' was released in 1984 by which Liverpool group?

_____

8. The Christmas time hit 'Do They Know It's Christmas' was by which collaboration of artists?

_____

9. Which group sang 'Do You Really Want To Hurt Me' in 1983?

_____

10. What was the title of Paul McCartney's hit of 1977?

Sport

1   At the 2012 Summer Olympics in London, which country finished at the top of the medal table?

2   At the 2014 Winter Olympics, which country finished at the top of the medal table?

3   What name is given to a two under par in golf?

4   The Milk Race is a former name of a multi-stage cycling race known today as what?

5   In the game of darts, what is the highest score attainable by one dart?

6   In fencing, three types of weapon can be used; epee and sabre are two, what is the third?

7   What were the forenames of father and son boxers, London, who held British Heavyweight Champion titles in the 1940s and 1950s?

8   Which Canadian sprinter broke the 100 metres world record in 1987 and 1988 but was later disqualified and stripped of his title?

9   Which English football star was the first player to receive the title of European Player of the Year?

10 Which two teams compete for golf's Ryder Cup?

Inventors

1. Which Russian-born U.S. aeronautical engineer invented the first successful helicopter?

2. The discovery/invention of which beverage was made by the Yemenis of southern Arabia during the 15th century?

3. Which Dutch lens grinder is credited with producing the first telescope?

4. Who invented dynamite?

5. Which artillery fragmentation shell is named after its inventor, an English artillery officer, and today broadly denotes any projectile fragments?

6. Who was the German physicist who invented the modern alcohol and mercury thermometers?

7. What type of camera was invented by Edwin Land in the 1940s?

8. What nationality was Adophe Sax, the inventor of the saxophone?

9. What was the name of the two French brothers who invented the first practical hot air balloon?

10. Who first stated the laws of gravitation and light and also constructed the first reflecting telescope?

Politics

1. In which European country did armed soldiers burst into the parliament building and attempt a right-wing coup in 1981?

2. Who was the socialist, anti-U.S. foreign and economic policy president of Venezuela from 1999 until his death in 2013?

3. By what name was the U.S.-sponsored postwar European Recovery Program known?

4. Name the U.S. Secretary of State who resigned in protest over President Carter's desperate plan to rescue U.S. embassy staff held hostage in Iran.

5. John Diefenbaker was prime minister of which country from 1957 to 1963?

6. Which Irish nationalist politician, who took part in the Easter Rising, formed Fianna Fáil in 1926?

7. Which political party did president Dwight D. Eisenhower represent?

8. By what acronym was the Council for Mutual Economic Assistance formed between communist countries in 1949 known?

9. In which West African country was president Samuel Doe captured by rebel forces and put to death in September 1990?

10. The Mount Rushmore National Memorial is a gigantic sculpture of the heads of four U.S. presidents. They are Washington, Jefferson, Lincoln and which other?

General Knowledge

1. Published in six volumes between 1776 and 1789, who wrote 'The History of the Decline and Fall of the Roman Empire'?

2. Ishtar was the goddess of war and love in Assyria and which other ancient civilisation?

3. A 'googol' is the number one, followed by how many zeroes?

4. In which TV series was the 'Village' monitored and patrolled by a white balloon-like device called 'Rover'?

5. 'Homo ad Circulum' is a study of the proportions of the human body, by which historical figure?

6. What is the name of the fibrous substance found in hair and nails?

7. The aria 'Che gelida manina' from Puccini's opera 'La Boheme' is commonly known by what English title?

8. In olden times, which plant with a forked root was said to scream when pulled out of the ground?

9. Which institution was satirized by Cardinals Ximinez, Fang, and Biggles in TVs 'Monty Python's Flying Circus'?

10. The Battle of the Three Emperors in 1805 is more commonly known by what name?

Travel and Transport

1 In which European city was the world's first urban underground railway built?

2 Who built the first successful petrol-driven car?

3 Which instrument, that often appears to defy the laws of gravity, consists in its most common form of a wheel within another wheel?

4 Thor Heyerdahl crossed the Atlantic twice in 1969/70 in papyrus boats. What name was given to both boats?

5 Which American railroad engineer became a folk hero after his death on the Cannonball Express in 1900?

6 What was the name of the first nuclear-powered submarine?

7 Which American test pilot was the first man to fly through the sound barrier?

8 Which vehicle takes its name from the Russian for a 'group of three'?

9 How many masts does a brig have?

10 What is the name of the corporation that operates intercity passenger trains in the United States?

Movies

1. Barbra Streisand produced, directed and starred in which 1991 movie featuring Nick Nolte as a man in a midlife crisis?

2. Also featuring Annette Bening, Harvey Keitel and Ben Kingsley, Warren Beatty co-produced and acted in which 1991 gangster movie?

3. Which Martin Scorcese movie looked at New York Mafia life and featured Robert De Niro, Joe Pesci and Ray Liotta?

4. Which movie was based on the true story of a young American's disappearance in Chile and starred Jack Lemmon and Sissy Spacek?

5. Which legendary Hollywood actress and dancer's real name was Margarita Carmen Cansino?

6. In which movie does Woody Allen play Alvy Singer?

7. Who sang the theme song for the Bond movie 'Thunderball'?

8. Which actress played Natalie Cook in the 2000 movie 'Charlie's Angels'?

9. 'We are Siamese, if you please' is sung by a pair of snooty cats in which Disney animated movie?

10. In which 1991 movie does actor Alan Rickman say the line: "I'll cut his heart out with a rusty spoon."?

Fictional Detectives

1. The Belgian writer, Georges Simenon was the creator of which sleuth?

2. In a 1970s TV series, which private eye lived in a trailer on Malibu Beach, California?

3. Which detective was played by Humphrey Bogart in the 1941 film 'The Maltese Falcon'?

4. Which American author created the French detective, Auguste Dupin?

5. Who was the inept police detective played by Leslie Nielsen in the 'Naked Gun' films and the TV series 'Police Squad'?

6. Who was Sherlock Holmes' astute assistant?

7. Richard Hart, George Nader and Jim Hutton, have all played TV or film roles of which fictional American sleuth?

8. Police sergeant Joe Friday was the main character in which early TV series?

9. Who created the fictional detective, Philip Marlowe?

10. Which famous sleuth has been played on TV and in film by Albert Finney, Peter Ustinov and David Suchet?

ROUND 143

Religion

1   What revolutionary 16th century religious movement resulted in the creation of Protestantism?

2   Marcus Garvey (1887-1940) was associated with which religious movement of Jamaica?

3   What is the name of the building which stands at the centre of Islam's most sacred mosque, in Mecca?

4   In which Middle East country is Mount Nebo, from where Moses is said to have first seen the Promised Land?

5   Shiva, Vishnu and Shakti are deities of which religion?

6   The symbol and the flag of which Eastern religion bears a swastika at their centres?

7   The Roman Catholic Church regards which saint and apostle of Jesus to be the first Bishop of Rome?

8   Religious reformer, Jan Hus, burned at the stake for heresy in 1415, was born in which present-day country?

9   St. Nicholas was born in which present-day country?

10 Who is the elephant-headed god of the Hindu religion?

General Knowledge

1. Which country has the word Hellas on its postage stamps?

2. In economics, what does G.D.P. stand for?

3. Which U.S. actor starred in 'A Streetcar Named Desire', 'On the Waterfront' and 'The Godfather'?

4. What is the capital city of Brazil?

5. What have to be interpreted in a Rorschach test?

6. Which academic discipline is the study of the individuals, groups and institutions that make up society?

7. Which American dancer and flautist starred in 'Riverdance' and 'Lord of the Dance'?

8. Which Italian city is famous for its leaning bell tower?

9. In law, what name is given to the unlawful entrance upon the property of another?

10. Auyuittuq National Park is located in which country?

Science

1 What is the main constituent in the manufacture of glass?

_____

2 Which element has the highest melting point?

_____

3 In radio transmission, what does the abbreviation AM stand for?

_____

4 What does an astrolabe measure the position of?

_____

5 Which element is the best conductor of electricity?

_____

6 What alloy consists of a mixture of copper, tin and zinc?

_____

7 Who, in 1884, patented the first practical fountain pen containing its own ink reservoir?

_____

8 What is the acronym for 'sound navigation and ranging'?

_____

9 What word, from a Greek word meaning 'to hear', is a term used for the science of sound in general?

_____

10 What subatomic particle was discovered by James Chadwick in 1932?

History

1 The naval fleet of which country was defeated by ships of the British navy off Cape Matapan in 1941?

2 Hibernia was the Roman name for which country?

3 Which fashionable hairstylist, along with Sharon Tate, was one of the victims of the Charles Manson killings in 1969?

4 Who was the American aviator who disappeared on the last half of her round-the-world flight in 1937?

5 What was the name of the German camp doctor at Auschwitz who was known as the Angel of Death?

6 Which household appliance was pioneered by Elias Howe and redesigned by Isaac M. Singer in 1857?

7 In which year did Elvis Presley and his wife Priscilla divorce, the U.S. dollar get devalued by 10 per cent, and a Libyan Boeing 727 get shot down by Israeli jets?

8 Whose 18th century exploration of Alaska prepared the way for a Russian foothold on the North American continent?

9 What was the name of the Republic of Sri Lanka prior to 1972?

10 Name the Vietnamese military leader whose tactics led to the Viet Minh victory over the French and an end to French colonialism, and later to the North Vietnamese victory over South Vietnam and the U.S.

Soap Operas

1. 'Knots Landing' was a spin-off of which earlier soap opera?

2. In Dallas, who was the father of J.R. and Bobby Ewing?

3. One of the most famous events in any soap, the 'Moldavian Massacre' was an episode of which soap opera?

4. Which U.S. soap was centred on the long-running feud between the Channing and Gioberti wine-growing families?

5. How did 'Dallas' patriarch, Jock Ewing, die in South America?

6. Which long-running soap is known as GH?

7. What was the name of the Ewing family ranch in 'Dallas'?

8. Which U.S. city was the setting for 'Dynasty'?

9. Which Australian soap is set in Ramsay Street, Erinsborough, a fictional part of Melbourne?

10. 'Dynasty' spawned which spin-off, which debuted in 1985?

Geography

1. In Africa, the Namib Desert merges with which other desert to the south?

2. Where in Colorado would you find the Old Faithful geyser?

3. Lake Tiberias is an alternative name for which Middle East sea?

4. Name the river in Belize whose name is also that of the title of a John Wayne western.

5. Some 2,700 miles in length, and flowing from the hills of Tibet, through China, Myanmar, Laos, Cambodia and Vietnam, which is the longest river in south-east Asia?

6. In which state of the U.S.A. is the city of Pasadena situated?

7. In which city are the headquarters of the University of California situated?

8. Cape Horn is the most southerly point of which continent?

9. Which is the highest cataract in the world?

10. Which city was made the capital of newly-independent Czechoslovakia in 1918?

General Knowledge

1. The 1989 overthrow of the Communist government of which country became known as the Velvet Revolution?

2. Who or what is the 'dumb witness' in Agatha Christie's book of the same name?

3. How many faces does a does a dodecahedron have?

4. Which planet orbits the Sun at a mean distance of about 143 million miles?

5. Ben Gunn is a character in which Robert Louis Stevenson novel?

6. What is the bitter-tasting ingredient extracted from the plant artimisia absinthium that is used to flavour absinthe?

7. Which Hindu goddess of wealth and prosperity is also the wife of Vishnu?

8. The pangolin, a mammal found in Africa and Asia, is more commonly known by what name?

9. In Charles Dickens's novel 'Great Expectations' who is the woman who locks herself away after she is jilted on her wedding day?

10. After Shanghai, which is China's second-largest city?

Sport

1. Which Austrian Formula One driver is the only one to posthumously win the driver's championship title (1970)?

2. The Indianapolis 500 race covers a distance of 500 miles, but how many laps?

3. The 1956 Olympic Games were held in which Australian city?

4. Who, with his sister Tracey, won the 1980 Wimbledon Mixed Doubles title?

5. What nationality is golfer, Gary Player?

6. Film star, Paul Newman, finished second in which motor race in 1979?

7. In which year was the first F.A. Cup Final held?

8. At 17, who became the youngest-ever player to win the Wimbledon Men's Singles title in 1985?

9. Which Finnish runner accumulated 12 Olympic medals (9 gold and 3 silver) from 1920 to 1928?

10. Which U.S. boxer held the World Heavyweight Champion title from 1919 to 1926?

Famous Women

1 Which African American became famous for her refusal to vacate her bus seat to a white passenger, bringing the civil rights cause to the attention of the American public?

2 Of which country did Sirimavo Bandaranaike become the world's first prime minister in 1960?

3 Most of the surface features of which planet are named after famous women?

4 Aung San Suu Kyi is a political figure and former activist of which Asian country?

5 In January 2005, who became the 66th United States Secretary of State?

6 Who was known as 'The Angel of Calcutta'?

7 Whose 'Diary of a Young Girl' catalogued her life in German-occupied Holland during World War II?

8 Making many contributions to astronomy in her own right, who was the sister of astronomer William Herschel?

9 Who was the illegitimate daughter of Pope Alexander VI?

10 Who was the wife of Peter III of Russia, later to become Empress of Russia on his death in 1762?

Rulers and Leaders

1. Who is missing from this list of Czar Nicholas II's children – Alexei, Olga, Tatiana, Maria and ...?

2. What was the name of the last emperor of the Incas, murdered by Pizarro in 1533?

3. Who was the first King of Saudi Arabia?

4. Which son of Charles Martel founded the Carolingian dynasty?

5. Which king of France was the husband of Catherine de' Medici?

6. Which French town is famous for its baroque palace, which was the residence of the French kings from 1678 to 1769?

7. Juan Carlos became king of which country in 1975?

8. Who was the prime minister of Canada from 1968 to 1979 and 1980 to 1984?

9. Who was Britain's prime minister from 1940 to 1945?

10. What surname did Turkish leader Mustafa Kemal receive in 1934?

General Knowledge

1 Which English explorer captained the 'Resolution' the 'Adventure' and the 'Endeavour' on voyages during the 18th century?

2 Who succeeded Nikita Khrushchev as prime minister of the Soviet Union in 1964?

3 Which British soldier and adventurer (1888-1935) wrote 'The Seven Pillars of Wisdom'

4 The Chinese philosopher, Lao Tze founded which religion in the 6th century B.C.?

5 Which kinds of animals are 'vulpine'?

6 Completed in 1930, which New York skyscraper was the first building to exceed 1,000 feet in height?

7 General Jaruzelski was the last communist leader of which country?

8 Which country made its first successful atomic weapon test in October 1964?

9 Which British king abdicated in 1936?

10 What term is used for a limb or tail of an animal that is capable of grasping?

Music

1. Which American lyricist wrote the words to the songs 'Moon River' and 'That Old Black Magic'?

2. Which symphony by Beethoven is the only one by him that does not contain the standard four movements?

3. Which 1960s group, whose hits include 'Be My Baby', was awarded $3m in missing royalties by a New York court in 2000?

4. Which Belfast-born musician became principal flautist with the Berlin Philharmonic in 1967 and later pursued a higher-profile solo career?

5. Which town in Northern Italy is famous for violins made there by the Stradivari family?

6. Who composed the music to Alphonse Daudet's play 'L'Arlesienne'?

7. Who wrote the operetta 'Bitter Sweet'?

8. Which Stephen Sondheim musical was based on an Ingmar Bergman movie 'Smiles of a Summer Night'?

9. Who composed the incidental music to Byron's play 'Manfred' of which the overture is most often performed?

10. Which symphony orchestra, considered by some to be the world's finest, is unusual for the fact that, since 1933, it has never had a principal conductor?

Art

1. What word is used to describe the art of decorating or carving shells or whale's teeth as practised by sailors, especially in days gone by?

2. What name is both the title of a song recorded by Nat 'King' Cole and Conway Twitty, and that of a Da Vinci painting?

3. In art, what name is given to a halo of light over a holy figure? It is also the word for a type of cloud.

4. Which art movement was founded in Munich in 1911; its founding members were Franz Marc and Wassily Kandinsky?

5. In which French city is the Pompidou Centre?

6. Which English sculptor married painter Ben Nicholson in 1933?

7. Which Welsh artist painted portraits of George Bernard Shaw, Dylan Thomas and James Joyce?

8. Which English artist is probably best known for 'A Rake's Progress'?

9. Name the Italian-born painter famous for his portraits of Queen Elizabeth II and John F. Kennedy.

10. Name the female American writer who went to live in Paris in 1903 and became the patron of avant garde artists such as Picasso and Braque.

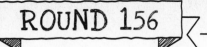

Space

1. Triton is the largest known satellite of which planet?

2. Which Polish astronomer formulated the modern heliocentric theory of the solar system?

3. Venus, Earth, Mars: which planet is the largest?

4. Of which planet is Charon a satellite?

5. Which is the brightest star in the night sky?

6. Which American astronomer predicted the existence of a planet beyond Neptune?

7. Of which constellation is Aldebaran the brightest star?

8. Which giant planet orbits between Saturn and Neptune?

9. The Great Red Spot can be seen in the atmosphere of which planet?

10. What is the largest and most luminous type of star?

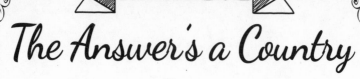

The Answer's a Country

1 From which country does Indian ink originate?

_____

2 Lake Garda is the largest lake in which country?

_____

3 In which European country can the Arlberg Pass be found?

_____

4 The city of Strasbourg was returned by Germany to which country after World War I?

_____

5 The Balearic and Canary Islands are part of which European country?

_____

6 In which country are Angel Falls, the world's highest waterfalls, situated?

_____

7 In which country is the extinct volcano Aconcagua?

_____

8 Which country demanded the return of the Elgin Marbles, relics which have been displayed in the British Museum, London, since 1816?

_____

9 In which African country is the Serengeti National Park?

_____

10 Sherpas are natives of which country?

General Knowledge

1. Which precious metal has the chemical symbol Ag?

2. Who provides the voice for Rocky the rooster in the movie 'Chicken Run'?

3. What name is given to the watering of land by artificial methods?

4. In computing, what does ISP stand for?

5. Which famous opera company is based at the Lincoln Center for the Performing Arts in New York?

6. What nationality was the conductor Karl Böhm?

7. What name is given to the skin of an animal treated for writing on, but untanned?

8. What name is given to a dome-shaped Inuit dwelling made of blocks of hard snow?

9. Which sign of the zodiac is symbolized by a ram?

10. Who directed the movies 'The Magnificent Ambersons' and 'Chimes at Midnight'?

History

1. On 29 May 1953 the summit of which mountain was reached by Edmund Hillary and Sherpa Tenzing Norgay?

2. Which Norwegian explorer and scientist won the Nobel Peace Prize in 1922?

3. What were the first names of aviation pioneers the Wright brothers?

4. Which major conflict was also called the War Between the States?

5. Who was the unsuccessful Republican candidate in the 1996 U.S. presidential election?

6. Which Soviet statesman signed a major arms limitation treaty with President Reagan in 1987?

7. The surname of which Norwegian army officer and Nazi collaborator during World War II has come to mean 'traitor'?

8. The Entente Cordiale of 1904 was an agreement between which two countries?

9. By what name was the policy of separate development of the white and non-white populations in South Africa known?

10. Who was the first chancellor of the Federal Republic of Germany?

Movies

1 The song 'Some Day My Prince Will Come' featured in which Disney full-length animated movie?

2 Released in 1976, 'Family Plot' was the last movie made by which famous director?

3 Name the director of 'Beetlejuice', 'Edward Scissorhands', 'Ed Wood' and 'Mars Attacks!'.

4 Following his death, Warner Brothers re-released which 1971 Stanley Kubrick movie that Kubrick himself had asked to be taken out of circulation some 20 years previously?

5 Famously played in movies by Peter Sellers, what's the first name of the bungling Inspector Clouseau?

6 Which actress appeared in the John Wayne movie 'Stagecoach' and won an Oscar for her performance as Edward G. Robinson's moll in 'Key Largo'?

7 In the 'Toy Story' movies, what is the name of Woody and Buzz Lightyear's owner?

8 The hero of 28 western novels written by Clarence E. Mulford, he was portrayed in over 60 feature movies by William Boyd. Name this fictional cowboy hero.

9 In which 1991 movie thriller does one of the main characters say: "I do wish we could chat longer, but I'm having an old friend for dinner."?

10 Which Walt Disney movie is based on a story about a deer by Felix Salten?

Food and Drink

1. What is the name of the Italian dessert made from coffee-soaked biscuits layered with a sweetened cream cheese?

2. In France, carbonade is a beef stew made with which type of drink?

3. What is the name of the pate made from goose or duck liver?

4. In Middle Eastern cooking, what is the name of thin lamb slices, flavoured with garlic and herbs, cut from a revolving spit?

5. In Spain, what P is a seasoned rice dish with chicken, shellfish and often vegetables?

6. What in Indian cooking is the name given to slightly leavened bread usually cooked in a clay oven?

7. What is the name of the Cajun dish, a type of paella containing shrimps, sausage, chicken and ham seasoned with chilli powder and cayenne?

8. Which rich, white sauce flavoured with herbs and seasonings takes its name from the French Marquis who invented it?

9. The name of which salad dish of shredded cabbage, mayonnaise, carrots and onions is derived from the Dutch for 'cabbage salad'?

10. Which island of the Netherlands Antilles gives its name to a liqueur flavoured with orange peel?

The Human Body

1 The hypothalamus is part of which organ of the body?

_____

2 What is the most common blood group in the world?

_____

3 How many teeth does an adult human have, assuming he has a full set?

_____

4 In psychoanalysis, which part of the unconscious mind is governed by irrational instinctive forces?

_____

5 How many pairs of ribs usually make up the human rib-cage?

_____

6 Which English physician discovered how blood circulates?

_____

7 What is the thickest and most powerful tendon in the human body?

_____

8 What name is given to the process of removing waste products from the blood?

_____

9 What name is given to inflammation of the mucous membrane of the nose?

_____

10 What name is given to the fluid that remains after blood has clotted?

General Knowledge

1. On which date in 1945 did Adolf Hitler commit suicide in his Berlin bunker?

2. In which country is Punta Gallinas, the most northerly point of South America?

3. Which English composer, of Swedish parentage, wrote the opera 'Savitri'?

4. In Alfred Hitchcock's 'North by Northwest' on which U.S. landmark does the climax of the film take place?

5. Which bird is the largest member of the crow family?

6. Of what was the German World War II 'V1' the first of its kind?

7. What is a hygrometer used to measure?

8. In the early days of domestic video film, two basic systems vied for supremacy. The result was that VHS eventually succeeded over which other system?

9. Where in London are the Royal Botanic Gardens?

10. Which major Mediterranean island lies south of Turkey and west of Syria?

Literature

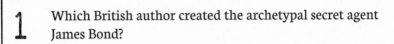

1. Which British author created the archetypal secret agent James Bond?

2. Which American author wrote 'The Case of Charles Dexter Ward'?

3. Which Indian novelist wrote 'A Suitable Boy'?

4. Whose first novel was called 'Kate Hannigan'?

5. Which Roman emperor was the subject of two novels by Robert Graves?

6. Which French author wrote 'Notre-Dame des Fleurs'?

7. Which story from 'The Thousand and One Nights' concerns a boy and a magic lamp?

8. Which Italian author wrote 'The Name of the Rose'?

9. Who wrote the Second World War epic novel 'The Winds of War'?

10. Which best-selling novelist wrote 'Birds Of Prey' and 'The Sound of Thunder'?

Geography

1 Which U.S. city associated with the motor industry was founded by Antoine de la Mothe Cadillac?

2 What is the highest active volcano in Europe?

3 Which famous square is on the east side of the Kremlin in Moscow?

4 Of which Italian island is Palermo the capital?

5 Which volcano between Java and Sumatra erupted catastrophically in 1883?

6 In which Turkish city is the former cathedral, Hagia Sophia?

7 Through which two European countries does the River Tagus flow?

8 In which country would you find Lake Baikal, the world's deepest lake?

9 Of which country is Damascus the capital?

10 What is the chief seaport of Tanzania?

Classical Music

1. Sir Edward Elgar composed an overture about London. What is its name?

2. Where exactly is 'Fingal's Cave' which inspired Mendelssohn to compose an overture named for it?

3. By what name is Beethoven's third symphony commonly known?

4. Which Puccini opera was unfinished at his death?

5. Which Czech composer wrote the symphonic poems 'The Wood Dove', 'The Noon Day Witch' and 'The Water Goblin'?

6. Which Czech composer wrote the 'Glagolitic Mass'?

7. Which French composer wrote 'The Sorcerer's Apprentice'?

8. Who composed 'The Academic Festival Overture'?

9. Who composed the overture 'Roman Carnival'?

10. Who composed the overture 'Calm Sea and Prosperous Voyage'?

News from 2014

1. The Soma mine disaster in May, which claimed over 300 lives, occurred in which country?

2. What is the name of the terrorist organization which kidnapped 234 schoolgirls in Nigeria in April?

3. General Prayuth Chan-ocha led a coup against the government of which country in May?

4. What is the name of the Islamic fundamentalist cleric, extradited from Britain to the U.S. in 2012? In 2014, he was convicted in New York on charges of terrorism.

5. The control of which southern region of Ukraine was contested by pro-Russian and pro-Ukrainian factions, resulting in the annexation of the region by Russia?

6. Flight MH370, which disappeared over the South China Sea in March involved which kind of plane?

7. In April, the passenger ferry MV 'Sewol' capsized off the coast of which country, causing over 300 fatalities?

8. Which Russian city hosted the 22nd Winter Olympics in February?

9. Which country hosted the FIFA World Cup tournament in June and July?

10. In February, which country became the first in the world to legalize euthanasia for terminally ill patients of any age?

General Knowledge

1. First introduced in 1937, which convenience food gets its name from 'spiced ham'?

2. Born Harry Webb, in Lucknow, India, in 1930, how is this man known to pop music fans?

3. The moons of which planet are named after water-gods in Greek and Roman mythology?

4. 'The Bride of the Wind' a 1914 painting by Oskar Kokoschka, is an expression of his unrequited love for the widow of which Austrian composer?

5. Ellesmere Island, in the Arctic, belongs to which country?

6. What name is given to a large landed estate in Spanish America?

7. The cathedral city of Reims in northeast France, lies in which famous wine-growing region?

8. Styria, Burgenland and Carinthia are provinces of which European country?

9. Dr Evil is the arch-enemy of which film series 'secret agent'?

10. Mozart's 'Serenade No 13 in G Major' is commonly known by what name?

Sport

1. At which sport was Jack Dempsey a world champion from 1919 to 1926?

2. Which sport is also known as freefall parachuting?

3. In which sport do people compete for the Admiral's Cup?

4. Greensome and four-ball are terms used in which sport?

5. Which sport involves the use of epees, sabres and foils?

6. Which American city hosted its first marathon in 1897?

7. At which Scottish resort was the famous Royal and Ancient Golf Club founded in 1754?

8. With which sport is Reggie Jackson associated?

9. What name is given to a two-hulled sailing vessel?

10. Which type of winter sport is divided into Alpine and Nordic varieties?

The Animal Kingdom

1   From the hair of which kind of creatures is mohair manufactured?

2   What sort of creature is a schipperke?

3   Which wild cat is also called a desert lynx?

4   What sort of creature is an addax?

5   What is the smallest of the anthropoid apes?

6   What sort of creature is an oriole?

7   Which word can refer to any bird of prey and to a small carnivorous dinosaur?

8   On which animal would you find fetlocks and withers?

9   What sort of creature is a frogmouth?

10   What sort of creature is a Lhasa apso?

Mythology

1 According to Greek legend, who was the father of Apollo?

2 According to Greek legend, which son of Priam abducted Helen of Troy?

3 Which legendary Greek king of Ithaca was the hero of Homer's 'Odyssey'?

4 According to Greek legend, which king of Thebes fulfilled the prophecy that he would kill his father and marry his mother?

5 According to Greek mythology, which wife of King Menelaus was abducted by Paris thus precipitating the Trojan War?

6 Who was the supreme god in Babylonian mythology?

7 Which Greek goddess of the underworld was the daughter of Zeus and Demeter?

8 Which god of love is the Roman counterpart of Eros?

9 According to Greek mythology, who was the goddess of epic poetry and the chief of the nine Muses?

10 In Greek mythology, which swift-footed huntress lost a race when she stopped to pick up golden apples?

Pop Music

1 'My Sharona' did quite well for ___?

_____

2 'Le Freak' was quite a hit for ___?

_____

3 From the album of the same name, 1970 was the year that Simon and Garfunkel released a single destined to become a classic. What was the title?

_____

4 In 1973, who asked us to 'Help Me Make It Through The Night'?

_____

5 'Let it Be' was a massive single hit for ___?

_____

6 'Tears of a Clown' was re-recorded in 1979 by which English ska outfit, featuring Dave Wakeling and Rankin' Roger?

_____

7 Who first sang 'The Hustle'?

_____

8 In 1973, 'Killing Me Softly' was a great success for the first time. It was sung by ___?

_____

9 George Michael had two big winners in 1984. One was 'Wake Me Up Before You Go Go'. What was his solo hit?

_____

10 What did Gloria Gaynor promise in her hit single of 1978?

General Knowledge

1. Which singer starred in the year 2000 film 'Dancer in the Dark'?

2. What is the common name for the bird 'Pica pica'?

3. Who edited the Italian political newspaper 'Avanti!' from 1912 to 1914?

4. A vexillologist studies and/or collects which kind of objects?

5. What does MSG, a flavour enhancer, often seen on the ingredients list on food packaging, stand for?

6. What is the name of the Norwegian man convicted in 2012 for the murder of 77 people in a mass-shooting and bombing during the previous year?

7. What is the most often used letter in the English language?

8. What was the name of the Lone Ranger's horse?

9. Which Beatles' single of 1963 was their first to reach No. 1 in both the U.K. and U.S.?

10. Former penal colony Robben Island, site of the imprisonment of Nelson Mandela for eighteen years, lies close to which South African city?

Rivers, Seas, Oceans

1   Which river, a major battleground during the American Civil War, joins the Potomac at Harpers Ferry?

2   The Russian city of St Petersburg stands on the delta of which river?

3   In geology, what is the term used to describe sands and gravels carried by rivers and deposited along the course of the river?

4   In which African country do both the Limpopo and Zambezi rivers reach the Indian Ocean?

5   Which North American river, it has the same name as a U.S. state, forms the state boundary between Vermont and New Hampshire and drains into the Long Island Sound at New Haven?

6   The Straits of Hormuz is the entrance from the Indian Ocean/Arabian Sea into which body of water?

7   The Kiel Canal links which two seas?

8   The remains of the Biblical towns of Sodom and Gomorrah are said to lie under which inland sea?

9   Which 16th century Spanish soldier was the first to explore the river Amazon?

10   The name of which ocean is derived from one of the Titans of Greek mythology?

Shakespeare

1. Which musical set in the slums of New York City is based on 'Romeo and Juliet'?

2. Which play is subtitled 'The Moor of Venice'?

3. Ethan Hawke played the title role in a 2000 movie version of which Shakespeare play?

4. In which play do three witches appear?

5. In which play does Lancelot Gobbo appear?

6. Shakespeare was born in which town in the county of Warwickshire in England?

7. What was the theatre in London that Shakespeare was associated with?

8. What was the name of William Shakespeare's eldest daughter?

9. In which year did William Shakespeare die?

10. "If music be the food of love, play on" is a quotation from which play?

History

1. What was the official currency unit of Belgium prior to the Euro?

2. Which French-born explorer was the first to map the eastern side of Canada and to give Canada its name?

3. In which year did India and Pakistan gain independence from Britain?

4. At the start of the Korean War, which U.S. general was the U.N. forces' commander?

5. In 1909, which Frenchman made the first crossing of the English Channel by plane?

6. The Klondike Gold Rush of 1896-1899, took place in which country?

7. Which charitable institution was founded by William Booth in 1865?

8. In which year did Italy surrender to the Allies in World War II?

9. The 'Titanic', which sank in 1912, was owned by which shipping company?

10. In 1789 which captain, along with some of his crew, were set adrift from HMS 'Bounty'?

Entertainment

1 Which late movie star and performer was once quoted as saying "If I'm such a legend, why am I so lonely?"

2 Ruby Keeler, who starred in some of the classic musicals of the 1930s, was married to which showbiz legend?

3 Which Hollywood actor published two volumes of autobiography during the 1970s entitled 'The Moon's A Balloon' and 'Bring On The Empty Horses'?

4 Name the writer whose first novel 'Valley Of The Dolls' was a best-seller.

5 What was the surname of the singer known as Mama Cass?

6 Of which singer was it once said: "If she burnt her bra, it would take three days for the fire to go out"?

7 Which 20th century American humorous writer is remembered for his outrageous lines such as: "A bit of talcum is walcum" and "Candy is dandy but liquor is quicker"?

8 Name the manager of Elvis Presley who died aged 87 in 1997.

9 By what name was the American striptease artiste Rose Louise Hovick better known?

10 First published in the U.S.A. in 1923, which international news and general interest magazine became famous for its 'Man of the Year' issue?

General Knowledge

1   What name is given to a place where coins are made?

2   By what name is the popular houseplant Monstera deliciosa better known?

3   Which French philosopher is famous for the statement "I think, therefore I am"?

4   Which five-sided building is the headquarters of the U.S. Defense Department?

5   Which cold dry northerly wind is funnelled down the Rhône Valley in southern France to the Mediterranean Sea?

6   Which fibrous protein is found in hair, nails, horns, hoofs and skin?

7   In law, what name is given to money a court orders one person to pay to another as compensation?

8   How many degrees are there in a right angle?

9   What name is given to a space devoid of matter?

10 What did the G stand for in the movie company MGM?

Science

1   Which British physicist and mathematician discovered the law of gravitation?

2   The name of which unit of work or energy is derived from a Greek word meaning 'work'?

3   How is acetylsalicylic acid commonly known when in tablet form?

4   Which word describes the reduction in the temperature of a liquid below its freezing point without its solidification?

5   Which American scientist is credited with the invention of the electric light bulb?

6   Of which common metal is bauxite the chief ore?

7   Which poison is represented by the letters CN?

8   What is the common name for the hallucinogenic drug Phencyclidine or P.C.P.?

9   What nickname was given to the M9A1 rocket launcher?

10 Which corrosive acid has the chemical formula HCl?

The Bible

1. Who is the traditional author of the third Gospel?

2. Which character in the Old Testament derived his strength from his long hair?

3. Which Hebrew prophet picked up the mantle as successor to Elijah?

4. According to the Old Testament, which founder of the Hebrew nation was commanded by God to sacrifice his son Isaac?

5. In 2012, the Ecclesia Society, through the publisher Thomas Nelson, produced a modern English language translation of the Bible. What was its title?

6. According to the New Testament, who baptized Jesus?

7. Who was the mother of Salome?

8. According to the Old Testament, which son of David was famous for his wisdom as the third King of Israel?

9. Which of the gifts brought by the Magi is also known as olibanum?

10. According to the Old Testament, which son of Nebuchadnezzar was the last King Of Babylon?

Sport

1. At the age of 14, who became the first female gymnast to score a perfect 10 in an Olympic gymnastics event at the 1976 Olympics in Montreal?

2. Which baseball legend from Ohio is commemorated in an award that bears his name, that honours the best major league pitcher each year?

3. Basketball legend Magic Johnson who played for Los Angeles Lakers had a close friend and rival who played for the Boston Celtics: what was his name?

4. Which former race walker was the 2006 Australian Male Athlete of the year, Australia's most prestigious sporting award across all sports?

5. Which tennis player won the Men's Singles in the Australia Open in 2014?

6. Which female French tennis player won the 2013 Wimbledon Championships singles title?

7. Which is the only nation to have won at least one gold medal at every Summer Olympic Games?

8. Which city will host the 2020 Summer Olympics?

9. 'Total Recall' is the autobiography of which former bodybuilder, weightlifter, and Governor of California?

10. To what did boxer Cassius Clay change his name in 1964?

Famous Buildings

1. The futuristic-looking Guggenheim Museum is in which Spanish city?

2. Which famous building stands at 1600 Pennsylvania Avenue, Washington DC?

3. When it was completed in 1931, which building was the tallest in the world?

4. Which controversial futuristic arts centre was designed by Joern Utzon and opened in 1973?

5. In 1891, which American philanthropist built the famous New York concert hall that bears his name?

6. On its completion in 2012, which London landmark became the tallest building in Europe?

7. Which steel and glass London building was built in 1851, relocated in 1854 and burned down in 1936?

8. Which U.S. complex is said to be the world's largest office building?

9. On which southern German cathedral was work started in 1377, but not completed until 1890, when it became the world's tallest cathedral?

10. Where is the Rungnado May Day Stadium, the largest stadium in the world, seating 150,000 people?

General Knowledge

1. Which British singer released the compilation album 'Universal Soldier' in 1967?

2. 'Planet' is a word derived from ancient Greek; what does the word mean?

3. Which species of tree form the majority of the Salix genus?

4. Standing in the state of California, what kind of tree is General Sherman, one time thought to be the oldest and largest tree in existence?

5. Who was Noah's grandfather, who according to tradition lived to the age of 969?

6. The medical condition, otitis, affects which part of the body?

7. What is the capital of the Canadian province, Manitoba?

8. King Gustavus Adolphus was a 17th century king in which country?

9. Who launched 'Playboy' magazine, in 1953?

10. Blue Mountain coffee originated in which country?

Movies

1. Which actor played double roles as the U.S. president and his look-alike in the 1994 movie 'Dave'?

2. Which actress appeared in the movies 'Sliding Doors', 'Shakespeare In Love' and 'The Talented Mr. Ripley'?

3. Which movie starring Esther Williams featured the song 'Baby It's Cold Outside'?

4. Which Italian actor, star of 'Three Coins in the Fountain', died at the end of 1994?

5. Who was the American vaudeville star known as the 'Last of the Red Hot Mamas'?

6. In which 1971 movie is Dennis Weaver terrorized and chased in his car by a large tank truck?

7. Which movie director said: "Drama is life with the dull bits cut out"?

8. Which national monument in Wyoming was featured in the movie 'Close Encounters of the Third Kind'?

9. Which gangster movie featured Burt Lancaster as a small time ageing mafia hood and Susan Sarandon as an ambitious young woman?

10. Directed by Alan Parker, and featuring Brad Davis, which movie is a sordid story about a young American busted for smuggling hash in Turkey and his subsequent harsh imprisonment and later escape?

History

1   During World War II, which part of the U.S.A. was invaded and held for a time by Japanese forces?

2   In which year did United Nations forces expel Iraqi troops from Kuwait, but refrained from removing Saddam Hussein from power?

3   In 1979, who was ousted as head of state by the Nicaraguan Sandinista rebel movement?

4   Which Pacific territory was annexed by the U.S. in 1898?

5   In 1904, a naval battle at Port Arthur was the start of a war between Russia and which other country?

6   In which year was the revolution in Russia that deposed Tsar Nicholas II?

7   Which road was built between Rome and Brindisi about 312 B.C. by the statesman Appius Claudius?

8   Which U.S. warship accidentally shot down Iran Air Flight 655 in 1988?

9   Which British field marshal was deputy commander of NATO forces from 1951 to 1958?

10 The meteorite impact which probably resulted in the extinction of the dinosaurs, occurred approximately how many million years ago?

Literature

1. Which English dramatist and poet, a contemporary of William Shakespeare, wrote the satirical plays 'Volpone' and 'The Alchemist'?

2. Which Norwegian playwright and poet wrote 'A Dolls House', 'The Master Builder', and 'Hedda Gabler'?

3. Which American novelist wrote 'The Deer Park', 'The Executioner's Song' and 'The American Dream'?

4. Which German philosopher, famous for his 'atheistic pessimism', wrote 'The World as Will and Representation'?

5. Which Scottish novelist wrote the novels 'Rob Roy', 'The Lady of the Lake', 'Ivanhoe', and 'Waverley'?

6. Which African-American historical author wrote 'The Foxes of Harrow' and 'McKenzie's Hundred'?

7. Which Canadian author won the 2000 Booker Prize for her novel 'The Blind Assassin'?

8. What is the name of Herge's cartoon character Tintin's dog?

9. Which American author wrote 'The Red Badge of Courage'?

10. Which statesman and World War II leader received the 1953 Nobel Literature Prize?

The Animal Kingdom

1   Is a chimpanzee a monkey or an ape?

2   What is the major endocrine gland of vertebrates?

3   Which fairly large rodent has spines or quills with which it defends itself?

4   What sort of creature is an argali?

5   What is the name for the sterile offspring of a female ass and a male horse?

6   What sort of animal is a Saluki?

7   What is a group of lions called?

8   What sort of creature is a gazelle?

9   What kind of creature is Injaz, an animal cloned in the United Arab Emirates in 2009?

10   What sort of creature is a Russian Blue?

Civil Aircraft

1   What was the world's first wide-body 'jumbo' jet?

_____

2   Introduced in 1952, what was the world's first jet-powered passenger aircraft?

_____

3   What was the first, but ultimately ill-fated, supersonic passenger aircraft?

_____

4   What is the name of the veteran Douglas DC-3, first flown in 1935 with many of the type still operating in 2014?

_____

5   Introduced in 1972, which U.S. manufacturer produced the Tristar passenger jet?

_____

6   The turbo-prop Vanguard and Viscount, and the jet-powered VC-10 were produced by which British company?

_____

7   The first American jet-powered airliner was the Boeing 707. Which airline was the first to use it, in 1958?

_____

8   What do/did the Boeing 727, the Hawker-Siddeley Trident and the Tupolev Tu-145 all have in common?

_____

9   The Boeing 787 has what name-tag?

_____

10   Which were the only two airlines to operate the Concorde supersonic passenger aircraft?

General Knowledge

1. The ritual in India where a widowed woman would join her husband on his funeral pyre was known by what name?

2. What kind of music was played by Kenny Ball and Chris Barber?

3. Which U.S. president resigned in 1974?

4. The members of the pop band, A-ha were from which country?

5. Most weather systems are formed and guided by high-speed winds at high altitudes where cold and warm air meet. What term is given to these winds?

6. According to the Roman Catholic church, who was the first pope?

7. Which U. K. airport has the three-letter code, LHR?

8. The mirabelle is a variety of which kind of fruit?

9. Who played Tony Soprano in the television series 'The Sopranos'?

10. Which Norwegian archipelago lies approximately 400 miles due north of that country?

Girl Singers

1   Who was dubbed 'The White Lady of Soul'?

2   Whose albums 'In Concert' and 'Pearl' were posthumously released in 1971?

3   'Big Yellow Taxi' and 'Woodstock' were big hits for which Canadian songstress?

4   Whose first big, international hit album was 'She's So Unusual'?

5   Whose albums, '19' and '21' have together sold over 36 million copies worldwide since their release in 2008 and 2011 respectively?

6   'What a Difference a Day Made' 'Mad About the Boy' and 'Unforgettable' are just some of the great songs recorded by which American singer?

7   Who had a big early hit with the single 'Genie in a Bottle'?

8   What do the initials in k.d. lang's name stand for?

9   Rihanna's smash hit 'Umbrella' was a track from which 2007 album?

10 Who were the two girl singers in ABBA?

Geography

1. In which city of Central Europe would you find the Schönbrunn Palace, Albertina Museum and Burgtheater?

_____

2. Which is the second largest of North America's Great Lakes?

_____

3. The territory previously known as Prussia is now part of which modern country?

_____

4. Lake Kariba, created by the Kariba Dam, is an expansion of which African river?

_____

5. Which river in Argentina has the same name as a river in the U.S.A.?

_____

6. What name is shared by a British river and a river in northwestern Ontario, Canada?

_____

7. Which Russian city is the world's largest city north of the Arctic circle?

_____

8. In which country is the city of Marrakesh?

_____

9. The second city and chief seaport of Egypt, Alexandria lies on which sea?

_____

10. What is the name of the seaport of Athens?

Politics

1. The phrase 'expletive deleted' widely used in the 1970s, entered popular use after the publication of transcripts relating to which scandal?

2. What three-word phrase was coined by militant Black Panther leader Stokely Carmichael in 1966?

3. Which former Middle East dictator was executed by hanging on 30th December 2006?

4. Killed by a bullet intended for president-elect Franklin D. Roosevelt in 1933, Anton Cermak was the mayor of which U.S. city?

5. Robert Kennedy was senator of which U.S. state?

6. By which name, meaning "Great Soul", was the Indian nationalist leader Mohandas Gandhi known?

7. Prior to reunification, what was the capital of West Germany?

8. Of which Caribbean country was François 'Papa Doc' Duvalier the president?

9. In 1852, which American statesman's famous last words were: "I still live."?

10. Who was the Democratic opponent whom Ronald Reagan defeated in the 1984 U.S. presidential elections?

Food and Drink

1. Stollen is a German fruit loaf traditionally eaten at which time of the year?

2. Mace is a spice made from the dried fleshy covering of which seed?

3. Caviare (the true, expensive variety) is the salted roe of which fish?

4. What name is given to a very large wine bottle, equivalent to twenty ordinary bottles?

5. Who was the Roman god of wine or intoxicating liquor, whose Greek counterpart was Dionysus?

6. Native to North America and having cultivars that include Catawba and Concord, what type of fruit is 'Vitis labrusca'?

7. What do the letters V.S.O.P. mean on a brandy bottle label?

8. The yellow-and-black-striped Colorado beetle (Leptinotarsa decemlineata) is a serious pest of which plant?

9. Which department of Normandy gives its name to an apple brandy originally made there?

10. Which expensive spice is obtained from the flower of the crocus, 'Crocus sativus'?

General Knowledge

1 Singer, Natalie Imbruglia is a national of which country?

2 Astraphobia is an irrational fear of which weather phenomenon?

3 What name is given to the vast region of dry, treeless grassland of Central Asia?

4 According to the Bible, which land lies to the east of Eden?

5 Artaxerxes and Xerxes were kings of which ancient empire?

6 Which cartoon character was 'smarter than the average bear'?

7 In geology, what term describes a vent or hole that emits gases in volcanic regions?

8 Who sang the theme song in the James Bond film 'From Russia with Love'?

9 Which Spanish opera singer duetted with Freddie Mercury in the song 'Barcelona'?

10 Which country did China invade and annex in 1949-1950?

Science

1 Which greenish, poisonous halogen gas is represented by the symbol Cl?

_____

2 Sphalerite is the principal ore of which metal with the chemical symbol Zn?

_____

3 In which field was British physicist William Henry Fox Talbot a pioneer?

_____

4 Which chemical element was discovered by Hennig Brand in the 17th century?

_____

5 With which branch of science was Edwin Powell Hubble associated?

_____

6 Which German physicist discovered X-rays while professor at the University of Würzburg, Bavaria?

_____

7 Which unit of mass is equal to one thousandth of a kilogram?

_____

8 By what abbreviation is polyvinyl chloride better known?

_____

9 Dry ice is a solid form of which gas?

_____

10 Which force occurring on a liquid makes it behave as if the surface has an elastic skin?

Entertainment

1. What was the name of the beautiful white stallion ridden by the cowboy matinee idol, Roy Rogers?

2. 'Blondie' of comic-strip fame has a dog who is frequently the most intelligent person in the strip. What is its name?

3. Which cartoon character has a 30-inch chest which increases to 60 inches when expanded?

4. Which star of the movie 'Grease' won Grammy Awards in 1973, 1974 and 1982?

5. Which singer and actress starred in the movie 'The Next Best Thing'?

6. Which Hollywood great won Best Actress Oscars for 'Dangerous' and 'Jezebel'?

7. Which actress stars in the movie '28 Days'?

8. Which actor performed his own stunts in the movie 'Mission: Impossible 2'?

9. What was the stage name of actress, singer and dancer Virginia McMath?

10. What was the nickname of the straightfaced American comedian Joseph Francis Keaton?

Art

1. What nationality was the painter Claude Monet?

2. What nationality was the painter and sculptor Edgar Degas?

3. Which famous 20th century artist said: "There is only one difference between a madman and me. I am not mad."?

4. What is the name of the museum in Amsterdam which houses one of the largest collections of Dutch and Flemish old masters?

5. Which artist's best-known painting is 'Nude Descending a Staircase No 2'?

6. What nationality was the painter Daniel Maclise?

7. What was the first name of the French Post-Impressionist painter Cezanne?

8. Which German artist and engraver is probably best known for his 1513 engraving on copper, 'Knight, Death and the Devil'?

9. Which one of the following art galleries is not located in its country's capital city: Prado, Tate, Uffizi?

10. Which one of the following was not an impressionist painter: Matisse, Monet, Pissarro?

The Olympics

1   Where was the location of the 1960 Summer Olympic Games?

2   Which Canadian city was the venue for the 1976 Olympics?

3   Which Japanese city hosted the 1998 Winter Olympics?

4   Which German became the first skier ever to retain an Olympic downhill title in 1998?

5   Which female American sprinter won Olympic gold medals in 1984, 1988 and 1992?

6   In which sport was the father of Grace Kelly an Olympic gold medallist?

7   Which winter sports resort hosted the 1960 Winter Olympics?

8   Which Finnish runner won gold medals in the 5,000 and 10,000 metres at both the 1972 and 1976 Olympics?

9   Which Canadian sprinter was stripped of his Olympic gold medal in 1988 for taking anabolic steroids?

10 Which Asian city hosted the 1988 Olympics?

General Knowledge

1 Which American movie star retired from acting after marrying Prince Rainier III of Monaco in 1956?

2 What name is given to a bird's entire covering of feathers?

3 What name is given to a party or dance at which masks are worn?

4 What name is given to a court order that forbids a person from doing something?

5 What is the Roman numeral for ten?

6 In publishing, what does the abbreviation ISBN stand for?

7 What name for a place of wild disorder and confusion is derived from the hospital of St. Mary of Bethlehem?

8 Which U.S. rapper and actor was murdered in a drive-by shooting in 1996?

9 What name is given to the deliberate and systematic destruction of a racial, religious or ethnic group?

10 Which presumed assassin of John F. Kennedy was killed by Jack Ruby?

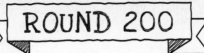

ROUND 200

Around the Islands

1 What was the former name of the island of Taiwan?

2 The ancient Minoan civilization city of Knossos is sited on which Greek island?

3 What is the former name of the island state of Sri Lanka?

4 The Indian Ocean island of Socotra lies off the easternmost point of which continent?

5 Which is the largest island of Japan?

6 Which island nation is located about 300 miles west of the westernmost point of Africa?

7 Which large Russian island in the Arctic Ocean was extensively used for nuclear testing during the 20th century?

8 Ellesmere Island is the most northerly part of which country?

9 Located between Antarctica, Africa and South America, what is unique about Bouvet Island?

10 Which Pacific atoll was cleared of its inhabitants in 1946 to enable its use for nuclear bomb testing?

History

1 Napoleon Bonaparte's ambitions in Russia were stopped at which battle of 1812?

2 Which space shuttle crashed in January 1986, killing all seven crew members?

3 In which year was Nelson Mandela released from imprisonment?

4 In 1865, what was abolished by the Thirteenth Amendment to the U.S. Constitution?

5 What substantial aid to world shipping was opened in November 1869?

6 What was the original nationality of Mexico's only king, Maximilian the First?

7 The Great Irish Famine of 1845-52 had its origins in the failure of which staple food crop?

8 In the mid-17th century, the areas of present-day Delaware, New York state, New Jersey state and other surrounding lands were claimed by Dutch settlers. What name was given to this territory?

9 Which Muslim race invaded Spain and Portugal in 711 A.D.?

10 Which military and religious order was founded in the 12th century to protect pilgrims going to the Holy Land?

Movies

1   In which 1961 Disney comedy movie was a substance called 'flubber' invented?

2   What was the professional name of Rodolpho Guglieni, who was born in Castellanteta, Italy in 1895 and died in New York in 1926?

3   Which movie director formed the United Artists Corporation in 1920 with Douglas Fairbanks, Mary Pickford and Charlie Chaplin?

4   Which American actor and director said: "Movies are fun, but they are not a cure for cancer."?

5   Which French woman said: "I started out as a lousy actress, and I have remained one."?

6   In which movie does Montgomery Clift play a priest who is told of a murder in confessional?

7   In the movie 'The Agony and the Ecstasy', which painter is played by Charlton Heston?

8   Which American actor starred in his first hit movie 'Barefoot in the Park' in 1967?

9   What is the breed of the dog who starred in 'Beethoven' in 1992 and the sequel in 1993?

10   The movie 'Something's Got To Give' was never completed because of the death of Marilyn Monroe. Who was to be the male lead opposite Monroe in that movie?

The Human Body

1. Which veins in the neck return blood from the head to the vena cava?

_____

2. Which joint in the human body is formed by the meeting of the humerus, radius and ulna?

_____

3. Which disease of the central nervous system is represented by the abbreviation MS?

_____

4. What name is given to the first part of the small intestine?

_____

5. What does someone suffering from dysphagia have difficulty doing?

_____

6. Which acute respiratory disease is also called pertussis?

_____

7. How is the bone, the clavicle commonly known?

_____

8. Which infectious disease is also called TB?

_____

9. What is the main artery of the human body called?

_____

10. Which part of the body is inflamed when one is suffering from gingivitis?

General Knowledge

1   Around which Russian city was the greatest-ever tank battle, in 1943?

2   In Scottish folklore, the Kelpie takes the form of which creature in order to fool its victims?

3   Which Monkees band member had a major role in the 1950/60s TV series 'Circus Boy'?

4   In Greek mythology, what was Morpheus the god of?

5   Which South American capital city's name roughly translates as 'See the mountain'?

6   Who famously quipped 'Hell is other people'?

7   In which U. S. state is Grand Teton National Park?

8   What are the names of the three musketeers in Alexander Dumas' eponymous novel?

9   Which metal is the greatest constituent of the alloy, pewter?

10   Who said 'I can resist anything except temptation'?

Myths and Legends

1 Who are the spirits in Arab legend, from where the word 'Genie' comes?

2 Stirling Castle is said to be haunted by which historical figure?

3 Who were the shield-maidens of Odin that collected the bodies of dead warriors and brought them to Valhalla?

4 Which hardy warrior fought and killed the monster, Grendel?

5 Which queen of Carthage committed suicide because of her unrequited love for Aeneas?

6 In Greek mythology, who was turned into a spider after she defeated Athena in a spinning contest?

7 Which hero killed the gorgon, Medusa?

8 To whom did Apollo give the power of prophesy, coupled with the curse of never being believed?

9 Sedna, Agloolik and Nanook are deities of which indigenous people?

10 The Rainbow Serpent and Dreamtime myths are part of the folklore of which people?

Quotations

1. In his autobiography, 'My Autobiography', who wrote: "All I need to make a comedy is a park, a policeman and a pretty girl"?

2. Who said: "Give a man a free hand and he'll run it all over you"?

3. Which U.S. president said: "There can be no whitewash at the White House"?

4. Who said: "I'm half-Irish, half-Dutch, and I was born in Belgium. If I was a dog, I'd be in a hell of a mess!"?

5. Who said: "In politics, if you want anything said, ask a man; if you want anything done, ask a woman"?

6. Which Canadian prime minister said: "The attainment of a just society is the cherished hope of civilized men"?

7. Who said: "Politicians only get to the top because they have no qualifications to detain them at the bottom"?

8. Which French Romantic writer of the 19th century said: "A day will come when there will be no battlefields, but markets opening to commerce and minds opening to ideas"?

9. Which former U.S. vice president said: "We don't want to go back to tomorrow, we want to move forward"?

10. Who said: "We only have to look at ourselves to see how intelligent life might develop into something we wouldn't want to meet"?

War

1. Which British historian wrote 'The Origins of the Second World War'?

2. In which German city were the trials of Nazi criminals held after World War II?

3. What nationality was the World War I spy Mata Hari?

4. Which Belgian village was the site of a famous battle on 18th June 1815 which ended the Napoleonic Wars?

5. In what year did the Second World War Siege of Leningrad begin?

6. Author of 'Slaughterhouse Five', which American novelist, as a prisoner-of-war, witnessed the 1945 carpet-bombing of the German city of Dresden?

7. What was the name of the airplane that dropped the first atomic bomb on Hiroshima?

8. In which year did World War I start?

9. Which organization was founded by the Geneva Convention of 1864 to provide care for the casualties of war?

10. Which war lasted from June 1950 to July 1953?

Geography

1 Which sea channel between Denmark and Sweden links the Kattegat and the Baltic Sea?

2 Which country was known as Dahomey until 1975?

3 Of which South American country is Caracas the capital?

4 Of which state of the U.S.A. is Phoenix the capital?

5 In which continent is the Republic of Senegal located?

6 Which is the third largest state of the U.S.A.?

7 Of which country is P'yongyang the capital?

8 In which South American country is the Atacama Desert?

9 By what name do we know the Bahia de los Cochinos on the Cuban coast?

10 In which country is the Kruger National Park?

General Knowledge

1   Which is the fourth planet from the Sun?

_____

2   Which British comedian, popular in North America, won two Emmys for his show 'Dress To Kill'?

_____

3   What does the abbreviation I.Q. stand for?

_____

4   Which flamboyant Russian-born ballet dancer died in Paris in 1993?

_____

5   Which Greek mathematician is famous for his geometry book, 'Elements'?

_____

6   What name is given to the oath taken by doctors?

_____

7   Which group won the 1994 Mercury Music Prize for their album 'Elegant Slumming'?

_____

8   Which sign of the zodiac is also called the Water Bearer?

_____

9   Agate is a semiprecious variety of what form of quartz?

_____

10   What nationality was the actress Sarah Bernhardt?

Pop Music

1 Whose opinion was it in 1962 that 'It Might As Well Rain Until September'?

2 Who released his hit single 'Are You Lonesome Tonight' in 1960?

3 Who had a hit single in 1961 with 'Let's Twist Again'?

4 Who released 'Surfin' Safari' in 1962?

5 The Beatles had two major hit singles in 1963. One was 'Twist and Shout'. What was the other?

6 Who, in 1965, complained that 'You've Lost That Lovin' Feelin''?

7 In 1965, who thought that 'It's Not Unusual'?

8 Who was the original 'King of the Road'?

9 Who first sang 'I Got You Babe'?

10 Who couldn't get no 'Satisfaction'?

Inventors

1 Which American engineer invented the cotton gin?

2 Which British engineer and pilot is credited with the invention of the jet engine?

3 Which British aeronautical engineer is best known for his invention in 1943 of a bouncing bomb, devised specifically to destroy German dams?

4 Which temperature scale is named after the inventor of the mercury thermometer?

5 Which British scientist and inventor patented the telephone in 1876?

6 Which British mathematician invented logarithms?

7 What did British inventor Trevor Bayliss develop in order to solve communication problems in the Third World?

8 Which British chemist and inventor had a waterproof garment named after him?

9 Which American astronomer and aviation pioneer invented the bolometer (1879-81) and contributed to the design of early aircraft?

10 What was invented by English clergyman Edmund Cartwright (1743-1823)?

Language

1. Which weather phenomenon takes its name from the Spanish for 'the child'?

2. Meaning 'he has sworn', what A is a sworn written statement?

3. What Latin phrase, meaning 'under a judge' means that something is under deliberation by the courts, and is not, therefore, open to public comment or discussion?

4. What Latin phrase means 'not in control of one's mind' or 'of unsound mind'?

5. What phrase meaning a social blunder comes from the French for 'false step'?

6. What name is both a type of Pacific salmon, a wind, and a type of helicopter?

7. The name of which city in China was used as a word meaning meant to kidnap someone for enforced service at sea?

8. Taken from the French for 'accomplished fact', what term means something already done and beyond alteration?

9. What six-letter word beginning with G is the name Latin Americans give to a person from an English-speaking country?

10. What word is an acknowledgement of a hit in fencing and also an acknowledgement of a witty reply?

Sport

1   Which Belgian driver once held the record for the greatest number of wins (six) at the Le Mans 24-hour race?

2   Robert Harting of Germany and Gerd Kanter of Estonia were Olympic gold medal winners in 2012 and 2008 respectively in which field event?

3   In 1934, U.S. boxer Jack Sharkey was disqualified from a World Heavyweight bout after he delivered a below-the-belt punch against which opponent?

4   Ukrainian pole-vaulter Sergei Bubka was the first man to clear which height, in 1985?

5   Tennis player Andre Agassi's father Emmanuel emigrated to the U.S. from which country?

6   Who beat Muhammad Ali at Caesar's Palace, Las Vegas in October 1980; Ali's trainer stopping the fight after the tenth round?

7   With which American sport is Mickey Mantle associated?

8   As of 2013, which team has won the Oxford-Cambridge boat race the most times?

9   Which golf trophy is awarded to competing teams of male amateur players from the U.K., Ireland and the U.S.A., in a contest played every two years?

10 When the Davis Cup was inaugurated in 1900, between which two nation's teams did the contest take place?

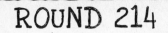

General Knowledge

1. According to Greek mythology, who is said to have created man?

2. Which passenger ship was torpedoed and sunk by a German U-boat on 7th May 1915, killing 1,200 of the 1,900 on board?

3. In which sport is the Copa America Cup (Americas Cup) awarded?

4. What is the name of the burrow-nesting, flightless bird of New Zealand?

5. Published in 1951, what was the title of J.D. Salinger's first full length novel?

6. Complete the quotation by Mae West: 'It's not the men in my life that counts, its ...'

7. Which town in Tuscany, Italy gives its name to a white marble?

8. Which American author once said "The report of my death was exaggerated"?

9. The berries of which tree are used in the flavouring of gin?

10. The world's first nuclear-powered submarine, U.S.S. 'Nautilus' achieved which feat in August 1958?

Classical Music

1 Dvorak composed a set of eight light pieces for the piano, Opus 101. What did he call them?

2 Who composed 'Ludus Tonalis' (Tonal Game) which he referred to as a 'play on keys'?

3 Who composed the 'Hungarian Dances' for piano?

4 Who composed the ' Hungarian Rhapsodies' for piano?

5 Who composed a suite of 12 pieces for piano which he called 'Iberia'?

6 Who composed a set of thirty piano pieces which he called 'Inventions'?

7 What nationality was the composer Jon Leifs?

8 Which outstanding concert pianist was born in a tent in a mining camp in Tasmania and didn't learn to read or write until she was twelve? The people of Kalgoorlie collected £1,000 to send her to the Leipzig Conservatoire.

9 What is the most famous composition by Claude Joseph Rouget de Lisle?

10 Who composed the piano suite for four hands entitled 'Mother Goose'?

History

1   In Roman times, what word meant a marketplace or public square, and place for public activity?

2   A turning point in the American War of Independence was the surrender of British troops on 17 October 1777. Where did that surrender take place?

3   Which year saw the Suez Canal re-open to international traffic after eight years, and the death of Spain's leader Franco?

4   What popular name was given to the German counter-offensive in the Ardennes in December 1944?

5   In which year did Martin Luther King make his famous 'I have a dream' speech, the Boeing 727 make its first test flight, and Alcatraz prison get closed?

6   Which French national holiday is celebrated on 14 July?

7   In the Christian era, What does the abbreviation A.D. stand for?

8   What was the federation of Serbia, Montenegro, Croatia, Slovenia and Bosnia-Herzegovina named in 1927?

9   To what did East Pakistan change its name in 1972?

10   By what name are the fleet of 130 ships sent by Philip II of Spain in 1588 to invade England usually known?

U.S. Tour

1. Largest in the state of Maryland, which port city stands at the northern end of Chesapeake Bay? It had a disastrous fire in 1904.

2. The towns of Great Falls, Billings and Bozeman are all in which Rocky Mountain state?

3. Which Rhode Island city has held an annual jazz festival since 1954?

4. Which Californian mountain range has a namesake in the south of Spain?

5. Which national park, sited on a potential supervolcano, is shared between Wyoming, Montana and Idaho?

6. The cities of Chicago and Milwaukee are sited on the shores of which lake?

7. Once the capital of the Republic of Texas, which coastal city, approximately 50 miles south-east of Houston, suffered a huge loss of life in a 1900 hurricane?

8. Which 1,500 mile-long mountain range extends from Georgia in the south to Maine in the north?

9. At over seven thousand feet above sea level, which is the United States' highest altitude state capital?

10. Close to the Grand Canyon National Park, the romantically-named Painted Desert lies in which state?

Literature

1. Which London theatre was rebuilt by a trust set up by the U.S. actor Sam Wanamaker?

2. Which German poet and dramatist wrote 'Mother Courage and Her Children'?

3. In which imaginary country was 'The Prisoner of Zenda' set?

4. What is the name of the whaling ship in Herman Melville's novel 'Moby Dick'?

5. Which U.S. author of 'hard-boiled' fiction had the middle name Mallahan?

6. Which U.S. novelist wrote 'The Turn of the Screw'?

7. Which children's author wrote about Tom Kitten and Squirrel Nutkin?

8. Which American author wrote 'The Scarlet Letter' and 'The House of the Seven Gables'?

9. Which American author wrote 'The Catcher in the Rye'?

10. Who wrote the adventure novel 'The Count of Monte Cristo'?

General Knowledge

1   Of which relation did Muhammad Ali once say that he'd had his toughest ever fight?

2   Jarlsberg cheese comes from which country?

3   Which disease is the world's largest cause of death?

4   Who wrote 'Travels in Africa', an account of her journeys of exploration during the 19th century?

5   American zoologist Dian Fossey studied gorillas in which African country?

6   Which paralympic athlete was put on trial in 2014 for the murder of his girlfriend Reeva Steenkamp?

7   According to the famous old saying, 'The road to hell is paved with … what?

8   Which high-end Italian motorcar company was formed by the brothers Alfieri, Bindo, Carlo, Ernesto and Ettore in 1914?

9   Which English city was given the name 'Jorvik' by the Vikings?

10 Which 1970s TV cop played the villain, Blofeld in the James Bond film 'On Her Majesty's Secret Service'?

Music

1. In 1904 which singer made his first American recording, 'La Donna e Mobile'?

2. In concert pitch, to what note are orchestral instruments tuned?

3. Which Icelandic pop star picked up a Best Actress award at Cannes in the year 2000?

4. What nationality was the operatic soprano Kirsten Flagstad?

5. Which lyricist collaborated with Richard Rodgers on the song 'My Funny Valentine'?

6. Which superstar singer and movie star died in May 1998 at the age of 82?

7. Who are the two sons of John Lennon who released albums on the same day in 1998?

8. Which former Beatle had a hit with the single 'My Sweet Lord'?

9. In recognition of the exceptionally large orchestral and choral forces used, by what name is Gustav Mahler's eighth symphony popularly known?

10. Which instrument of the violin family when played is held between the knees?

ROUND 221

Space

1. In which constellation are the stars Castor and Pollux?

2. What name is given to a star that explodes and increases in brightness by a million times or more?

3. Which German-born British astronomer discovered the planet Uranus?

4. Which early 20th century theory on the nature of the Universe was superseded by the currently accepted Big Bang Theory?

5. Which is the third planet from the Sun?

6. Which manned Soviet space stations were first launched into Earth orbit in 1971?

7. Onto which planet did the Vega probe drop a helium balloon and land module in 1985?

8. What name is given to a cosmic body of immense gravity from which nothing can escape?

9. What is the second-brightest star in the night sky?

10. By what name were the two identical spacecraft that went into orbit around Mars in 1976 known?

Religion

1. In which Saudi Arabian city can the tomb of Mohammed be found?

2. What name is given to the announcement to Mary that she was to be the mother of Jesus?

3. What is the more common name for metempsychosis in which the soul is born again in another body?

4. On which hill, also known as Golgotha, was Christ crucified?

5. Kol Nidre is a prayer chanted in synagogues on the eve of which Jewish holiday?

6. In Indian philosophy, what term is used for the sum of a person's actions, carried forward into his next life?

7. In Christianity, what name is given to the cup used in the celebration of the Eucharist?

8. Who became Holy Roman Emperor in 1519 on the death of his grandfather Maximilian I?

9. According to Jewish tradition, who was Adam's first wife?

10. According to Genesis 19:24-25 in the Christian Bible, which two cities were destroyed by 'brimstone and fire'?

General Knowledge

1 What is the proper name for your Adam's apple?

2 Who became the sixth 'James Bond' in 2006?

3 'Knowledge is power' is a quotation often attributed to which British philosopher?

4 In which make and model of car did James Dean meet his death in 1955?

5 In 1984, London policewoman Yvonne Fletcher was killed by shots fired from the embassy of which country?

6 "Life is what happens to you while you're busy making other plans" is a quote by which pop music superstar?

7 Which 'greenhouse gas' is absorbed by the leaves of trees?

8 Who did John F. Kennedy succeed as U. S. president in 1961?

9 According to legend, who was struck blind by Lady Godiva?

10 Which organ of the human body regulates the level of glucose?

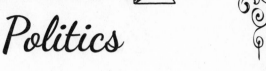

Politics

1. Who became head of the Soviet secret police in 1938 and a member of the politburo in 1946?

2. Which former Defense Secretary did George W. Bush choose as his running-mate?

3. Which committee was established by the U.S. House of Representatives in 1935 to investigate subversive organizations?

4. What name is given to the practice of rearranging voting boundaries to favour the party in power?

5. In which London street is the official residence of the British prime minister?

6. Of which country was David Ben-Gurion the first prime minister?

7. Which Middle East political group is represented by the initials P.L.O.?

8. Which communist movement ruled Cambodia from 1975 to 1979?

9. Who was prime minister of South Africa from 1919 to 1924 and from 1939 to 1948?

10. Of which country did Kurt Waldheim become president in 1986?

Geography

1 What is the capital of South Korea?

_____

2 What is the capital of Poland?

_____

3 In which U.S. state is the city of Peoria?

_____

4 Which of Canada's provinces extends furthest west?

_____

5 The Canadian city of Thunder Bay lies on the shore of which of the Great Lakes?

_____

6 Of which European country is the Cote d'Azur a part?

_____

7 What is the southernmost cape of Africa?

_____

8 Which U.S. state lies furthest south?

_____

9 After Russia, what was the largest state of the former U.S.S.R.?

_____

10 What is the capital of Thailand?

Movies

1. Which fictional character has been portrayed in the movies more than any other?

2. Who was responsible for the distinctive laugh of cartoon character Woody Woodpecker?

3. The actress Susan Blackline played the first victim in which 1975 blockbuster movie?

4. What was the nickname of Jimmy Doyle, played by Gene Hackman in 'The French Connection'?

5. Who, in a 1942 Disney feature length cartoon movie, became the Great Prince of the Forest?

6. In which prison is Steve McQueen held in solitary confinement in the movie 'Papillon'?

7. Which actor won a posthumous Oscar for the movie 'Network'?

8. Which U.S. actor won an Oscar for his role in the movie 'True Grit'?

9. Who won an Oscar for directing the movie 'My Fair Lady'?

10. Which controversial movie rewrote history to give the Americans credit for capturing an Enigma decoding machine?

Food and Drink

1. In which country is the port of Mocha, which gives its name to a type of coffee?

2. Which carbohydrate is also called milk sugar?

3. What heat treatment of milk to destroy germs was named after the French microbiologist who devised it?

4. What name is given to the Mexican dish consisting of a tortilla filled with meat or cheese and served with a chilli sauce?

5. What name is given to Italian dumplings made from potato, semolina or flour and served with a cheese sauce?

6. Which narcotic was removed from Coca-Cola's formula in 1905?

7. In which country is the headquarters of the multinational company Nestlé?

8. What variety of apple was originally cultivated by Maria Ann Smith?

9. From which country does Gorgonzola cheese come?

10. Which food item takes its name from the French for 'twice cooked'?

General Knowledge

1. What name is given to a water spout in the shape of a grotesque person or animal, associated with Gothic architecture?

2. What name is given to a force of mounted soldiers?

3. What name is given to a court that tries offences against military discipline?

4. What is the oldest U.S. military decoration?

5. What name was given to the American equivalent of British Music Hall?

6. Which eccentric creation of Hugh Lofting can talk to animals?

7. Which sign of the zodiac governs the period from July 23 to August 22?

8. The 1947 movie 'Forever Amber' was set during which century?

9. Which zodiac sign is between Aquarius and Aries?

10. What name is given to a group of witches?

Poetry

1 Which British poet wrote 'Endymion' and the 'Ode to a Nightingale'?

2 Which British poet wrote the verse drama 'Prometheus Unbound'?

3 Which Roman writer is famous for his love poems addressed to a married woman named Lesbia?

4 Which French poet wrote 'Une Saison en Enfer'?

5 What nationality was the 8th century poet Tu Fu?

6 Which poet and dramatist wrote 'The Waste Land' and 'The Cocktail Party'?

7 Which American poet drowned off the coast of Florida in 1932, shortly after he completed probably his most famous work, 'The Bridge'?

8 Which Italian poet wrote the epic 'Rinaldo' and the pastoral drama 'Aminta'?

9 Which English poet wrote 'The Rime of the Ancient Mariner'?

10 What nationality was the poet Gabriela Mistral who won the 1945 Nobel Prize for Literature?

Sport

1. At which race did the world's worst motor racing accident occur in 1955?

2. As of 2013, who was the longest-reigning World Heavyweight boxing champion; holding the title from 1937 to 1949?

3. Assiniboia Downs, Hastings, and Northlands Park are racecourses in which country?

4. In North America, what is known as 'The Fastest Game on Earth'?

5. Which Frenchman founded the International Olympic Committee in 1894?

6. The U.S. Masters golf tournament is held annually at which U.S. venue?

7. As of 2014, which country has won the World Indoor Bowls Championships the most times?

8. Which award is given to the top scorer in a Fifa World Cup competition?

9. Set up by U.S. businessman, Ted Turner, which international games event ran from 1986 (Moscow) to 2001 (Brisbane)?

10. The 1956 Olympic Games equestrian events were not held in the host city, Melbourne, but in which European city?

History

1   Which war started in 1618, raged across much of Europe and ended with the Peace of Westphalia in 1648?

2   One of the Seven Wonders of the Ancient World, in which present-day country was the Mausoleum at Halicarnassus?

3   Which epidemic, having spread from Asia, reached Europe in 1347?

4   The 12th-13th century emperor, Genghis Khan, ruled over which people?

5   Six thousand followers of which Roman rebel slave were crucified in 71 A.D.?

6   Owain Glyndwr was a 12th-13th century revolutionary in which country?

7   The Carthaginian civilization was centred on which present-day country?

8   Which infamous ecclesiastical court was established in 1478?

9   What was the name of the raft used by Thor Heyerdahl in his Pacific journey of 1947?

10   Which ancient city is believed to have been sited at present-day Hisarlik, in Turkey?

Jazz

1 Which leading lady of the British jazz scene, who first came to notice in the 1950s with the Johnny Dankworth Seven?

2 Who was the talented jazz singer renowned for her 'scat singing' as well as her mellow treatment of love songs?

3 Born Marian Maud Runnells in Mississippi in 1934, which jazz singer is possibly best remembered for her song 'Maybe in the Morning' and album 'Sometimes in the Night'?

4 Who composed 'Jazz Me Blues'?

5 Who composed 'Ain't Misbehavin''?

6 Who was the singer, pianist and composer who developed the modern concept of a trio with piano, guitar and double bass. Sang 'Unforgettable', 'Stardust' and 'Too Young'?

7 Which singer and guitarist and a very relaxed style led to recordings such as 'Boogie Chillen' and ' Boogie With The Hook'?

8 Who composed 'Stormy Weather'?

9 With which instrument is jazz musician Humphrey Lyttelton primarily associated?

10 Who succeeded Thelonius Monk as pianist with the Dizzy Gillespie band, and went on to be a founder of the Modern Jazz Quartet?

General Knowledge

1. What is the name of NASA's Mars rover which landed on the Red Planet on 6th August 2012?

2. In Egyptian mythology, who was the falcon-headed god of the sky?

3. Which German engineer invented the rotary car engine?

4. Regarding atmospheric pressure, what is the metric equivalent of millibars?

5. Who became the president of France after the resignation of Charles de Gaulle in 1969?

6. Before she embarked on a solo career in 1993, who was the lead singer of the band, The Sugarcubes?

7. The building at No. 30 St. Mary Axe, London is commonly known by what name, due to its resemblance to the object?

8. What nationality was Sir Edmund Hillary, who with Sherpa Tenzing Norgay, was the first man to climb Mt. Everest?

9. Which weather phenomenon results when rain falls from a warm layer of atmosphere into a layer at ground level which is below zero degrees Celsius, causing severe icing to occur?

10. Which cartoon mouse duo always outwitted their feline arch-enemy, Mr Jinks?

The Answer's a Country

1 In which European country is the city of Gerona located?

_____

2 In which country are the Plains of Abraham?

_____

3 In which European country is Lake Lucerne situated?

_____

4 In which country did the Rottweiler dog breed originate?

_____

5 Which European country became the first to legalize euthanasia?

_____

6 In which European country is the city of Modena?

_____

7 Of which former Soviet republic is Tbilisi the capital?

_____

8 Of which country is Seoul the capital?

_____

9 Of which country is Windhoek the capital?

_____

10 In which Caribbean country is the port and tourist resort of Montego Bay?

Nature

1   What name is given to a tree of the genus Taxus?

2   Of which natural phenomena are cirrus, altostratus and stratocumulus examples?

3   To which continent is the plant, poison ivy, native?

4   Which severe viral disease was named after the Nigerian village in which it was first described in 1969?

5   What name is given to the dried excrement of fish-eating birds that is used as a fertilizer?

6   How is lignite commonly known?

7   Which mite causes scabies in man and mange in animals?

8   Which natural substance is formed by pedogenesis?

9   Which creature has between 14 and 77 pairs of legs?

10   What name is given to trees of the genus Platanus?

Famous People

1. Who was the wife of President Ferdinand Marcos of the Philippines, remembered as a symbol of excess because of her collection of more than a thousand pairs of shoes?

2. By what professional name was the musician Ferdinand Joseph LaMothe better known?

3. A poet and a leading figure in the Romantic movement, described by one contemporary as 'mad, bad and dangerous to know', what was the first name of Lord Byron?

4. Executed by the Bolsheviks in 1918, who was the last tsar of Russia?

5. Which Victorian pioneer of nursing was born in 1820 and is famous for her work in the military hospitals of the Crimea?

6. Who was the first wife of King Henry VIII of England?

7. Which Egyptian ruler, the last of the Ptolemys, was the lover of both Julius Caesar and Mark Antony?

8. Che Guevara, a Cuban revolutionary leader who became a left-wing hero, was born in which country?

9. Along with Le Duc Tho of North Vietnam, which American academic and politician received the 1973 Nobel Peace Prize for his part in bringing an end to U.S. involvement in Vietnam?

10. Who led the first successful expedition to the South Pole?

Astronomy

1 Which planet has moons all named after water deities in Greek mythology?

2 What is the brightest star in the constellation of Lyra?

3 On what is the distance-measurement, the astronomical unit (AU) based?

4 The so-called 'belt' of which constellation is made up of the stars Alnilam, Alnitak and Mintaka?

5 Which planet has ice at the poles even though the surface temperature averages 170 degrees Centigrade?

6 What kind of star is Algol, in the constellation of Perseus, the first star of its kind to be discovered?

7 Which astronomer is generally credited with inventing the term 'Big Bang' to describe the origin of the universe?

8 To which constellation would you have to look to find the Crab Nebula?

9 The small constellation known in English as The Northern Crown, is better known to astronomers by what name?

10 Although it had been seen many times before, which astronomer was the first to identify Uranus as a planet, in 1781?

General Knowledge

1   What number represents 'hurricane force' on the Beaufort wind measurement scale?

2   The anthem of the European Union is derived from the final movement which composer's ninth symphony?

3   Which 5th - 6th century Irish monk made several voyages into the Atlantic Ocean and is believed by some to have discovered North America?

4   Which British symphony orchestra was conducted by Sir John Barbirolli from 1943 until his death in 1970?

5   American industrialist and philanthropist Andrew Carnegie was actually born in which country?

6   In which year was the first Russian Revolution?

7   The town of Churchill, Manitoba stands on the shore of which great Canadian bay?

8   How is the tune to the United States' patriotic anthem 'My Country, 'Tis of Thee' known in Britain?

9   Which British army officer organised a coalition of Arab groups to fight against Turkey during the First World War?

10 Which present-day European country was ruled by Sweden during the 12th to the 19th centuries and then by Russia until 1917?

Movies

1   The song 'Windmills of Your Mind' is from the soundtrack of which 1968 movie?

2   In a 1943 movie a future U.S. Senator played the father of a future U.S. president. Can you name the two actors?

3   Better known for her role in another television series, who played Chris Cagney in the pilot movie of 'Cagney and Lacey'?

4   Who played the wheelchair-bound character in the 1998 made-for-television remake of Hitchcock's movie 'Rear Window'?

5   In which movie does Donald O'Conner perform the classic number 'Make 'Em Laugh'?

6   In which movie does Olivia Newton-John sing 'Hopelessly Devoted To You'?

7   In which 1995 blockbuster movie does Kevin Costner play 'The Mariner' and Dennis Hopper play 'The Deacon'?

8   Which U.S. author wrote the book on which the movie 'The Grinch' is based?

9   Which married couple starred in 'Who's Afraid of Virginia Woolf' in 1966?

10 Which star of Hitchcock's 1944 movie 'Lifeboat' said: "The only thing I regret about my past is the length of it. If I had it to live over again, I'd make the same mistakes, only sooner."?

U.S. Presidents

1 Which U.S. president delivered the Gettysburg Address in 1863?

2 Which statesman acquired California for the U.S.A. whilst serving as president from 1845 to 1849?

3 Which U.S. president founded the Peace Corps in 1961?

4 Which U.S. president was associated with the 'Square Deal'?

5 Which U.S. president was known as 'Old Hickory'?

6 Who was the last Democrat President before Bill Clinton to be re-elected for a second term?

7 Who was U.S. president throughout World War I?

8 Which sculptor is famous for his gigantic heads of U.S. presidents at Mount Rushmore National Memorial?

9 In which year did Richard Nixon get sworn in as U.S. president?

10 Who succeeded as 30th President of the United States when Warren Harding died in 1923?

Who Wrote ...?

1 ... the short story 'The Pit and the Pendulum'.

_____

2 ... the plays 'Death of a Salesman' and 'The Crucible'.

_____

3 ... 'All Quiet on the Western Front'.

_____

4 ... the oratorio 'The Dream of Gerontius'.

_____

5 ... the spy novel 'The Scarlatti Inheritance'.

_____

6 ... the thriller trio 'The Millennium Trilogy'.

_____

7 ... the 'James Bond' books.

_____

8 ... the ghost story 'The Legend of Sleepy Hollow'.

_____

9 ... the fantasy novel 'The White Dragon' and other 'Dragon' books.

_____

10 ... the 'Eroica' symphony.

Geography

1 Of which country is Marrakesh the second largest city?

_____

2 In which continent are the pampas located?

_____

3 In which country is the ancient Inca city of Machu Picchu?

_____

4 In which European country is the region of Transylvania?

_____

5 In which European country is the city of Maastricht?

_____

6 Of which former Soviet state is Yerevan the capital?

_____

7 Of which Asian country is Vientiane the capital?

_____

8 Which African country was formerly called Upper Volta?

_____

9 Of which South American country is Rosario a major city?

_____

10 Which U.S. city is nicknamed the Windy City?

General Knowledge

1. In which African country can the Matopo Hills be found?

2. What is the capital of Egypt?

3. The kimono is the traditional costume of which country?

4. Which unit, equal to 1 gram per 9000 metres, is used to measure the fineness of materials?

5. Which Austrian psychiatrist wrote 'The Interpretation of Dreams'?

6. What name is given to the offspring of a male donkey and a female horse?

7. What is a balalaika?

8. Which former Soviet republic has Tallinn as its capital?

9. Which number is represented by the symbol M in Roman numerals?

10. Which unit of power is often abbreviated to hp?

Inventions

1. Which household aid did Hubert Cecil Booth invent in 1901?

2. What was invented by Gustav Eric Pasch and later produced by Johan Edvard Lundström in the 1850s?

3. In 1930, Frank Whittle submitted a patent application for which invention?

4. Which kind of early plastic material was invented by Leo Baekeland in 1907?

5. The invention of the printing press is often credited to Gutenberg, but where had printing by the use of movable type originated in the 11th century?

6. In 1712, who invented the first successful working steam engine?

7. The 13th century philosopher, Roger Bacon perfected which optical device that has its origins in ancient Greece?

8. Nils Bohlin invented which safety device while he was employed by the car firm, Volvo?

9. What was the invention that made David Gestetner a big name during the early 20th century?

10. What nationality was Erno Rubik, inventor of the Rubik's Cube?

Classical Music

1. Of whom was Beethoven speaking when he said 'We shall hear more from him' after a concert in Vienna on December 1st, 1823?

2. Who was the French court musician and composer who created the French National Opera?

3. How did Grieg refer to his 47 immensely popular 'Lyric Pieces'?

4. Who was the composer of the 'Songs Without Words'?

5. Tchaikovsky composed a suite of twelve pieces for piano, Opus 37a, on a particular theme. What is it called?

6. Beethoven's piano sonata in C sharp minor, Opus 27, No. 2, is better known as what?

7. Who was the British pianist who achieved world fame as the greatest accompanist to singers of lieder? His autobiography was entitled 'The Unashamed Accompanist'.

8. Chopin composed a suite of 24 piano pieces, Opus 28 which he called what?

9. What is unusual about Maurice Ravel's Piano Concerto in D?

10. Who, in 1945, composed 'Metamorphosen', an elegy in response to the bombing of his home city, Munich?

Mythology

1 Mithras, a major deity popular with Roman soldiers because it was believed he could give eternal life, originated in which Asian country?

2 Cronus, Oceanus, Hyperion and Atlas were all which kind of being in Greek mythology?

3 What is the collective name for the 40 sea-nymph daughters of Oceanus, of whom the composer Sibelius wrote an evocative symphonic poem?

4 What was the name of the savage, three-headed dog which guarded the entrance to Hades?

5 In Hindu mythology, who was the goddess of death and destruction?

6 Who was the principal Roman sea god, identified with the Greek god, Poseidon?

7 Which stringed musical instrument is named after the Greek wind god Aeolus?

8 In Greek mythology, which brother of Prometheus was forced to support the sky?

9 Which mythological daughter of Oedipus and Jocasta was the subject of a tragedy by Sophocles?

10 Who was the ferryman who transported the dead across the River Styx and into Hades?

General Knowledge

1. Who played Jason Colby in the 1980s soap opera 'The Colbys'

_____

2. What name is given to an aquatic mammal with four limbs modified into flippers?

_____

3. The extinct animal, the quagga, was related to which African equine animal?

_____

4. Riboflavin is the name for which vitamin?

_____

5. Which island group was once known as the Spice Islands?

_____

6. Which Formula One driver was badly injured in a skiing accident near Méribel, France in December 2013?

_____

7. In terms of size, which planet is closest to that of Earth?

_____

8. Which U. S. architect (1867-1959) was famous for his 'prairie style' of design?

_____

9. Which manufacturer has produced the 'Fireblade' series of sports motorcycles since 1992?

_____

10. Beethoven's 'Triple Concerto' features the violin, the cello and which other solo instrument?

History

1. The Anschluss of 1938 was a union between which two countries?

2. How many North American colonies originally became the United States of America in 1776?

3. What name is given to the night of anti-Jewish rioting in Germany on the night of November 9th, 1938?

4. Which Turkish city has also been formerly called both Constantinople and Byzantium?

5. In what year was there an unofficial spontaneous truce on Christmas Day during World War I?

6. What name is given to the period from about 476 to 1000 A.D. in western Europe?

7. What title was given to the eldest son of a French king from 1350 to 1830?

8. By what name is 16th century astrologer Michel de Notredame better known?

9. Which two countries agreed to the Alcock Convention of 1869?

10. How was the Strategic Defense Initiative announced by Ronald Reagan in 1983 popularly known?

Sport

1 Which U.S. tennis player was the first to win all four major singles titles (Australian, French, U.S. and Wimbledon)?

2 With which sport is Alain Prost associated?

3 Which great Czech distance runner died in 2000 at the age of 78?

4 Which tennis player was stabbed by a spectator in 1993?

5 By what name are the Kentucky Derby, the Preakness Stakes, and the Belmont Stakes collectively known?

6 With which sport are Oksana Baiul and Elvis Stojko associated?

7 In which athletics event might one see a Fosbury flop or Western roll?

8 Which American tennis player won the women's singles at the 2001 Australian Open?

9 By what first name was the baseball player Henry Aaron known?

10 What name is given to the traditional Japanese art of fencing with bamboo swords?

Travel and Transport

1 What name is given to any device used to moor a vessel to the bottom of a body of water?

2 The Turtle, designed by David Bushnell, was an early example of what sort of vessel?

3 Which device in a jet engine provides extra thrust for takeoff or supersonic flight?

4 Which dog is the trademark of the main providers of intercity bus transportation in the U.S.?

5 In which country is the airline KLM based?

6 Aer Lingus is the national airline of which country?

7 With which Italian motor company is the Agnelli family associated?

8 What was a galleon?

9 What type of vehicle was a penny-farthing?

10 In 1947, what achievement was attained by the Bell X-1 experimental aircraft?

Pop Music

1 'Sounds of Silence' was a 1966 hit album for whom?

_____

2 Which group first recorded the hit single 'I'm A Believer'?

_____

3 Which group had a hit single with 'Light My Fire'?

_____

4 Which father/daughter pairing had a hit with 'Something Stupid'?

_____

5 Who wooed the girls with hits like 'Maybelline', 'Nadine' and 'Sweet Little Sixteen'?

_____

6 1968 produced a wonderful hit single 'Those Were The Days' for which singer?

_____

7 September 1968 produced which hit single for the Beatles?

_____

8 Which Beatles song mentions two people: the first was the song's title, and the second the name of a priest?

_____

9 The Beach Boys had a U.K. Top Ten hit single in 1964. It was ___?

_____

10 'I Only Want To Be With You' made an international star of ___?

General Knowledge

1   In ancient times, what was a 'dromond' (or dromon)?

2   In which wooded region of Germany does the River Danube have its source?

3   The architect born Charles Edouard Jeanneret-Gris is better known by what name?

4   The DAX Index relates to the stock market of which country?

5   Which Indian city was devastated by a poisonous gas release from a Union Carbide pesticide site in 1984?

6   What is the scientific name for the human voice-box?

7   What is the literal translation of the French term 'déjà vu'?

8   Which German air-ace was shot down and killed on 21st April 1918?

9   The Fire of Rome in 64 A.D., occurred during the reign of which emperor?

10   The term 'Helvetic' refers to which European country?

Computing

1 What does GUI stand for?

_____

2 What does the abbreviation DBMS stand for?

_____

3 What does the abbreviation OCR stand for?

_____

4 Who is the heroine of the 'Tomb Raider' series of computer games?

_____

5 Which number system uses only two digits: 1 and 0?

_____

6 What are Basic, FORTRAN, COBOL and Pascal examples of?

_____

7 Along with whom did Bill Gates found Microsoft?

_____

8 Kenneth Lane Thompson was the principal inventor of which operating system?

_____

9 To what do the initial DNS refer?

_____

10 One byte is equivalent to how many bits?

Literature

1 Which early science fiction novel tells of a future where humans have evolved into two species: the savage Morlocks and the effete Eloi?

2 Which author of the detective novel 'Trent's Last Case' invented a humorous verse form consisting of two rhyming couplets?

3 How is the classic Chinese work on divination the 'Book of Changes' otherwise known?

4 Which French dramatist wrote 'Le Bourgeois Gentilhomme' and 'Le Malade Imaginaire'?

5 From which country do the 13th century books known as the Eddas come?

6 Which English novelist wrote 'The Ipcress File' and 'Funeral in Berlin'?

7 Who wrote the novel 'Roots: The Saga of an American Family'?

8 What was the name of the lion in the 'Chronicles of Narnia'?

9 Which Anglo-Irish novelist wrote 'Good Behaviour' and 'Time After Time'?

10 Which Booker Prize-winning novel by Michael Ondaatje was adapted into an Oscar-winning movie?

Politics

1 Which German Nazi politician became head of the S.S. in 1929 and also directed the Gestapo from 1936?

2 Who was the first African-American mayor of New York City?

3 At the end of World War II, which two countries were divided by the Oder-Neisse Line?

4 In which political scandal of the 1970s was John D. Ehrlichman involved?

5 Which electrician became leader of the Polish trade union Solidarity in 1980, and was awarded the 1983 Nobel Peace Prize?

6 Which Democratic politician ran for the U.S. presidency in 1952 and 1956, but was defeated both times by Eisenhower?

7 Which pollster successfully predicted the result of the 1936 U.S. presidential election?

8 What nationality was the singer and political activist Fela Kuti?

9 Of which East European country did General Jaruzelski become leader in 1981?

10 Of which country was Adnan Menderes prime minister from 1950 to 1960?

General Knowledge

1. Which 19th century British reformer invented the device (that bears his name) to ensure that ships were not overloaded?

2. Which U. S. gay rights activist was shot and killed in San Francisco in 1978?

3. Who was the Russian cosmonaut who made the very first space-walk in 1965?

4. In population terms, which is the largest city in Texas?

5. In which country is the 'Jyllands Posten' newspaper published? It became notorious in 2005 after it printed cartoons depicting the prophet, Muhammad.

6. Which sea creature has the Latin name 'hippocampus'?

7. Which British jazz musician was married to singer Cleo Laine?

8. Who became the first Czar of Russia in 1547?

9. The supervolcano, Toba, which erupted around 70,000 years ago, lies on which Indonesian island?

10. Which international relief charity was founded by Jean Henry Dunant after he saw the awful results of the 1859 Battle of Solferino?

Movies

1   In which movie does Gary Cooper play an about-to-retire sheriff, Will Kane?

2   Which Scottish actor won an Oscar for his performance in the movie 'The Untouchables'?

3   Joel Grey won an Oscar for Best Actor in a Supporting Role in 1972 for his performance in which musical?

4   What is the name of the saloon owned and run by Frenchy (Marlene Dietrich) in the 1939 movie 'Destry Rides Again'?

5   In which movie musical does Ethel Merman play the U.S. Ambassador to the country of Lichtenburg?

6   In which 1998 movie does Annette Bening play a book illustrator who uses her psychic powers to discover where a child murderer is to strike next?

7   What song from their 1937 movie 'Way Out West' was a surprise hit for Laurel and Hardy in 1975?

8   Which Oscar-winning actor plays Benjamin Martin in the movie 'The Patriot'?

9   Which German directed the movies 'Doctor Mabuse', 'The Gambler' and 'Metropolis'?

10 In which movie did Fred Astaire first team up with Ginger Rogers?

Military Aircraft

1 What was the first operational jet-powered aircraft of World War II?

2 What was the first U.S. jet-powered fighter aircraft?

3 What was the name for the gull-winged German Ju87 dive-bomber of World War II?

4 The A10 Thunderbolt ground-attack aircraft was given which nickname due to its ugly appearance?

5 What was the first Russian-built jet fighter, used extensively during the Korean War?

6 The F4 Phantom fighter-bomber, was manufactured by which company?

7 Which bomber aircraft first entered U.S. Air Force service in 1955 and is expected to operate, in updated form, until 2045?

8 The World War II North American P-51 fighter plane is better known by what name?

9 Which present-day multi-role aircraft, in service with several European air forces, shares its name with a British World War II fighter-bomber?

10 The Viggen, the Draken and the Gripen are/were fighter-bombers made by which company?

Geography

1. What is the name of the body of water which forms the southern arm of Canada's Hudson Bay?

2. Of which Asian kingdom is Kathmandu the capital?

3. Of which Asian country is Vientiane the capital?

4. What is the largest city in Alabama?

5. Maoris make up about 10 per cent of the population of which country?

6. Of which African country is Maputo the capital?

7. In which country can the dormant volcano Mount Popocatépetl be found?

8. In which Middle Eastern country is the Negev Desert situated?

9. Of which country is Bulawayo the second largest city?

10. In which former Yugoslav republic is the port of Pula situated?

The Bible

1   What was discovered at Qumran, in present-day Israel, in 1946?

2   Where was Jesus arrested following his betrayal by Judas Iscariot?

3   On the road to where did the conversion of Saul (later to become Paul the Apostle), take place?

4   On which body of water did Jesus 'walk on the water'?

5   Jebel Musa is today the name of which mountain?

6   On the side of which mountain is Noah's Ark said to have come to rest after the Great Flood?

7   The burial site of Moses is said to be on which mountain in present-day Jordan?

8   Which archangel told Mary of the imminent birth of Jesus?

9   Who was the brother of Mary and Martha that Jesus 'raised from the dead'?

10 At the Last Supper, of which disciple did Jesus state that he would deny him three times?

General Knowledge

1. In which year were the Band Aid charity events first performed?

2. Which city is the financial capital of Switzerland?

3. In which Asian country is the ancient city of Harappa, thought to have been built in the late Bronze Age?

4. The fictional hero, Sir Percy Blakeney, who assisted many a French aristocrat in avoiding the guillotine during the French Revolution, is better known by which alias?

5. What do Hermes and Mercury have in common?

6. The words 'magic' and 'bazaar' come from Farsi, the language of which present day country?

7. Which U. S. Army officer was held responsible for the murders of hundreds of unarmed civilians, mostly women and children, at the My Lai (Vietnam) Massacre of 1968?

8. The Battle of the Coral Sea was fought in which war?

9. Film star Grace Kelly married which royal in 1956?

10. In Norse mythology, who was the god of mischief?

Music

1. Which American conductor commissioned George Gershwin's 'Rhapsody in Blue'?

2. Which brass musical instrument has the lowest pitch?

3. In a symphony orchestra, what is a tam-tam?

4. In music, what name is given to a combination of notes that sounds harsh to the ear?

5. Which style of music is associated with the Jamaican cult of Rastafarianism?

6. Which musical instrument is associated with David and Igor Oistrakh?

7. Which left-handed American rock guitarist died in 1970 at the age of 27?

8. With which musical instrument is Larry Adler associated?

9. What is a lyre?

10. With which musical instrument was Jascha Heifetz associated?

Nature

1 The young of which animal is called a leveret?

2 How many humps has a dromedary camel?

3 Which heavily built monitor lizard is the world's largest species of living lizard?

4 What name is given to the offspring of a female donkey and a male horse?

5 What name is given to the natural environment of an organism?

6 What is studied by a conchologist?

7 By what name is the tree 'Ficus elastica' known?

8 Which fly transmits trypanosomiasis, more commonly known as sleeping sickness?

9 Which large South American amphibious rodent has partly webbed feet and is the world's largest living rodent?

10 Formerly widely used as an antimalarial drug, which bitter alkaloid is extracted from the bark of the South American cinchona tree?

Art

1. In which year was the first Cannes Film Festival held?

2. Which gigantic statue of the Sun god Helios was one of the Seven Wonders of the World?

3. Which type of artistic image was named after an 18th century French finance minister?

4. By what name was Italian painter Michelangelo Merisi known?

5. Which British portrait painter became the first president of the Royal Academy in 1768?

6. For which art form is Donatello famous?

7. Which English modern artist painted 'Mr and Mrs Clark and Percy'?

8. Which Spanish painter was noted for his 'blue period' in the early 20th century?

9. Which Flemish artist painted the ceiling of the Banqueting House, Whitehall, London for King Charles I?

10. Which Spanish surrealist artist painted 'The Crucifixion' in 1951?

History

1 After whom is the month of July named?

_____

2 What nationality was the navigator Christopher Columbus?

_____

3 Which U.S. industrialist founded the oil-refining company, Standard Oil, in 1870?

_____

4 Which Italian astronomer upset the 17th century establishment by claiming that the Earth moved round the Sun?

_____

5 What was the apt middle name of union leader Jimmy Hoffa who mysteriously disappeared in 1975?

_____

6 Who became leader of the Palestine Liberation Organization in 1969?

_____

7 What name is given to the study of fossilized remains?

_____

8 What nationality was the famous 16th century astronomer Tycho Brahe?

_____

9 Which Roman emperor murdered his wife Octavia in order to marry Poppaea?

_____

10 From 1510 to 1961, the Indian state of Goa was an overseas territory of which European country?

General Knowledge

1. The name of which constellation of means 'bull' in Latin?

2. What is the Latin name for the constellation The Great Bear?

3. In geometry, what name is given to a straight line that touches a curve at one point?

4. Which unit used to express depths of water is equal to six feet?

5. In clocks and digital displays, what does the abbreviation LCD stand for?

6. What does a philatelist collect?

7. How many millimetres are there in a kilometre?

8. Which system of healing is based on the belief that disease results from a lack of normal nerve function?

9. What colour are emeralds?

10. In mathematics, what name is given to the likelihood that something will occur?

Sport

1 The first game of American Football was played between which two university teams?

2 Which motor sport 1000-mile endurance race over public roads was last run in Italy in 1957?

3 What was the site of the first Olympic Games, thought to date from the eighth century B.C.?

4 Which English football team's home ground is sited at Elland Road?

5 How many on-court players are there in a netball team?

6 Which U.S. basketball team were NBA champions every year in the 1960s except 1967 when it was won by the Philadelphia 76ers?

7 Near to which U.S. city is Churchill Downs, the home of the Kentucky Derby?

8 Which Puerto Rican boxer became the world's youngest-ever world title-holder at age 17 in 1976?

9 Which tennis player was nicknamed 'Little Mo'?

10 As of 2014, which team has made the most appearances at the Superbowl?

Rivers and Mountains

1   In which American state is North America's highest mountain situated?

2   Which river flows through Paris to the English Channel?

3   What is the chief river of British Columbia?

4   What peak on the French-Italian border is the highest mountain in the Alps?

5   What is the chief river in Burma?

6   In which U.S. state are the Adirondack Mountains?

7   On which continent can the Zambezi River be found?

8   Along which continent does the Andes mountain system extend?

9   Which river is known as Tevere in Italy?

10 Which is the highest mountain in the Western Hemisphere?

Entertainment

1 Name the duo who created the cartoon characters Tom and Jerry, Huckleberry Hound, The Flintstones and Scooby Doo.

2 Name the U.S. actor with the Greek sounding name who appeared in 'West-Side Story', '633 Squadron' and 'Kings Of The Sun'.

3 Which actor, star of the movie 'Matrix', appeared with his rock band at the 1999 Glastonbury festival?

4 Famous for her legs, which Hollywood star of the 1940s and 1950s once said: "There are two reasons why I'm in the movies - and I'm standing on both of them."?

5 Which Hollywood tough-guy actor was involved in the first ever 'palimony' case in 1979?

6 An Italian movie director, he made the movie 'Shoeshine' among others. As an actor he appeared in the TV series 'The Four Just Men'. Name him.

7 Henry, Jane, Peter and Bridget - what is the surname of this family of actors?

8 At the 1998 Golden Raspberry Awards, who won the award for worst actress for her performance in the movie 'GI Jane'?

9 Which famous Italian actress was married to movie producer Carlo Ponti?

10 Who created the voices of Porky Pig, Daffy Duck, Sylvester, Tweety Pie and Bugs Bunny?

Science

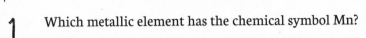

1. Which metallic element has the chemical symbol Mn?

2. By what name is sodium hydroxide commonly known?

3. Which metal is added to copper to make brass?

4. Permalloy is an alloy of which two metals?

5. Which chemical element has the symbol P?

6. Which reddish-brown metal is represented by the symbol Cu?

7. Which alkaloid extracted from deadly nightshade is used during anaesthesia to decrease lung secretions?

8. How is the anaesthetic trichloromethane more commonly known?

9. Which system of treating illness was developed by Samuel Hahnemann, based on the principle of 'like cures like'?

10. Which pH number indicates neither acidity nor alkalinity?

General Knowledge

1 Which Mexican volcano didn't exist before 1943, but now stands at over 9,000 feet high?

2 To the nearest half billion years, how old is planet Earth?

3 Which country did the Dutch call New Holland during the 17th century?

4 The Gulf of Venice is located in which sea?

5 Which American cyclist was stripped of seven Tour de France race titles in 2012?

6 The astronomical observations of Giovanni Schiaparelli mistakenly 'discovered' non-existent features on which planet?

7 In electronics, what is a MOSFET?

8 Born of Irish immigrants in 1854, which Australian outlaw was hanged for murder in 1880?

9 Which animation technique is used in the Wallace and Gromit films?

10 Excepting Pluto, which is now regarded as not being a true planet, which is the smallest planet of the Solar System?

Food and Drink

1. Which evergreen tree's berries are used to flavour gin?

2. What acid is found in milk and other dairy products that have turned sour?

3. Whey is a by-product of the manufacture of which dairy product?

4. In which country was chewing gum first patented?

5. From which tree are cocoa and chocolate derived?

6. For which drink is the Indian town of Darjeeling famous?

7. What sort of peas are used to make the dish, hummus?

8. What fruit is hollowed out to make jack-o'-lantern decorations for Halloween?

9. Which fruit comes from the tree Prunus armeniaca?

10. Which vegetable comes from the plant Brassica napus napobrassica?

History

1. What name is given to the hypothetical intermediate form between human beings and their anthropoid ancestors?

2. Which English monarch was known as the Virgin Queen?

3. Which King of England was nicknamed 'The Lionheart'?

4. Which Swiss national hero is reputed to have shot an apple from his son's head with a crossbow at 80 paces?

5. Which child movie star of the 1930s was appointed U.S. ambassador to Ghana in 1974?

6. Of which South American country was Getulio Vargas president from 1930 to 1945?

7. In which year did the U.S.A. enter World War II?

8. Which European country colonized Martinique in 1635?

9. The manufacture, sale and transportation of which products were banned during the U.S.A.'s Prohibition of 1919 to 1933?

10. Which international environmental pressure group was founded in British Columbia in 1971?

The Answer's a Number

1   Add together the number of sides on a square, a heptagon, an octagon and a pentagon. What is the answer?

2   A Balthazar is very large wine bottle, in capacity usually taken to equal how many regular bottles?

3   What is the square root of 1225?

4   In Genesis Chapter 7 of the Bible, for how many days and nights did God tell Moses it would rain?

5   In 'Star Wars Episode III: Revenge of the Sith', The Great Jedi Purge began with what number Order, Supreme Chancellor Palpatine's directive to the Clone Army to wipe out the Jedi?

6   Amy Winehouse, Janis Joplin, Kurt Cobain, Jim Morrison and Jimi Hendrix all died at what age?

7   What number is represented by the Roman numerals XLV?

8   What number is the only palindromic prime with an even number of digits?

9   How many dominoes are in a standard set (that is, one with tiles ranging from 0-0 to 6-6)?

10 What number lies directly opposite the number 2 on a standard dartboard?

Movies

1   In the movie 'The Jazz Singer', who declared: "You ain't heard nothin' yet folks."?

2   Which Disney movie features the voices of Julianna Margulies and Joan Plowright?

3   In Alfred Hitchcock's 1951 movie 'Strangers on a Train', one of the strangers was played by Farley Granger, who played the other?

4   What nationality was the movie director Ingmar Bergman?

5   What 'does A.E. stand for in the sci-fi movie 'Titan A.E.'?

6   In the 1951 movie 'Quo Vadis', which Roman emperor was played by Peter Ustinov?

7   Which song by Jimmy Durante was played on the soundtrack of 'Sleepless in Seattle'?

8   In the remake of which movie does Jessica Lange recreate the role made famous by Fay Wray?

9   Who was the director of the movie 'The Ninth Gate'?

10 Which American actress starred in the movies 'I'm No Angel' and 'She Done Him Wrong'?

General Knowledge

1. Who was the Kaiser of Germany on the outbreak of World War I?

2. What was the name for present-day New York in the mid 17th century?

3. According to legend, who was the arch-enemy of Robin Hood?

4. In which year did the famous Roswell UFO incident occur?

5. In which U. S. state is the town of Roswell, where the UFO incident occurred?

6. In 1968, at which Greenland airbase did a U.S.A.F. B-52 bomber crash, nearly detonating the four nuclear weapons that the plane carried?

7. By what name is the 'Gendarmerie Royale du Canada' better known?

8. Which Austrian philosopher (1889-1951), who moved to Britain in 1938, wrote the 'Philosophical Investigations'?

9. Of which African country is Harare the capital?

10. What do the initials CGI stand for in reference to animated films?

Geography

1. What is the science of map and chart making known as?

2. Of which former Yugoslavian republic is Ljubljana the capital?

3. Which country claimed the area of Antarctica known as the Ross Dependency from 1923?

4. By what name is the SE coast of India between the Krishna Delta and Point Calimere usually known?

5. In which Asian country is the city of Pondicherry?

6. What is the capital of Sri Lanka?

7. In which state of the U.S.A. are the ports of New Orleans and Baton Rouge situated?

8. In which Italian port can the cathedral of San Lorenzo be found?

9. What is the state capital of Utah?

10. In which Asian country can the city of Lahore be found?

Books

1. Who wrote 'The Janus Man' and 'The Leader and the Damned'?

2. Which popular American writer's books include 'A Walk In the Woods' and 'The Lost Continent'?

3. 'Steppenwolf' and 'The Glass Bead Game' are titles among the novels of which German writer?

4. 'The Gulag Archipelago' and 'One Day In the Life of Ivan Denisovich' are probably the best-known works by which dissident Russian author?

5. Which Swedish author's works include the Inspector Wallander novels?

6. Which nineteenth-century Irish writer's works include the horror novels 'Uncle Silas' and 'Carmilla'?

7. Who was the young British Navy officer of the twelve books set in the Napoleonic Wars, by C.S. Forester?

8. Which thriller by Frederick Forsyth tells of one man's mission to assassinate French president Charles de Gaulle?

9. 'All the President's Men' is a 1974 non-fiction book based on which 1970s-era scandal?

10. 'Childhood's End' and 'Rendezvous With Rama' are two science fiction novels by which writer?

The Animal Kingdom

1   What sort of creature is a gannet?

_____

2   Which small round beetles are mainly yellow or red with black spots?

_____

3   What sort of creature is a cormorant?

_____

4   What sort of creature is an Affenpinscher?

_____

5   From which kind of animal do we get cashmere wool?

_____

6   What sort of creature is an opossum?

_____

7   What sort of creature is a gourami?

_____

8   What sort of creature is a mud puppy?

_____

9   To which continent is the chickadee native?

_____

10 What sort of creature is a bichon frise?

Classical Music

1   What is unusual about the way Haydn's 'Farewell' Symphony ends?

2   By what collective name are Haydn's symphonies Nos. 93-104 known?

3   What did Haydn do which affected the way most symphonies were written ever afterwards?

4   Mendelssohn's 4th Symphony in A, Opus 90, is known by what name?

5   Mozart's last symphony, in C major, (K. 551) was given what name, many years after his death?

6   Who, other than Haydn, composed a 'London Symphony'?

7   Who composed the orchestral suites 'Karelia' and 'King Kristian II'?

8   Why was Gustav Mahler reluctant to give his ninth symphony a number?

9   Robert Schumann composed 12 short, light fluttery pieces for the piano, his Opus 2. What did he call these pieces?

10 What was Rachmaninov's last major work for piano and orchestra?

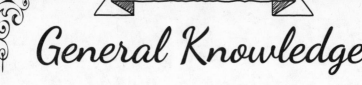

General Knowledge

1 What form of exercise was popularized by Bill Bowerman in a 1967 book?

2 Which French couturier was the first to show a collection for men?

3 In ethology, what name is given to the form of learning in the first hours of life identified by Konrad Lorenz?

4 What name is given to the inability to read and write?

5 What name is given to the carved and painted poles erected by Native North American tribes?

6 What sort of creature is a kudu?

7 What letter is represented by three dots in Morse code?

8 What name is given to the amount a borrower is charged for a loan, usually expressed as a percentage?

9 Which British-born American comedian was awarded an honorary knighthood in 1998?

10 What name is given to fog containing a high proportion of smoke?

Rulers and Leaders

1 Who was the Archduchess of Austria from 1740 to 1780?

2 What was the title of the ruler of Egypt from 1867 to 1914?

3 Which Mongol emperor was the grandson of Genghis Khan?

4 By what name was Russian tsar Ivan IV known?

5 Which country was ruled by Kemal Atatürk from 1923 to 1938?

6 Which daughter of Henry VIII and Anne Boleyn was the Queen of England from 1558 to 1603?

7 Which hereditary military Japanese title was Tokugawa Keiki the last to have?

8 What was the family name of the French emperors Napoleon I, Napoleon II, and Napoleon III?

9 Which nomadic people were ruled by Attila from 434 to 453 A.D.?

10 Goodluck Jonathan was elected president of which West African country in 2011?

Sport and Games

1 Who made golfing history in 1997 by becoming the youngest-ever U.S. Masters champion?

2 Which team game was originally called Mintonette?

3 With which sport is Kareem Abdul-Jabbar associated?

4 Who beat Lindsay Davenport to win the women's tennis singles at the 2000 U.S. Open?

5 In which equestrian event do horses perform complex manoeuvres in response to their rider's body signals?

6 How many gold medals did the U.S.A. win at the Moscow Olympics in 1980?

7 What number wood in golf was formerly known as a spoon?

8 A luge is a type of what?

9 Which former Olympic swimming champion played Flash Gordon and Buck Rogers in movies?

10 Which four-time world superbike champion announced his retirement in 2000?

Around the Islands

1. Of which island country is Antananarivo the capital?

2. Of which Asian country is Honshu the largest island?

3. Gotland is a large island in the Baltic Sea. To which country does it belong?

4. Which Indonesian island is the largest of the Nusa Tenggara group?

5. In which ocean are the Line Islands situated?

6. The Mediterranean island of Corsica is a region of which country?

7. Which Mediterranean island was invaded by Turkish troops in 1974?

8. Of which group of islands is Espiritu Santo the largest?

9. In which sea are the Cayman Islands?

10. Which country is the smallest island in the Greater Antilles?

Literature

1. Which Nigerian dramatist and poet was awarded the 1986 Nobel Prize for Literature?

2. From which collection of stories do Aladdin and Ali Baba come?

3. Which Nobel Prize-winning American novelist wrote 'The Good Earth'?

4. Which American novelist wrote 'The Naked Lunch'?

5. Which British novelist wrote 'The French Lieutenant's Woman'?

6. Which Greek novelist wrote 'Zorba the Greek'?

7. Which French feminist and companion of Jean-Paul Sartre wrote 'The Second Sex'?

8. What is the first name of the South African author J.M. Coetzee?

9. Which Indian writer and activist won the 1997 Booker Prize for her novel 'The God of Small Things'?

10. Which French dramatist wrote the 1897 play 'Cyrano de Bergerac'?

General Knowledge

1   Which holy book consists of 114 chapters called the 'surahs'?

2   Garry Shandling played the character of which fictitious TV chat show host?

3   What term is given to the part of the human skull that encloses the brain?

4   In photography, what is represented by a number 8 lying on its side?

5   Which kind of lager-style beer takes its name from the town in the Czech Republic where it was originally brewed in 1842?

6   To what colour does litmus paper turn in acidic solutions?

7   Dutch is the official language of which South American country?

8   In which capital city did the famous 'defenestration' of 1618 (when several noblemen were thrown out of a third floor window) occur?

9   The NASDAQ is a stock exchange in which country?

10 In computing, what do the initials HTML stand for?

ROUND 287

Movies

1 Which French naval officer and underwater explorer is famous for such movies as 'The Silent World' and 'The Living Sea'?

2 Which American singer and actress starred in the movies 'Calamity Jane' and 'Pillow Talk'?

3 Which comic actor starred in the movie 'Me, Myself and Irene'?

4 What was the name of the character played by Gene Hackman in 'The French Connection'?

5 Which French actress and animal rights activist starred in the movie 'And God Created Woman'?

6 Which 2009 movie, set in Mumbai, India, scooped up eight Academy Awards?

7 Which American actress starred in 'You Can't Take It With You' and 'Shane'?

8 Which former silent movie star is best known for her portrayal of Norma Desmond in the 1950 movie 'Sunset Boulevard'?

9 Which unconventional director made the movies 'M*A*S*H', 'Nashville' and 'The Player'?

10 Which Austrian-born moviemaker directed 'Anatomy of a Murder'?

Science

1   Which chemical element is represented by the symbol Sr?

2   Which term describes the time taken for half the atoms in a sample of a radioactive isotope to decay?

3   Which Russian physiologist is famous for his use of dogs in demonstrations of the conditioned reflex?

4   What is the SI unit of work or energy named after a 19th century British physicist?

5   Which French chemist and microbiologist was the first to produce an effective rabies vaccine?

6   What is the formula for the toxic gas carbon monoxide?

7   In mathematics, what name is given to a quantity that has both magnitude and direction?

8   Which two acids are present in aqua regia?

9   Which metal makes up the majority of the alloy bronze?

10 Which Italian electrical engineer shared the 1909 Nobel Prize for Physics for his work on the transmission of radio waves?

Mythology

1 According to Greek mythology, who was the twin sister of Apollo?

_____

2 According to Greek legend, which prophet advised the Greeks to build the wooden horse by which they gained entry to Troy?

_____

3 Which Roman goddess was identified with the Greek Aphrodite as goddess of love?

_____

4 According to Greek legend, which sorceress helped Jason to steal the Golden Fleece?

_____

5 According to Greek mythology, which brother of Prometheus was forced to hold up the pillars separating heaven from Earth?

_____

6 Who was the Roman god of fire?

_____

7 According to Greek legend, which Cretan monster had a bull's head and a man's body?

_____

8 According to Greek legend, which dryad was the wife of Orpheus?

_____

9 According to legend, which courtier did Dionysius seat at a banquet beneath a sword suspended by a single hair?

_____

10 Who was the daughter of Cepheus who was chained to a cliff for a monster to devour, but was rescued by Perseus?

General Knowledge

1   What kind of material is 'iroko'?

2   The wreck of which German battleship, sunk by the British Navy on 27th May 1941, was located and surveyed in 1989?

3   Which organization was originally formed by Saudi Arabia, Iraq, Iran, Kuwait and Venezuela in 1960?

4   To the nearest whole number, how many inches are there in a metre?

5   Which hero of German mythology was made invincible after he bathed in dragon's blood?

6   Which ancient Middle East city was described by poet John Burgon as 'rose-red, half as old as time'?

7   What are Canada's two official languages?

8   Which date did President F. D. Roosevelt say "will live in infamy"?

9   Which two contrasting but complementary principles lie at the root of traditional Chinese cosmology?

10   In which island country did the Tamil Tiger militant separatist organization operate from the mid-1970s?

History

1. The battles at Roanoke Island and Shiloh were fought during which war?

2. What nationality was Trygve Lie, the first Secretary General of the United Nations?

3. In 1932, the baby son of which aviator was kidnapped and murdered by Bruno Hauptmann?

4. Which general of the American Civil War was the country's president from 1869 to 1877?

5. King Zog was the king of which Balkan country until he was deposed in 1939?

6. The Battle of Actium in 31 B.C., was fought between Octavian for Rome, and Mark Antony for which country?

7. Where did German amateur aviator Mathias Rust illegally land his Cessna light aircraft on 28th May 1987?

8. The Battle of Navarino in 1827 was fought by Britain and France against forces of which empire?

9. What trade was abolished in Britain in 1807 and in the U. S. in 1865?

10. During the French Revolution, which French king was guillotined in 1793?

Pop Music

1 Who was the American singer with many hits to his name, like 'Dream Baby' and 'Pretty Woman'?

_____

2 'The Man Who Shot Liberty Valance' was a hit for ___?

_____

3 'One Night' was a big hit for ___?

_____

4 Who sang 'This Is Not A Love Song' in 1981, but it sold anyway?

_____

5 Who had a big, big hit with a single called 'Cry'?

_____

6 Who took 'A Walk On The Wild Side'?

_____

7 Some time in the mid-sixties, who suggested 'Let's Spend The Night Together'?

_____

8 Who first sang about 'The Leader of the Pack'?

_____

9 Whose hits included 'Annie's Song' and 'Take Me Home Country Road'?

_____

10 Who shared the big, big hit 'You Don't Bring Me Flowers' with Barbra Streisand?

Geography

1. Marie Byrd Land is an unclaimed region of which continent?

2. In which American state is Kent State University?

3. In which European country is the resort of Biarritz?

4. Which channel between Spain and Africa connects the Mediterranean Sea with the Atlantic Ocean?

5. What name is given to the promontory of basalt columns on the coast of Antrim in Northern Ireland?

6. Which tower in Chicago became the world's tallest building in 1973?

7. In which African country is the city of Aswan situated?

8. Of which African country is Mogadishu the capital?

9. Which German city was formerly called Karl-Marx-Stadt?

10. Of which country is Brisbane the third largest city?

General Knowledge

1 Which former Formula 1 racing driver was nicknamed 'the clockwork mouse'?

2 Of which European country is Piedmont a region?

3 What are the five colours of the rings on the Olympic flag?

4 Which poet's best-known work was his first, 'Seven Types of Ambiguity', published in 1930?

5 What was the name of John Travolta's character in the 2010 movie 'From Paris with Love'?

6 Pico de Orizaba, or Citlaltépetl, is a stratovolcano, and is the highest mountain in which country?

7 What creatures are the main pollinators of *Agave tequilana* (otherwise known as the century plant), which is used to make tequila?

8 Phobos and Deimos are two moons orbiting which planet?

9 In which ocean are the Maldives and the Cocos Islands?

10 Of which country was John Joseph Curtin the 14th prime minister, from 1941 to 1945?

The Human Body

1. Which organ of the body is inflamed when suffering from the disease nephritis?

2. Which bone is also called the thighbone?

3. What name is given to the natural painkillers secreted by the brain that resemble opiates?

4. What name is given to scurf that forms on the scalp and comes off in flakes?

5. What part of the body is affected by glaucoma?

6. What is the organ that supplies oxygen and nutrients to a foetus called?

7. Which parts of the body do doctors known as ophthalmologists specialize in?

8. Which body tissue consists of the dermis and the epidermis?

9. Which degenerative brain disorder is the most common form of dementia?

10. What name is given to painful involuntary contraction of muscle?

Religion

1. Which leader of the Israelites anointed Saul as king and chose David as his successor?

2. Who is the patron saint of Russia?

3. Which meeting place for the College of Cardinals in the Vatican had its ceiling painted by Michelangelo?

4. Which Jewish festival commemorates the revolt of the Maccabees?

5. Followers of which religion worship the Trimurti?

6. Which Spanish Dominican friar was appointed head of the Spanish Inquisition in 1483?

7. Of which European country is St. Stanislaw the patron saint?

8. Ko ji ki and Nihon Shoki are scriptures of which native Japanese religion?

9. Which contemplative Roman Catholic religious order was founded in 1084 by St. Bruno?

10. To which religion do the Sunnites belong?

Heroes and Villains

1 Journalist Jim McGuire became which superhero after he fell into a tank full of chemicals?

_____

2 Who played the part of villain, Lex Luthor in the Superman films?

_____

3 Peter Parker turned into which superhero?

_____

4 Diana Prince was the real name of which superhero?

_____

5 Played by Frank Gorshin in the 1960s TV series, who was Batman's puzzling, word-bending enemy?

_____

6 Barry Allen transforms from ordinary human into which super-fast hero?

_____

7 Who gained super-powers after he was given a power-ring by a dying alien?

_____

8 Who played the part of Lois Lane in the 'Superman' films of the 1970s and 80s?

_____

9 The Invisible Woman, The Human Torch, Mr Fantastic and The Thing are collectively known by what name?

_____

10 Who is Batman's female arch-enemy?

Entertainment

1 In the 'Popeye' cartoon series who is Popeye's hamburger-loving friend who has an I.Q. of 326?

2 Which symphonic fairy tale with narration by Prokofiev uses different instruments to represent characters in the story?

3 Who was born Allan Stewart Konigsberg?

4 Which American actor played Andy Hardy in a series of movies beginning in 1937?

5 Which American singer and actor starred in the movies 'Carmen Jones' and 'Island in the Sun'?

6 Which American actor was born Marion Michael Morrison?

7 Which 2000 comedy western movie featured martial arts star Jackie Chan?

8 Which bespectacled young wizard does Daniel Radcliffe play in movies?

9 Who wrote the musicals 'Company', 'Follies' and 'A Little Night Music'?

10 Which two young actors starred in and co-wrote the movie 'Good Will Hunting'?

General Knowledge

1 What is a hygrometer used to measure?

2 By what name is the United Nation's Children's Fund commonly known?

3 The Sorbonne is part of which European city's university?

4 Which piece of laboratory equipment did German chemist Robert Bunsen give his name to?

5 Which famous comet reappears every 76 years, its last appearance being in 1986?

6 Which natural red dye is obtained from the dried bodies of certain Mexican insects?

7 Which incendiary liquid is a mixture of naphthenic and palmitic acids?

8 Which shrub of the genus Philadelphus is also called syringa?

9 Cocker spaniels were originally bred to hunt which birds?

10 Which American actor starred in 'Men in Black' and 'The Fugitive'?

Politics

1. Established in 1961, The Sandinista National Liberation Front is a socialist political party in which country?

2. Corazon Aquino, universally known as Cory, who died of colon cancer in 2009, was a former president of which country?

3. Which political leader who twice ruled Cuba was overthrown in 1958 by rebel forces led by Fidel Castro?

4. Supporter of both Colonel Gaddafi and Saddam Hussein, Jorg Haider (1950-2008) was a controversial far-right wing political figure in the government of which country?

5. In 1901, who became the first prime minister of Australia?

6. The French Revolution took place in the latter part of which century?

7. Which year saw the 100th anniversary of the start of the Great War (also known as World War I)?

8. Prior to Margaret Thatcher, who was prime minister of the United Kingdom?

9. Who was U.S. president when Margaret Thatcher first became prime minister of the United Kingdom?

10. What name is given to the parliament of the State of Israel?

Tunnels and Bridges

1 In which year was the Channel Tunnel opened to rail traffic?

_____

2 The infamous bridge over the River Kwai is located in which country?

_____

3 The alpine Mont Blanc tunnel connects which two countries?

_____

4 The Seikan Tunnel connects Hokkaido with which other Japanese island?

_____

5 Which is the U.K.'s most famous hydraulically-operated bascule bridge?

_____

6 Which Scottish bridge collapsed in 1879, causing the deaths of all 75 people who were on the train crossing the bridge at the time?

_____

7 Which west-coast U.S. bridge opened in 1937, and was the world's longest suspension bridge at that time?

_____

8 In which country is the Laerdal Tunnel, at 15.3 miles long the world's longest road tunnel?

_____

9 Proposals to construct a tunnel under the Strait of Gibraltar have been ongoing between which two countries for several years?

_____

10 The Thousand Islands Bridge, which connects New York State with Ontario, Canada, spans which major river?

Sport

1. Who was the first UK winner of the U.S. Women's golf tournament?

2. In terms of revenue, which football club is the world's richest?

3. Hilda Johnstone is, as of 2014, the oldest woman ever to take part in the Olympics (1972 Games, aged 69): in which event did she compete?

4. For which U.S. soccer team did David Beckham play from 2007-2012?

5. In which year was the first Rugby World Cup held?

6. Eric Heiden, who accumulated no less than 15 world records, is a former ace in which sport?

7. Which female Soviet gymnast, dubbed 'The Sparrow from Minsk', gained three gold medals at the 1972 Olympics and one at the 1976 Games?

8. Which water sport was introduced for women for the first time at the year 2000 Olympic Games?

9. The 'Big Three' golf players are Arnold Palmer, Jack Nicklaus and which other?

10. Who won the World Heavyweight boxing title when he knocked out Joe Frazier in 1973?

Food and Drink

1 Which substance gives tea its colour and astringency?

2 From which Italian city does Parmesan cheese take its name?

3 Scotch, rye and bourbon are types of which alcoholic drink?

4 Which gas is used to make drinks 'fizzy'?

5 Which starchy foodstuff is the main ingredient of the Japanese drink saké?

6 Which spirit is mixed with tomato juice to make a Bloody Mary?

7 Kale is a variety of which vegetable?

8 Which country is associated with the alcoholic drink ouzo?

9 Which substance found in coffee and tea acts as a stimulant?

10 What form of Indian cookery takes its name from the cylindrical clay oven used?

General Knowledge

1 How many stars appear on the flag of New Zealand?

2 The eruption of which volcano in August 1883 was one of the most deadly of modern history?

3 Which country lies to the north and to the west of Bosnia and Herzegovina?

4 Casablanca and Marrakesh are cities in which country?

5 Which airline company operated flight MH370 that went missing on 8 March 2014 as it flew from Kuala Lumpur to Beijing?

6 Which British Celtic warrior queen led a revolt against Roman occupation in the first century?

7 What is the nationality of Tiki Gelana, who won the gold medal in the women's marathon at the 2012 London Olympics?

8 Reigning from 1951 to 1969, King Idris I was the first and only king of which country?

9 Triton is the largest moon of which planet?

10 The Taj Mahal, located in Agra, Uttar Pradesh, India, stands on the banks of which river?

Instruments

1. The Gibson company introduced which radically shaped electric guitar in 1958?

2. What was Larry Adler's instrument?

3. Russian cellist/engineer, Leon Termen invented which electronic instrument?

4. Which three solo instruments are played in Beethoven's 'Triple Concerto'?

5. Alison Balsom and Håkan Hardenberger are virtuosos of which brass instrument?

6. The Italian Guarneri family were distinguished makers of which kinds of instruments?

7. The Greek word 'kithara' is the origin of the modern-day English word for which instrument?

8. Which tuba-like instrument, often seen in marching bands, is named after a famous American composer of marches?

9. Which modern-day woodwind instrument is descended from the earlier 'hautbois'?

10. Made famous for its appearance in the main theme to the film, 'The Third Man', which instrument is formed of strings stretched across a flat sound-board?

Space

1. Which Apollo mission was aborted after an in-flight explosion?

2. In which year did the Apollo 11 lunar module land on the Moon?

3. Which spacecraft sent a probe into Jupiter's atmosphere in 1995?

4. The Moon's gravity is approximately what percentage of Earth's?

5. The name of which constellation near Orion means 'Great Dog' in Latin?

6. Which planet, like Earth, has only one moon?

7. In 2012 which space vehicle was the first to leave the region of the solar system and enter interstellar space?

8. What was the name of the Russian space station that orbited Earth from 1986 to 2001?

9. What term describes two suns which orbit each other around a common centre of gravity?

10. Iapetus, Dione and Tethys are moons of which planet?

Language

1. What English word, meaning suave and affable, is derived from Old French, literally 'of good temper'?

2. Which adjective means 'relating to the Moon'?

3. What clay-like material used in pottery means, in Italian, literally 'baked earth'?

4. What is the Russian word for 'fist', given to prosperous peasant farmers in pre-revolutionary Russia?

5. Used mainly in the U.S. states on the Gulf of Mexico, what is the meaning of the word 'Bayou'?

6. What name is given to a word that has the same meaning as another word?

7. Which European country is known as Sverige in its native language?

8. Which letter of the English alphabet is derived from the sixth letter of the Greek alphabet?

9. For which old Spanish coin was a piece of eight another name?

10. What does Descartes' famous Latin phrase 'cogito, ergo sum' mean?

History

1. Which volcano in Italy erupted in 79 A.D., engulfing the towns of Herculaneum and Pompeii?

2. What nationality was the explorer Ferdinand Magellan?

3. In which decade was the 'Treaty on the Non-proliferation of Nuclear Weapons' signed?

4. Between which two European countries was South America divided during the 16th century?

5. Which 1952 Charlie Chaplin movie was banned by many U.S. theatres due to Chaplin being an alleged communist sympathizer?

6. By what name was William F. Cody better known?

7. Which South African surgeon performed the first successful heart transplant operation?

8. What was the Greek name for Khufu, builder of the Great Pyramid at Giza?

9. Which ancient Greek physician is regarded as the father of medicine?

10. Which two countries joined with Austria-Hungary for the Triple Alliance of 1882?

General Knowledge

1. What is the name, of Dutch/Afrikaans origin, for meat that is cut into strips and dried in the sun?

2. Thomas Bowdler is famous mostly for his censorship of the works of which playwright?

3. In 1991, which U.S. general commanded the forces that liberated Kuwait from Iraqi occupation?

4. Tsuen Wan and Kowloon are urban areas of which Chinese territory?

5. Believed to have been the event which caused the extinction of the dinosaurs; the point at which a huge meteorite struck Earth around sixty-five million years ago lies off the coast of which country?

6. Just about every European state can stake a claim to being the 'Sick Man of Europe' at some time, but which Empire was the first to be so-called, in 1853?

7. The fjord-like Milford Sound is a geographical feature, and tourist hot-spot, of which country?

8. The medieval 'Mappa Mundi' displayed in Hereford Cathedral, England, shows which city at its centre?

9. The Gulf of California is bordered on all of its three sides by which country?

10. Which small city stands at the southernmost point of the 48 contiguous states of the U.S.A.?

Geography

1. The autostrade are a national system of motorways (mainly toll roads) in which European country?

2. Which country lies between Spain and France?

3. São Tomé and Príncipe is a Portuguese-speaking island nation in which gulf off the western coast of Africa?

4. Which major mountain range of North America extends from southern British Columbia to northern California?

5. Which country lies to the south of Slovakia?

6. The Sella, the Nervión, the Loire, the Garonne and the Adour rivers all empty into which bay?

7. Which is the most north-eastern state of the U.S.A.?

8. Which country lies to the west of the former Yugoslav Republic of Macedonia?

9. Which is the longest river in New Zealand?

10. Which hiking trail passes through Georgia, North Carolina, Tennessee, Virginia, West Virginia, Maryland, Pennsylvania, New Jersey, New York, Connecticut, Massachusetts, Vermont, New Hampshire, and Maine?

Movies

1. Which actress won Oscars for 'Norma Rae' and 'Places in the Heart'?

2. Who directed the movies 'Midnight Cowboy', 'Marathon Man' and 'Yanks'?

3. Which Hungarian-born actor played Dracula in a 1931 movie?

4. Which former star of 'ER' appeared in the movie 'The Perfect Storm'?

5. Which American actor won Oscars for his performances in the movies 'Philadelphia' and 'Forrest Gump'?

6. Who sang 'Stormy Weather' in the 1943 movie of the same name?

7. Who directed the movies 'Double Indemnity', 'The Lost Weekend' and 'The Apartment'?

8. What kind of creature was Chewbacca in the 'Star Wars' movie?

9. Who played Trapper John in the movie 'M*A*S*H'?

10. Directed by Rob Reiner and also starring Tom Cruise and Demi Moore, Jack Nicholson was nominated for the Oscar for Best Supporting Actor for his performance as a U.S. marine commander in which 1992 movie about the trial of two marines charged with murder?

Literature

1. Which detective died in Agatha Christie's 1975 novel 'Curtain'?

2. What is the name of the captain in Jules Verne's novel 'Twenty Thousand Leagues Under the Sea'?

3. Which American novelist wrote 'Little Women'?

4. Which philosopher and mathematician collaborated with Bertrand Russell on 'Principia Mathematica'?

5. Which Swedish author wrote 'Confessions of a Fool' and 'The Dance of Death'?

6. Which American soldier and diplomat wrote the bestseller 'Ben-Hur'?

7. Which Spanish novelist wrote 'The Four Horsemen of the Apocalypse'?

8. Who is the hero of John Buchan's novel 'The Thirty-Nine Steps'?

9. What was the title of actor David Niven's first autobiography?

10. Which fictional character made his first appearance in the novel 'The Little White Bird'?

Famous Russians

1 Who became the world chess champion in 1969 but lost the title to the American, Bobby Fischer in 1972?

2 In 1991, who succeeded Mikhail Gorbachev as the president of the Russian Federation?

3 Which nuclear scientist, and winner of the 1975 Nobel Peace Prize, was exiled in 1980, following his criticism of the Soviet occupation of Afghanistan?

4 Who was born Vladimir Ilyich Ulyanov in 1870?

5 Cosmonaut, Yuri Gagarin was the first person to travel into outer space, in 1961, but how did he die in 1968?

6 According to Forbes Magazine, in 2013 which Russian displaced Barack Obama as the world's most powerful person?

7 Who was the Russian (i.e. Soviet) leader at the time of the 1962 Cuban Missile Crisis?

8 Assassinated in Mexico in 1940, who was the first leader of the post-revolutionary Red Army?

9 In 1963, which Russian became the first woman to travel in outer space?

10 Which Russian-born engineer founded an aircraft manufacturing corporation in the U.S.A. in 1923?

General Knowledge

1 Bauxite is a clay-like compound which is the main ore of which corrosion-resistant metal?

2 What is the capital of Tasmania, an island state, part of the Commonwealth of Australia?

3 On 9 August 1965, Singapore broke away from which country to become a fully independent nation?

4 How many letters of the alphabet are not the initial letters of a U.S. state?

5 What was the name of the dog who in the painting titled 'His Master's Voice', which was the basis for the logo used by several audio recording and associated brands?

6 Which violinist made her Winter Olympics debut in Sochi in 2014, in the Alpine Skiing Giant Slalom, and was the only woman representing Thailand?

7 Known officially as Casa de Gobierno, and also known as La Casa Rosada, The Pink House is the executive mansion and office of the president of which country?

8 What name is commonly given to the medical condition hypermetropia?

9 Which Canadian singer represented Switzerland in the 1988 Eurovision Song Contest?

10 James Earl (Jimmy) Carter served as the 39th president of the United States and was awarded the 2002 Nobel Peace: in which year was he born?

The Animal Kingdom

1 Which is the only seal that feeds on penguins?

2 What sort of creature is a moccasin?

3 What sort of creature is a murex?

4 Ambergris is derived from the intestines of which creatures?

5 What sort of creature is a prairie dog?

6 Which lizard is noted for its ability to change colour?

7 What sort of creature is a looper?

8 What the largest New World member of the cat family?

9 Which marine creature has hermit, spider and king varieties?

10 Which insects are the principal food of the aardwolf?

Sport

1. Which German tennis player won his first Wimbledon title in 1985?

2. How many events are there in the modern pentathlon?

3. Which year saw New Zealander Peter Snell break the world record for the mile?

4. According to tradition, which games were first held in 776 B.C.?

5. Which British runner refused to compete in the 100m at the 1924 Olympics because it was held on a Sunday?

6. In which Japanese martial art do combatants fence with bamboo sticks?

7. Which Russian tennis player beat Pete Sampras to win the men's singles at the 2000 U.S. Open?

8. What nationality was the 1979 Formula 1 world champion Jody Scheckter?

9. In which sport did Audley Harrison win gold at the Sydney Olympics?

10. Which American golfer won the first of his six U.S. Masters titles in 1963?

Music of the 70s

1 Who sang 'You're So Vain' with great results?

_____

2 'Wuthering Heights' was a 1978 hit for which solo female artist?

_____

3 In 1977, the Bee Gees released which hit single?

_____

4 In 1972, the most unlikely 'Long Haired Lover from Liverpool' was a hit single for ___?

_____

5 In 1972, 'Let's Stay Together' did quite well for ___?

_____

6 In 1976, punk music arrived with 'Anarchy in the U.K.' by ___?

_____

7 In 1976, 'Bohemian Rhapsody' was a hit for ___?

_____

8 In 1978, 'Night Fever' did well for ___?

_____

9 Who in 1978 thought you were not once, not twice, but 'Three Times A Lady'?

_____

10 Who, in 1972, confessed 'I Shot The Sheriff'?

War

1. Which British general commanded British, German and Dutch forces to victory at Waterloo in 1815?

2. On which Japanese port was the second atomic bomb dropped in 1945?

3. In which country did the Boer Wars take place?

4. Which word for an anti-aircraft gun was originally an abbreviation of the German word Fliegerabwehrkanone?

5. Encouraged by the successful Japanese attack on Pearl Harbor four days earlier, what was Adolf Hitler's rash decision of 11th December 1941?

6. Which Australian city was heavily damaged by Japanese bombing on 19th February 1942 and on several later occasions?

7. In January 1943, Operation Ring was implemented to surround and eliminate German forces around which Russian city?

8. What is the common name for Operation Neptune, the largest-ever seaborne invasion that took place in June 1944?

9. In which year did the first Arab-Israeli war occur?

10. Which American fighter aircraft is also called the Fighting Falcon?

General Knowledge

1 Composed of the Rajya Sabha (Council of States) and the Lok Sabha (House of the People), the parliament of which country is popularly known as Sansad?

2 One half of one half of one half is more commonly expressed as what fraction?

3 Patrick Floyd "Pat" Garrett, who became famous for killing Billy the Kid, was also the sheriff of Lincoln County, as well as Doña Ana County, in which U.S. state?

4 Viswanathan Anand, Magnus Carlsen and Vladimir Kramnik have all become World Champions in which sport or game?

5 How many countries share a border with Switzerland?

6 How many horizontal red and white stripes appear on the national flag of the United States of America?

7 Which planet was discovered by William Herschel in March 1781?

8 "Toto, I've a feeling we're not in Kansas anymore" is a line from which movie?

9 Big Diomede and Little Diomede are islands in which strait, which separates Russia from Alaska?

10 Rotokas is a language spoken in Bougainville, an island to the east of New Guinea. How many letters are in the modern Rotokas alphabet, the smallest alphabet in use today?

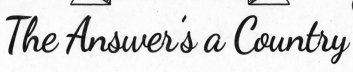

The Answer's a Country

1 The 'Marseillaise' is the national anthem of which European country?

2 Of which country was Brian Mulroney the prime minister from 1984 to 1993?

3 Of which country is the shekel the basic monetary unit?

4 Which is the only Western country not to have movie censorship?

5 Which European country has French, German, Italian, and Romansch as its official languages?

6 In which European country is the port of Bilbao?

7 In which country is the Baltic port of Gdansk situated?

8 Of which African country is Kigali the capital?

9 In which country did a volcano called Laki erupt in 1996?

10 In which country was the basketball star Patrick Ewing born?

Airlines

1. Garuda is the national airline of which Asian country?

2. Of which country was the low-cost airline, Loftleidir a carrier during the 1940s to late 1970s?

3. What kinds of aircraft were operated by DELAG of Germany, the world's first airline?

4. Which airline commenced services as Western Air Express in 1925 and ceased in 2001, when it was merged with American Airlines?

5. Scandinavian Airlines is operated by which three countries?

6. What was the name of Freddie Laker's 1970s transatlantic service which undercut the fares of established carriers?

7. Sabena was the national airline of which country from 1923 until bankruptcy in 2001?

8. Having operated for fifty-two years, which Dallas-based airline, noted for its garishly painted aircraft during the 1970s, went out of business in 1982?

9. Imperial Airways, launched in 1924, was a forerunner of which present-day airline?

10. Which airline is the world's oldest and still in existence? Although it merged with Air France in 2004, it still keeps its original name.

Catchphrases

1. 'Big brother is watching you' comes from which dystopian novel of 1949?

2. 'Frankly my dear, I don't give a damn' was said by which actor in the film 'Gone With the Wind'?

3. What Spanish phrase is often exclaimed by Bart in 'The Simpsons'?

4. In which film did Arnold Schwarzenegger utter the phrase 'I'll be back'?

5. In 'Apocalypse Now' what is Lieutenant Colonel Kilgore's famous response to certain olfactory stimulations at the start of the day?

6. 'Go ahead, make my day' is the challenge thrown down by Harry Callahan (Clint Eastwood) in which film?

7. 'Blistering barnacles' is the phrase often uttered by which character in the 'Tintin' comic books?

8. 'Here's looking at you kid' and 'Play it again Sam' were said by which actor in the 1942 film 'Casablanca'?

9. Which German POW camp guard often uttered a nervous 'I know nothing' in the TV series 'Hogan's Heroes'?

10. 'And now for something completely different' was an often-heard catchphrase in which classic British TV series?

Movies

1 What was the name of the 1944 movie starring Cary Grant about two sweet old ladies who poison lonely old men and bury them in the cellar?

2 Who won the Oscar in the supporting actor category in 1981 for his performance as Dudley Moore's butler in 'Arthur'?

3 Who played the part of Austin Powers in movies in 1997 and again in 1999?

4 Who were the two male stars who appeared in all three 'Back to the Future' movies?

5 What was the name of the 1988 movie which was an unexpected success and gave rise to a television series, in which a middle-aged Bavarian woman left stranded in the Mojave desert, transforms a seedy motel she happens across?

6 Who played the male and female leads in the 1997 movie 'As Good as it Gets'?

7 Who were the male and female leads in the 1960 movie 'The Apartment'?

8 What was so unusual about the 1992 movie 'Another Girl, Another Planet'?

9 Which actor whose movies include 'M', 'Casablanca' and 'The Maltese Falcon' was born Laszlo Loewenstein?

10 Which veteran actor starred in the 2000 movie 'Where the Money Is'?

General Knowledge

1   Which high-kicking dance originated in Paris in about 1830?

2   Which breed of working dog is sometimes known as a bobtail?

3   Which legal holiday is celebrated in America on the first Monday in September?

4   Which red hair dye is obtained from the shrub Lawsonia inermis?

5   To what is the drug lysergic acid diethylamide usually abbreviated?

6   Which sign of the zodiac is between Leo and Libra?

7   What is the study of the movements of the heavenly bodies in relation to their presumed influence upon human affairs?

8   In which South American country did the tango originate?

9   What is removed from seawater in a desalination plant?

10   Which zodiac sign governs the period from February 19 to March 20?

Science

1 Which element is represented by the symbol K?

2 Which metallic element is represented by the symbol Sb?

3 Which Italian physicist gave his name to the SI unit of electromotive force?

4 Which light metal has the chemical symbol Al?

5 Which rare-earth metal is represented by the symbol La?

6 What is defined by Ohm's law as the ratio of the potential difference between the ends of a conductor to the current flowing through it?

7 Which disease is prevented by the Sabin vaccine?

8 Hydrochloric acid is a solution of which gas?

9 Which unit, equal to one tenth of a bel, is often used to express a sound intensity?

10 Which theoretical temperature corresponds to -273.15 degrees on the Celsius scale?

History

1. During the 18th century, what was a 'Brown Bess' to a soldier?

2. Which general led the Prussian army at the Battle of Waterloo?

3. Which Chilean president died during the coup that brought General Pinochet to power in 1973?

4. Which American trades union activist disappeared in mysterious circumstances in July 1975?

5. In 1189, which English king left for the Holy Land as a participant in the Third Crusade?

6. What was the better-known name of the Scottish folk hero and outlaw, Robert McGregor (1671-1734)?

7. General James Wolfe was killed at the Battle of the Plains of Abraham, in 1759. Near to which present-day Canadian city did the battle take place?

8. The series of U.S. economic programmes known as the New Deal, were instigated by which president?

9. The U.S. Prohibition era started in 1920. In which year did it end, when the Act was repealed under the 21st Amendment?

10. Which country's first gold rush started after a prospector found gold at Bathurst, in 1851?

Distinguished Duos

1 Which two actors starred in the TV series 'The Persuaders'?

2 Which iconic dance-duo appeared in films such as 'Top Hat', 'Swing Time' and 'Follow the Fleet'?

3 Don and Phil are/were the first names of which singing duo?

4 Pam Dawber was Mindy; who was Mork, in the 1970s-80s TV series, 'Mork and Mindy'?

5 Singer/actor Dean Martin teamed up with which actor in several comedy films?

6 What were the stage names of comedy duo, Abbott and Costello?

7 What were the first names of the husband and wife Nobel Prize-winning couple, the Curies?

8 Which musical duo wrote and produced operettas such as 'The Mikado' and 'Trial by Jury'?

9 'Sons of the Desert' was one of the first feature-length films to star which comedy pair?

10 Who was the actress who appeared in the 'Road to...' series of films, starring Bob Hope and Bing Crosby?

'Friends'

1 Whose boyfriend is David, a scientist who went off to Minsk in Belarus on a research grant?

2 Who played the part of Emily Waltham, Ross Geller's English wife?

3 What was the name of the TV series in which Joey Tribbiani played the part of Dr Drake Ramoray?

4 Of Ross Geller's three wives through the various series, which one turns out to be a lesbian?

5 The part of Rachel Green is played by which actress?

6 Which character has a career as a masseuse?

7 Released in 2003, what was the final season of 'Friends'?

8 What was the name of Ross and Rachel's daughter?

9 Which two characters are brother and sister?

10 Who plays the part of Monica's boyfriend, Dr Richard Burke?

General Knowledge

1. USB is a means of connecting a device to a computer so they can communicate and exchange data. What do the initials USB stand for?

2. At the inauguration of the Third Republic in 1989, 23 October was declared a national holiday in which country?

3. What temperature has the same value in both Centigrade (Celsius) and Fahrenheit?

4. Which letter of the Greek alphabet is written as a circle with a vertical line running through the centre?

5. Which book of the Old Testament comes between Isaiah and Lamentations?

6. Peridot is a gemstone of which colour?

7. Not including any under water, which is the world's longest mountain range?

8. 'All You Need is Love' was a 1967 Beatles song that began with the national anthem of which country?

9. How many ancient galleys (representing sea trade) are depicted vertically in the centre of the New Zealand Coat of Arms?

10. In 'Star Wars' stories, Darth Vader was the name given to whom after he turned to the dark side of the force and became a Sith lord?

Geography

1 What is the capital of the U.S. state of Florida?

_____

2 Which port is the largest city in New Zealand?

_____

3 Which is the world's second largest ocean?

_____

4 Which ocean reaches its maximum depth in the Marianas Trench?

_____

5 Of which country is Gelderland a province?

_____

6 Which two countries comprise the Iberian Peninsula?

_____

7 Of which country is Riyadh the capital?

_____

8 Of which state of the U.S.A. is Columbia the capital?

_____

9 Of which U.S. state is Helena the capital?

_____

10 Of which African country is Luanda the capital?

The Human Body

1   By what name is the trachea commonly known?

2   Naevus is the medically correct term for which area of darkly pigmented skin?

3   Which organ of the body is affected by pyelitis?

4   What is the medical term for loss of memory?

5   A deficiency of which protein hormone causes the symptoms of diabetes mellitus?

6   Which muscular tube, also known as the gullet, runs from the pharynx to the stomach?

7   Which branch of medicine is concerned with the problems of infants and children?

8   Which skin condition caused by inflammation around the sweat glands is also called miliaria?

9   Of which organ is the tricuspid valve a part?

10 What is inflamed in a case of the medical condition, dermatitis?

Literature

1. Which novel by Sir Laurens van der Post was filmed as 'Merry Christmas Mr. Lawrence'?

2. Which Irish authoress wrote the novels 'Casualties of Peace', 'Country Girls' and 'Wild Decembers'?

3. Which American author wrote 'The Big Sleep' and 'The Long Goodbye'?

4. Which Hollywood great was the subject of the book 'Mommie Dearest'?

5. Which American novelist wrote 'Goodbye Columbus'?

6. Which Scottish explorer wrote 'Travels in the Interior Districts of Africa'?

7. Which American author wrote the novels 'Presumed Innocent' and 'Burden of Proof'?

8. The movie 'Apocalypse Now' is based on the book 'Heart of Darkness' by which author?

9. Which 15th century English author wrote 'Morte d'Arthur', a work based on the legend of King Arthur?

10. Which novel by Charles Dickens features a raven called Grip?

Sport

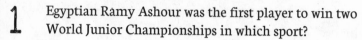

1. Egyptian Ramy Ashour was the first player to win two World Junior Championships in which sport?

2. What nationality is Sebastian Vettel, Formula One driver and multiple world champion?

3. Which Australian horse race takes place at three o'clock on the first Tuesday in November?

4. In which Japanese martial art can a fighter score a Waza-ari, a yuko and an ippon?

5. In which sport did Tom Daley earn the title of Britain's youngest ever world champion in any sport when he took 10-metre individual gold in Rome in 2009?

6. Who won the 2013 Tour de France road cycling race?

7. In the Triple Jump, who achieved a world record in 1995, with a jump of 18.29 metres?

8. In which sport is Clergé credited with being the first world champion of any sport, holding the title from 1740 until 1765, until Raymond Mason succeeded him?

9. Who won the 800m, 1500m, 5000m and marathon gold medals at the 2012 Paralympics?

10. The Olympic motto is made up of three Latin words: Citius, Altius, Fortius. What is the English translation of the motto?

The Great Composers

1 Who was the composer of 'The London Overture'?

_____

2 Which Russian composer wrote the famous piano concerto No. 1 in B flat minor?

_____

3 Who composed the operas 'The Thieving Magpie' and 'William Tell' with their famous overtures?

_____

4 Who composed the overture 'Portsmouth Point'?

_____

5 Who composed the operas 'Susanna's Secret' and 'The Jewels of the Madonna' of which only the overtures are played today?

_____

6 Which Austrian composer's free-spirited fourth symphony is known as the 'Romantic'?

_____

7 Which German composer wrote the opera 'Der Freischutz' and 'Oberon'?

_____

8 Which German composer wrote the Mass in D, 'Missa Solemnis'?

_____

9 Which U.S. composer wrote 'Star Dust' and 'In the Cool, Cool, Cool of the Evening'?

_____

10 Which composer wrote the 'Kullervo Symphony', a work based on an ancient Finnish legend?

Which Year?

1   PanAm 103 explodes over Lockerbie; Winter Olympics in Calgary; singer, Roy Orbison dies.

2   Start of the collapse of communism in eastern Europe; death of Ayatollah Khomeini; George Bush succeeds Ronald Reagan as U.S. president.

3   Soviet blockade of Berlin begins; Mahatma Ghandi assassinated; Jewish state of Israel founded.

4   Invasion of Iraq deposes Saddam Hussain; Seven astronauts killed when space shuttle 'Columbia' breaks up on re-entry; earthquake in Bam, Iran kills 40,000.

5   Egypt and Israeli leaders meet at Camp David; release of film 'Grease'; Chris Evert wins her fourth U.S. Open title.

6   John F Kennedy elected U.S. president; U2 plane shot down over U.S.S.R., pilot Gary Powers captured; Israeli agents capture German war criminal Adolf Eichmann in Argentina.

7   Elvis Presley dies; space-probes Voyagers 1 and 2 launched; Film, 'Network' picks up four Oscars.

8   Sarin gas attack on Tokyo subway; Tommy Lee marries Pamela Anderson; release of 'Toy Story' and 'Apollo 13'.

9   Deaths of F.D. Roosevelt and Benito Mussolini; Winston Churchill defeated in British General Election.

10   Films 'Titanic' and 'Men in Black' released; deaths of Princess Diana, Mother Teresa and conductor Georg Solti.

Sport

1. Cyclist, Eddie Merckx was a native of which country?

2. What are the fastest and slowest-paced styles in competitive swimming?

3. In 1922, which swimmer (and actor) was the first to swim 100 metres in less than a minute?

4. In which sport is the Eisenhower Trophy awarded?

5. 'Lutz', 'loop', 'salchow' and 'axel' are all terms used in which sport?

6. 'Joltin' Joe' was a nickname for which American baseball player?

7. Which U.S. welterweight/middleweight boxer had a 91-match winning streak that lasted from 1943 to 1951?

8. Which former West Ham United footballer played for U.S. soccer team Tampa Bay Rowdies from 1976-1979?

9. Long distance runner Miruts Yifter, winner of two Golds at the 1980 Olympics, is from which country?

10. Father and son racing drivers, Gilles and Jacques Villeneuve, were/are natives of which country?

Food and Drink

1 What type of creature is Bombay duck, or bummalo, dried and eaten as an accompaniment to curries?

2 What is the principal ingredient of laver bread, a traditional Welsh dish?

3 Mornay is a creamy white sauce flavoured with what?

4 Made originally in the Middle East, what name is given to puréed chickpeas mixed with garlic and lemon juice, and served as a starter or dip?

5 What are the four main ingredients of a Waldorf salad?

6 From what is tofu made?

7 Which fruit is used to make the dish known as guacamole?

8 Which nuts are used to make marzipan?

9 Which Mexican spirit made by distilling the fermented sap of an agave plant?

10 Which soft blue cheese from France is made from ewes' milk, ripened in limestone caves and has a strong flavour?

General Knowledge

1   The volcanic island of Karakatoa lies in the Sunda Strait, between Sumatra and which other Indonesian island?

2   In tennis, which year saw Chris Evert win her fourth U.S. Open title and Björn Borg win his third Wimbledon title?

3   The High Atlas mountain range is located in which North African country?

4   Which Carthaginian general defeated the Romans at the Battle of Cannae in 216 B.C.?

5   How many layers of filling are there in the traditional club sandwich?

6   In which present-day country did Saint Nicholas have his origins?

7   In revenge for the 1942 assassination of top Nazi, Reinhard Heydrich, which Czechoslovakian village was ordered by Hitler to be destroyed and erased from maps and all its inhabitants executed?

8   Who is Donald Duck's 'significant other'?

9   Which Russian composer wrote symphonic works based on Shakespeare's 'The Tempest', 'Romeo and Juliet' and 'Hamlet' and Dante's 'Francesca da Rimini'?

10 Which European capital city's name translates as 'Black Lake'?

Travel and Transport

1   Which U.S. nuclear-powered submarine was the first vessel to circumnavigate the world underwater?

2   Which two countries collaborated on the supersonic aircraft, Concorde?

3   What was the name of the ship in which Captain Cook discovered Australia?

4   Which vehicle derives its name from the U.S. Army's General Purpose vehicle or GP?

5   What kind of transport is the 'felucca' of northeast Africa?

6   Maersk is a transportation group with headquarters in which country?

7   Which airline was the first to operate the world's first wide-body jet passenger aircraft, the Boeing 747?

8   Which Italian city has airports at Malpensa and Linate?

9   Introduced in 1922, after which Norwegian explorer and humanitarian was the first 'stateless person's' passport named?

10 In 1964, which country introduced the Bullet Train, the world's first high-speed passenger train?

Movies

1. Who played the male and female leads in the 1988 movie 'Dangerous Liaisons'?

2. Power and Welles shared the lead in a costume drama movie in 1949, about an adventurer at the court of the Borgias in medieval Italy. What was it called?

3. Who played the chief pilot and the air hostess in the 1970 movie 'Airport'?

4. Who played the air hostess who had to take over the controls of a jumbo jet in the 1975 sequel to the movie 'Airport'?

5. Who were the two actors who played the leading roles in the 1976 movie 'All the Presidents Men' about the breaking of the Watergate affair?

6. Who played the part of 'the highest paid lover in Beverley Hills' in the 1980 movie 'American Gigolo'?

7. Who played the male and female leads in the 1956 movie 'Anastasia'?

8. Who played the lead in the 1995 movie 'Apollo 13' which recounted the story of that ill-fated space flight?

9. Based on a James Hilton novel, which 1942 movie starred Ronald Colman as Charles Rainier, a prosperous man who loses his memory as a result of shell-shock in World War I?

10. Made in 1957, Lana Turner, Arthur Kennedy, Russ Tamblyn and Hope Lange all appeared in which movie (based on a novel) about sex in a little American town?

ROUND 341

Science

1. Which gas is the main constituent of natural gas and marsh gas?

2. How is the insecticide dichlorodiphenyltrichloroethane commonly known?

3. Which British physician developed the first effective vaccine against smallpox?

4. What is the heaviest alkali metal?

5. On which temperature scale is the temperature of boiling water 212 degrees?

6. Which type of acid gets its name from the Latin word for ant?

7. What is a galvanometer used to measure?

8. Of which chemical element is graphite a form?

9. What name is given to the study of sound waves inaudible to the human ear?

10. Which unit of measurement is equivalent to an explosion of 1000 tons of TNT?

History

1. Which organization was founded by Peter Benenson in 1961 with the aim of defending freedom of speech throughout the world?

2. Which South African clergyman won the Nobel Peace Prize in 1984?

3. What was built in 1961 to curb the flow of refugees from East Germany to West Germany?

4. Which Swedish chemist left £75 million as a foundation for annual awards for Peace, Physics, Chemistry, Literature and Medicine?

5. What was the kingdom of the Serbs, Croats, and Slovenes, formed in 1918, subsequently named?

6. What was the surname of the brothers who made the first successful hot-air balloon flight in 1783?

7. Which island country in the West Indies did the U.S.A. invade in 1983?

8. In which British city was a cathedral consecrated in 1962, retaining the ruins of the original cathedral that was destroyed by German bombs in 1940?

9. Which republic on the north coast of South America was once known as Dutch Guiana?

10. Which South American soldier and statesman was Bolivia named in honour of?

General Knowledge

1   Which American actress married Humphrey Bogart in 1945?

2   In which country did the dance, the turkey trot, originate?

3   Who was the first actress to receive two Oscars before the age of thirty?

4   What is the chief addictive ingredient of tobacco?

5   Which soft white clay is also known as china clay?

6   What was the basic monetary unit of Italy before the Euro?

7   What form of ESP takes its name from the French for 'clear seeing'?

8   What is the name for the movie colour process introduced in movies in 1932?

9   Which unit of mass is abbreviated to kg?

10   What is a dulcimer?

Art

1. Derived from the title of the 1925 Paris Exhibition, what name is given to the decorative style that found its way into architecture and design during the 1920s to 1940s?

2. Which 20th century American artist worked at various New York locations, each known as 'The Factory'?

3. Which English artist was working on illustrations for Dante's 'Divine Comedy' when he died in 1827?

4. 'The Hunters in the Snow' and 'Landscape with the Fall of Icarus' are two famous paintings by which Flemish master?

5. Which Dutch-born artist became painter to the English court in the 17th century and is famous for his portraits of King Charles I?

6. What painting medium was produced from mixing egg-yolk with dyes to give fast-drying paints?

7. 'The Night Watch', a renowned masterpiece by Rembrandt van Rijn, is displayed in which eminent European museum?

8. Which Spanish master painted the famous 'Portrait of Pope Innocent X'?

9. The artist, Tiziano Vecelli is better known by which name in English-speaking countries?

10. The painting 'Portrait of Adele Bloch-Bauer I', sold for $135 million at an auction in 2006. Which Austrian artist painted this in 1907?

Music

1 Which Puccini opera was completed by Franco Alfano?

2 Which word describes the art of combining two or more melodic lines simultaneously in music?

3 Which girl band featuring the twins Edele and Keavy Lynch went straight to number one with their first single 'C'est La Vie'?

4 With which musical instrument is Julian Lloyd Webber associated?

5 Which U.S. guitarist and composer was the leader of the Mothers of Invention?

6 Which American singer had hits with 'Only the Lonely', 'It's Over' and 'Pretty Woman'?

7 Which of Gustav Holst's 'Planets' is 'The Bringer of Old Age'?

8 Which Roman Christian martyr is the patron saint of music?

9 Which British composer wrote the music for the musicals 'Evita' and 'Jesus Christ Superstar'?

10 Of which American orchestra was Sir Georg Solti the music director from 1969 to 1991?

The Bible

1 Which book of the Bible records many of the hymns written by David?

2 In which of the gospels of the New Testament is the verse "Jesus wept", famous for being the shortest verse in the King James Version of the Bible?

3 What did God produce as a sign of his covenant with Noah and all living creatures?

4 Esau's twin brother Jacob was seen to be gripping which part of Esau's body when he was born?

5 What did Jacob name the place where he dreamt of a ladder reaching to heaven, with the angels of God ascending and descending on it?

6 What form did God take when encountered by Moses on Mount Horeb?

7 "The Lord is my shepherd; I shall not want" are the opening words of which Psalm?

8 According to both Mark and Luke, how many devils were cast out of Mary Magdalene by Jesus?

9 After Abraham left Egypt and returned to Canaan, he was rich in what three things?

10 What was the first thing built by Noah after he left the ark?

Mythology

1. In Egyptian mythology, the Sphinx has the body of which animal?

2. The Vodyanoy is a water-spirit from the folklore of which country?

3. In the western part of Alexandria in Egypt there are two great temples, the Serapeion and the Poseidonium: to which gods were they dedicated?

4. Which legendary Spartan king was the husband of Helen and the brother of Agamemnon?

5. In Greek mythology, what name was given to a one-eyed giant?

6. In Greek mythology, who was drowned as an end result of flying too close to the Sun?

7. Which legendary Greek hero and son of Telamon fought Hector in single combat?

8. According to Greek mythology, into which vulnerable part of Achilles' body did Paris shoot a poisoned arrow?

9. According to Greek mythology, who was the sister and wife of Zeus?

10. In Greek mythology, which mountain nymph fell in love with Narcissus?

General Knowledge

1. Fuglestad, Soya and Merino are all breeds of which animal?

2. What six colours appear on the national flag of South Africa?

3. Which is the only Grand Prix that does not adhere to the FIA's mandated 305 kilometres (190 miles) minimum race distance?

4. The Galápagos Islands are a part of which country?

5. The Vince Lombardi Trophy, the Ed Thorp Memorial Trophy and the Brunswick-Balke Collender Cup are all team trophies awarded in which sport?

6. In the 1937 Disney film 'Snow White and the Seven Dwarfs', which one of the seven dwarfs does not have a beard?

7. Known for being one of the largest distributors of humanitarian aid, which organization was founded in London by William Booth?

8. Nicknamed the King of Pop, what was the middle name of Michael Jackson, the U.S. singer-songwriter who died at the age of 50 in June 2009?

9. What meat would you be eating if you ordered 'estofado de pollo' in Spain?

10. Which two planets of our solar system have no moons?

Geography

1 Santa Cruz and Las Palmas are the co-capitals of which Atlantic island group?

2 One of the world's most famous challenges for expert rock-climbers, the monolithic mountain, El Capitan is located in which U.S. national park?

3 Tashkent is the capital city of which Central Asian country?

4 To which country do the North Atlantic island group, the Faroes belong?

5 København is the local name for which capital city?

6 Which Middle Eastern country would be landlocked except for a five-mile strip of coast on the Red Sea's Gulf of Aqaba?

7 The city of Oakland is connected by a bridge to which other Californian city?

8 The Camargue region of southern France lies on the delta of which great river?

9 What is the name of the 3,700-mile geological fault/trench that stretches from Mozambique in Africa northwards as far as Syria?

10 Across which three Nordic countries does the region of Lapland extend?

Politics

1   Who was the U.S. secretary of state from 1993 to 1997?

2   Which building complex in Washington DC gave its name to a political scandal leading to the resignation of Richard Nixon?

3   By what first name was Nelson Mandela's second wife known?

4   Which former Soviet leader was head of the KGB from 1967 to 1982?

5   Who was president of France from 1981 to 1995?

6   Patrice Lumumba, ousted in a coup in 1960 and executed the following year, was the first democratically-elected prime minister of which African country; a region that still suffers from political strife in 2014?

7   Of which country did Nicolae Ceausescu become president in 1974?

8   Who was prime minister of the Union of South Africa from 1924 to 1939?

9   With whom did Marx collaborate on The Communist Manifesto of 1848?

10 Of which country was Menachem Begin prime minister from 1977 to 1983?

Music of the 90s

1 In 1994 which group claimed that 'Love Is All Around'?

_____

2 Who had a hit with 'All I Wanna Do' in 1994?

_____

3 Which group suggested in the 90s that 'Things Can Only Get Better'?

_____

4 'Firestarter' was something of a winner in 1996 for ___?

_____

5 One of the biggest hit singles of 1996 was the Spice Girls' first single, ___?

_____

6 In 1991, 'Everything I Do (I do it for you)' was a huge hit for ___?

_____

7 The massive hit single of 1992 was 'I Will Always Love You' from the movie 'The Bodyguard' sung by ___?

_____

8 Popular in 1992 was 'Achy Breaky Heart' by ___?

_____

9 In 1997, 'Don't Speak' was a hit for ___?

_____

10 The biggest hit of all in 1997, for all the wrong reasons, was 'Candle In The Wind' reworked and sung by ___?

Fictional Places

1 Created by Terry Pratchett, Ankh-Morpork is the most populous city of which fictional world?

2 The Californian town of Sunnydale was home to which vanquisher of bloodsucking beings?

3 Which fictional seaside town was the setting for the novel, 'Jaws'?

4 Maycomb, Alabama was the setting for which novel?

5 Which city does Dorothy find at the end of the yellow brick road in 'The Wizard of Oz'?

6 Ruritania was the country featured in which novel by Anthony Hope?

7 In which U.S. state is South Park?

8 What is the name of the town that neighbours, and rivals, Springfield in TV's 'The Simpsons'?

9 Which cartoon duo lived in Frostbite Falls, Minnesota?

10 The village of Hobbiton was created by which English author?

General Knowledge

1   Einstein's formula for relativity is 'E = mc²', where E = energy, m = mass, and c = ... what?

2   The boiling point of water (at normal pressure) is 100 degrees Celsius (centigrade), but what is the equivalent of this in degrees Fahrenheit?

3   Which is further north: Istanbul or New York City?

4   Fictional hero Superman's alter ego Clark Kent worked for which newspaper?

5   What was the standard monetary unit (equal to 100 pfennig) of East Germany prior to German unification?

6   The Feyenoord football team play their home matches in which European city?

7   What colour is the smoke from the chimney of the Sistine Chapel to signify that a new pope has been chosen?

8   The Vosges are a range of low mountains in the eastern part of which country?

9   The standard writing pencil is graded HB: what do the initials H and B stand for?

10 Which chemical element of atomic number 19 has the chemical symbol K?

General Knowledge

1 To the nearest two years, how long was The Hundred Years War between England and France?

2 Who was the first Roman emperor?

3 What name is given to an Australian Aboriginal stick used to throw a spear more forcibly?

4 The Welland Canal connects which two of the Great Lakes of North America?

5 Whose abduction by Paris brought about the Trojan War?

6 Which Hollywood actor married Calista Flockhart in June 2010?

7 By what name was Russian and Soviet writer Alexei Maximovich Peshkov better known?

8 Which day of the week is named after the chief god of the pagan Anglo-Saxons?

9 Donated in 1892 by Sir Frederick Arthur Stanley, The Stanley Cup is associated with which sport?

10 Confirmed in later treaties, the Kingdom of Castile formally ceded which territory near the southernmost tip of the Iberian Peninsula in perpetuity to the British Crown in 1713, under Article X of the Treaty of Utrecht?

Nature

1 What is the hardest naturally-occurring substance known?

2 What name is given to the winter dormancy of certain mammals?

3 Which volcano in Washington state spectacularly exploded in 1980 resulting in the deaths of 57 people?

4 Which bird, nicknamed 'laughing jackass', is often heard on television and motion picture soundtracks to typify jungle sounds?

5 Which tailless primate has 'slender' and 'slow' varieties?

6 What is the only gem that is of animal origin?

7 Which alkaloid poison is derived from plants of the genus Strychnos?

8 By what name is the aquatic larva of frogs and toads known?

9 Where can polar bears be found, the North Pole or the South Pole?

10 What common substance is obtained from latex-producing tropical trees?

Television

1   Played by Richard Roundtree in the 1970's television detective series, what is the first name of Shaft?

2   What did The A Team's B.A. Baracus' initials stand for?

3   Which star of the TV series 'Friends' married actor Brad Pitt in 2000?

4   What were the names of the policemen in the TV series 'Chips'?

5   What were the surnames of the animators who created Tom and Jerry, The Flintstones and Scooby-Doo?

6   What was the name of the character played by Telly Savalas' brother George in 'Kojak'?

7   Which American television personality successfully defended a libel action brought against her by a consortium of cattlemen in 1998?

8   Which cartoon series is set in the town of Bedrock?

9   Which comic actress starred in the TV series 'I Love Lucy'?

10 The Seattle-based television comedy 'Frasier' is a spin-off from 'Cheers' - which was set where?

Around the Islands

1   Of which country is Sumatra the second largest island?

2   Which Pacific island is also called Rapa Nui and Isla de Pascua?

3   Which island state in the West Indies has Bridgetown as its capital?

4   What is the largest island of the Canadian Arctic?

5   To which country does the Atlantic island of Bermuda belong?

6   Baffin Bay and the Davis Strait lie between Canada and which large island?

7   Surtsey is a volcano which rose from the sea off the coast of which Atlantic island in 1963?

8   The African country of Tanzania partly consists of the former republic of Tanganyika and which island?

9   Which atoll in the Marshall Islands gave its name to a form of swimwear?

10 How are the Friendly Islands otherwise known?

General Knowledge

1. What word describes the longest side of a right-angled triangle, opposite the right angle?

2. Karl Hans Albrecht is a German entrepreneur who, together with his brother Theo, founded which supermarket chain?

3. Which Internet company was founded by Sergey Brin and Larry Page in 1998?

4. What instrument is used to measure the distance travelled by a wheeled vehicle?

5. Which Australian publisher and journalist is best known as the editor-in-chief of the whistleblower website WikiLeaks?

6. What is the name of the French cartoon skunk in the Warner Bros. Looney Tunes and Merrie Melodies series of cartoons?

7. Ojani Noa, Cris Judd, and Marc Anthony are all former husbands of which actress, dancer, producer, and recording artist?

8. Who was Don Quixote's squire in the novel 'Don Quixote' by Miguel de Cervantes?

9. Carlo Lorenzini, better known by the pen name Carlo Collodi, was an Italian children's writer known for the world-renowned fairy tale novel 'The Adventures of...' whom?

10. Which Greek hero rode on the winged horse Pegasus, killed the Chimera monster, and tried to fly Pegasus to Olympus?

History

1. In which former colony did Robert Clive of Plassey establish British supremacy in the 18th century?

2. Which British navigator discovered and charted New Zealand and the east coast of Australia in his ship the 'Endeavour'?

3. At which ancient capital of Normandy was Joan of Arc tried and burned?

4. Which explorer and journalist was sent to Africa by the 'New York Herald' in 1871 to search for David Livingstone?

5. Named after the German valley where skeletal remains were found in 1856, which human sub-species first appeared around 600,000 years ago?

6. Which U.S. general devised the European Recovery Programme for which he won a Nobel peace prize in 1953?

7. Which ancient African city was said to have been founded by Dido?

8. What is the colloquial name for the Fasci di Combattimento, founded in 1919 by Mussolini?

9. Which two countries were first to sign the Anti-Comintern Pact in 1936?

10. On which date in which year did the U.S.A.'s Declaration of Independence take place?

Language

1. What name is given to the inability of a person or company to pay their debts?

2. Which termite-eating nocturnal mammal has a name which means 'earth pig' in Afrikaans?

3. Which wood means 'wood of life' in Latin?

4. By what name is the vitamin B1 also known?

5. What name is given to a verbal device for aiding the memory, such as 'i before e, except after c'?

6. What is the official language of Costa Rica?

7. Which is the most widely-spoken language of India?

8. In the language of the country, German, which capital city is known as Wien?

9. What is the name of the alphabet used for writing Russian?

10. What is the official language of the Co-principality of Andorra?

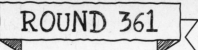

Crime

1. The death penalty was abolished in French law in which decade of the 20th century?

2. What first name is shared by the first and last of the women whose murders were attributed to Jack the Ripper?

3. Lady Justice, the figure atop the Central Criminal Court (otherwise known as the Old Bailey) in London holds a set of scales in her left hand. What is in her right hand?

4. What was the name of the woman who was tried and acquitted of the hatchet murders of her father and stepmother in Fall River, Massachusetts in 1892?

5. The Brink's-MAT robbery took place when robbers broke into a warehouse at Heathrow Airport, London, in November of which year?

6. Which notorious strangler of women lived at 10 Rillington Place, Notting Hill, London?

7. By what names are robbers Robert Leroy Parker and Harry Alonzo Longabaugh better remembered?

8. What was the nickname given to British murderer Peter Sutcliffe, who killed 13 women between 1975 and 1980?

9. In 1995, who bombed a federal building in Oklahoma City, USA, killing 168 people and injuring several hundred?

10. What was the name of the derivatives broker working in Singapore whose fraudulent speculative trading caused the spectacular collapse of Barings Bank in 1995?

General Knowledge

1 Which song, written and originally made famous by Roy Orbison in 1961, was a top ten hit in the U.S. and a number one hit in the U.K. for Don McLean in 1980?

2 In astrology, what is the sign of the 'crab'?

3 What is the human body's largest internal organ?

4 In which year did the following events take place? The Chernobyl nuclear plant meltdown and the 'Challenger' space shuttle disaster.

5 Which country is the world's largest producer of cork: Portugal, India or Italy?

6 Esso, the petroleum brand, is so-named after which company, incorporated in 1870?

7 What do the initials OPEC, the oil cartel, stand for?

8 Which country is known as 'The land of the long white cloud'?

9 Which two words complete Winston Churchill's famous quotation: "I like pigs. Dogs look up to you, cats look down on you, but pigs treat us ...''?

10 Which European capital city gets its hot water and heating energy from nearby hot springs?

Movies

1. Which 2000 movie based on a comic starred Patrick Stewart and Ian McKellen?

2. 'Goodness Had Nothing To Do With It' was the title of which Hollywood sex symbol's autobiography?

3. Which movie star is known as the 'Muscles from Brussels'?

4. Actress Angelina Jolie is the daughter of which actor?

5. Name the actor/singer, often compared with Sinatra, who appeared in the movies 'Memphis Belle', 'Little Man Tate', 'Hope Floats' and 'Copycat'.

6. Which actor was born Bernard Schwartz in New York in 1925?

7. Which actress was born in Japan, raised in Norway and appeared in several movies directed by the Swede, Ingmar Bergman?

8. Who starred as the vigilante in the 'Death Wish' movies?

9. Which 2000 movie starred Samuel L Jackson and Tommy Lee Jones?

10. In which of his movies did River Phoenix play an American marine?

Literature

1. Which English novelist wrote 'Brave New World' and 'Eyeless in Gaza'?

2. Which popular American author wrote 'The Carpetbaggers', 'Heat of Passion' and 'The Betsy'?

3. Which novel by Mary Norton first featured the Clock family?

4. Who wrote 'The Old Men at the Zoo' and 'Anglo-Saxon Attitudes'?

5. In which country is the Paul Theroux novel 'Saint Jack' set?

6. In literature and drama, what name is given to an extended speech by one person?

7. Which Canadian novelist wrote 'What's Bred in the Bone'?

8. Which English-born writer wrote 'The American Way of Death'?

9. Which Irish-American novelist wrote 'The Ginger Man' and 'The Onion Eaters'?

10. Who wrote the novels 'A Summer Bird-Cage' and 'The Ice Age'?

Seas and Oceans

1. Australia and New Zealand are located to either side of which sea?

2. Which is the northernmost sea of the Pacific Ocean?

3. The Sea of Azov is connected by the Kerch Strait to which larger sea to the south?

4. Which Indian Ocean bay is bounded by India, Bangladesh and Burma?

5. Which sea lies between Greece and Italy?

6. The Weddell and the Bellingshausen seas are located off the coast of which continent?

7. The peninsulas of the U.S. state of Florida and Mexico's Yucatan, form which great bay?

8. Which region of popular culture is more or less centred on the Sargasso Sea region of the western Atlantic Ocean?

9. The Bay of Biscay lies between the western coast of France and the northern coast of which other country?

10. Bounded on three sides by coasts of Russia, which sea lies directly to the north of Japan?

Science

1. By what acronym is radio detection and ranging commonly known?

2. Which adjective describes elements with a higher atomic number than uranium?

3. Which explosive plastic solid consists of 75% nitroglycerine and 25% kieselguhr?

4. Which colourless, odourless gas is represented by the symbol N?

5. What sort of alloy is melted to form a joint between other metals?

6. How is polymethyl methacrylate better known?

7. What is the name of the Scottish site of the world's first experimental fast-breeder nuclear reactor?

8. Laudanum is an alcoholic solution of which drug?

9. For which vitamin is cyanocobalamin the chemical name?

10. What is the trade name of the heat-resistant plastic PTFE?

General Knowledge

1   What is the capital of Colombia?

2   Which Russian ballet impresario founded the Ballets Russes?

3   Which tubes between the ovary and uterus are also called oviducts?

4   In which country is 'Le Figaro' a daily newspaper?

5   Santa Claus is a modification of which saint's name?

6   How many months of the year have 31 days?

7   By what first name was Gabrielle Chanel known?

8   For what sort of fabric is the town of Chantilly famous?

9   Which country developed the Polaris missile?

10 Which pets are paraded at the annual British show, Cruft's?

Classical Music

1   Who composed the concert overture 'Carnival' Opus 92?

2   Who composed the 48 preludes and fugues which are collectively known as 'The Well-Tempered Clavier'?

3   Who composed the 80 pieces of piano music collectively entitled 'For Children'?

4   Beethoven wrote five piano concertos, only one of which, the 5th in E flat major was given a name. What is it?

5   By what name is Beethoven's piano sonata in C minor, Opus 13 better known?

6   By what name is Chopin's Etude No 12 in C minor, Opus 10, better known?

7   The third movement of the 'Suite Bergamasque' for piano by Debussy is better known as what?

8   Who is called 'the father of modern piano playing'?

9   Who composed 'An Alpine Symphony' and the symphonic poem 'Death and Transfiguration'?

10 What is the English-language name for Wagner's opera 'Der Fliegende Holländer'?

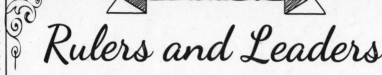

Rulers and Leaders

1 Of which South American country was Juan Peron president from 1946 to 1955?

2 Of which country was Ferdinand Marcos president from 1965 to 1986?

3 After which king of Macedon was Egypt's chief port named?

4 Of which country did Ayatollah Khomeini become leader in 1979?

5 Which Caribbean country was ruled by Dr. Francois Duvalier from 1957 to 1971?

6 Of which country did P.W. Botha become president in 1984?

7 Who did Hitler marry shortly before committing suicide in 1945?

8 Which Chinese statesman, was chairman of the Communist Party of the Chinese People's Republic 1949–76 and head of state 1949–59?

9 Who was the 28th president of the U.S.A., 1913-21?

10 Who succeeded Tony Blair as prime minister of the U.K.?

ROUND 370

The Olympics

1 Which swimmer won four golds and two silver medals at the Summer Olympics in London in 2012?

2 Who or what is depicted on the obverse face of an Olympic medal?

3 A bronze Olympic medal is comprised of approximately 97 per cent of which metallic element?

4 What did President Putin award to each medal-winning Russian Olympic athlete after the 2012 Summer Olympics?

5 Which Australian swimmer took the gold medal for the Women's 4 x 100m Freestyle Relay at the 2012 Summer Olympics?

6 Which country won the highest number of gold medals at the 2008 Summer Olympics?

7 After racing to victory in the Women's Skeleton, who was Team GB's lone gold medallist at the Winter Olympics held in Sochi in 2014?

8 For which country did Matthias Mayer win the Men's Downhill Alpine Skiing at the Winter Olympics in 2014?

9 Which US swimmer won a gold medal in the Men's 200m Backstroke at the 2012 Summer Olympics?

10 At the 2012 Summer Olympics, who won the Decathlon gold medal, finishing 198 points ahead of United States team-mate Trey Hardee?

Food and Drink

1 What name is commonly given to the ground thick green root used in Japanese cookery, usually as an accompaniment to raw fish?

2 What type of meat is stewed in wine with vegetables to create the Italian dish osso buco?

3 What is the main ingredient of the German dish sauerkraut?

4 Invented in 1934 at Harry's Bar in Venice, a Bellini cocktail is made with champagne and the juice of which fruit?

5 A rich creamy liqueur made from eggs, sugar and brandy, in which country did advocaat originate?

6 What name is given to small hollow cases of choux pastry usually filled with cream and covered with chocolate sauce?

7 Eggs Florentine is a dish of eggs served on a bed of which vegetable?

8 What colour is Chablis, a dry wine from Chablis in eastern France?

9 What type of fruit is used to make Calvados, traditionally made in the Calvados region of Normandy, France?

10 The discovery of which kind of meat in burgers and other food products caused a food scandal in Europe in 2012-13?

General Knowledge

1 Everest is first, K2 second; what is third?

2 Grenadine, used in cocktail drinks to add flavour and colour, is made from which fruit?

3 The 'baiji' which could only be found in China's River Yangtse, until its extinction around 2005, was what kind of aquatic creature?

4 In Greek mythology, which adventurer was delayed on his homeward journey by the nymphs Circe and Calypso?

5 What is the English translation of the Latin-derived word 'Cornucopia' as in 'a cornucopia of possibilities'?

6 Which war does Russia call the 'Great Patriotic War'?

7 Which drink is made from orange juice and champagne?

8 Founded around 3000 B.C., Memphis was the capital of which country at that time?

9 The traditional mythology of which country features the heroes Lemminkäinen and Kullervo and the deities Tapio and Luonnotar?

10 Which Swiss mountain was the subject of a 1975 film starring, and directed by, Clint Eastwood?

Geography

1   Of which ocean is the Davis Strait a section?

2   Which sea connects with the Atlantic Ocean at Gibraltar, the Black Sea via the Sea of Marmara, and the Red Sea via the Suez Canal?

3   Which is the world's largest and deepest ocean?

4   In which U.S. state is the city of Tacoma?

5   What is the capital of Portugal?

6   Of which country was Karachi the first capital?

7   In which U.S. state is the city of Branson?

8   In which state of the U.S.A. is the fashionable resort of Palm Beach situated?

9   Of which European country was Coimbra the capital from 1139 to 1260?

10 What is the name of the equatorial belt of light variable winds within which the trade-wind zones converge?

'The Simpsons'

1 What number Evergreen Terrace is home to the Simpson family?

_____

2 Which broadcasting company produces 'The Simpsons'?

_____

3 After more than 20 seasons, Simpsons creator Matt Groening finally revealed that the town of Springfield, in which U.S. state, was the inspiration for the show's setting?

_____

4 Before marrying Homer, what was Marge Simpson's last name?

_____

5 In which sector of the Springfield Nuclear Power Plant does Homer Simpson work?

_____

6 Marge's twin sister Selma has a pet iguana: what is its name?

_____

7 What is the name of the youngest son of Ned Flanders?

_____

8 What is Doctor Hibbert's first name?

_____

9 Who provides the voice of Lisa Simpson?

_____

10 Who directed 'The Simpsons Movie', an animated film that was released on 27 July, 2007?

Fairy Stories

1. According to the tale by Hans Christian Andersen, how many mattresses did the princess in 'The Princess and the Pea' need to sleep on?

2. Which fair maiden let down her hair for the prince to climb up into the tower in which she was imprisoned?

3. Who is said to have slept in a cradle made from a walnut-shell when she was a baby?

4. Which Hans Andersen story is a parable about trickery, self-delusion and the truthful innocence of childhood?

5. German composer Engelbert Humperdinck wrote an opera on the subject of which Grimms' fairy tale?

6. Which animal helped, then later ate, the Gingerbread Man?

7. The story of Little Red Riding Hood originated in which European country?

8. Whose hysterical claim that "the sky is falling down" leads a whole poultry population to the jaws of Foxy Loxy?

9. In 'Rumpelstiltskin', what is the miller's daughter commanded to do to make the king rich?

10. Though she pleads for help from the other farmyard animals, who gets no help with her efforts to produce bread, later taking revenge by refusing to share the loaf?

History

1 Which two countries signed the 1569 'Union of Lublin'?

2 How many wives did King Henry VIII of England have?

3 According to legend, which Greek mathematician shouted "Eureka!" after discovering a scientific principle whilst in the bath?

4 Who is the only First Lady of the U.S.A. to have won a Grammy award?

5 Which product did soap salesman William Wrigley Jr. begin distributing in 1892?

6 In which New Mexico city was the atomic bomb developed in the Manhattan Project?

7 Which assault rifle adopted by the U.S. Army in 1967 is also called AR-15?

8 Which English logician and philosopher wrote 'The Principles of Mathematics' in 1903?

9 In which year was the Berlin Wall built?

10 What was the official currency unit of Portugal before the Euro?

General Knowledge

1. The last letter of the Russian alphabet looks like a mirror image of which letter of the English alphabet?

2. Which is the longest river in Canada?

3. What is the middle name of Catherine, Duchess of Cambridge, née Middleton, who married Prince William in April 2011?

4. In Judaism, what name is given to the candelabra used in religious ceremonies, that typically has seven, eight or nine branches?

5. What colour is the belt worn by junior students in the sport of judo?

6. What word designates a gland which secretes hormones or other products directly into the blood?

7. Who won the Tour de France every year from 1999 to 2005 before being disqualified for doping offences from all those races and banned from competitive cycling for life?

8. What name is given to the canticle of the Virgin Mary (Luke 1:46-55) used as a canticle in Christian liturgy, especially at vespers and evensong?

9. Which international organization, founded in the UK in 1946, is open to people with a high IQ rating?

10. What is the capital of New York state?

Civil Aircraft

1 Which 1950s turbo-prop passenger aircraft was known as 'The Whispering Giant', due to its low levels of in-cabin noise?

2 Which British airliner, similar to the Boeing 727, first flew in 1963 and was later produced in a stretch-body 500 Series version?

3 The Friendship and Fellowship airliners were produced by which manufacturer?

4 As of 2014, which is the world's largest passenger transport aircraft?

5 Produced by the French company Sud Aviation, what was the world's first short to medium-range jet airliner?

6 Which tri-jet airliner design was modified into the KC-10 Extender, a tanker for the U.S. Air Force?

7 The NASA Space Shuttle was piggy-backed onto which commercial airliner type?

8 Which Canadian-based company produced the light passenger aircraft, the Otter and the Beaver?

9 Which U. S. company produced the Coronado four-engined jet-powered airliner in the 1950s and 60s?

10 The British, Bristol Britannia turbo-prop airliner was built under license by Canadair of Canada under what name?

Jazz

1 Who is the Algerian-born pianist, composer and bandleader, renowned for his imagination and capacity for improvization?

2 Who is the Canadian-born piano virtuoso, great accompanist and flamboyant soloist, who has many recordings to his name including 'Oscar's Blues'?

3 Who was called 'Lady Day'?

4 Who was the highly regarded 1930's blues singer who had such hits as 'Stormy Weather'?

5 Who started his career with Tommy Dorsey and went on to movie and concert fame. He was known as 'The Voice'?

6 Who was the pianist, composer and bandleader who sang his own songs like 'Ain't Misbehavin'' and 'Honeysuckle Rose'?

7 Who composed 'Bugle Call Rag'?

8 Who sang bebop with Charlie Parker and Dizzy Gillespie, and was known as 'Sassy'?

9 Which charismatic guitarist accompanied himself on recordings like 'Sweet Black Angel' and the 1981 Grammy winner 'There Must Be A Better World Somewhere'?

10 Which one of the following jazz musicians was a saxophonist and not a trumpeter: Louis Armstrong, John Coltrane, Dizzy Gillespie?

U.S. States

1 Which three states have names of just four letters?

_____

2 What is the state capital of Oregon?

_____

3 Which state has the largest population?

_____

4 Of which state is Cheyenne the capital?

_____

5 Which is the largest state by land area?

_____

6 The lowest point in the U.S.A., in which state is Death Valley?

_____

7 Which state shares borders with Alabama, Arkansas, Georgia, Kentucky, Mississippi, Missouri, North Carolina, and Virginia?

_____

8 In which U.S. state is Wichita?

_____

9 Which state lies directly west of Idaho?

_____

10 Which state's nickname is The Old Line State?

_____

General Knowledge

1. What was the name of the character played by Patrick Stewart in the successor to the original 'Star Trek' series?

2. Which dancer died in September 1927, when her trailing scarf became entangled in the wheels of a car in which she was travelling?

3. Which former U.S. president was nicknamed 'The Peanut Farmer'?

4. Laurence Tureaud is a U.S. actor and wrestler, better known by what name?

5. Once a Greek Orthodox patriarchal basilica, later an imperial mosque, and now a museum, Hagia Sophia is in which Middle Eastern city?

6. A prince in India in the 6th century B.C., by what name is Siddhārtha Gautama better known?

7. Which fictional city in Providence County, Rhode Island is home to 'Family Guy' Peter Griffin and his relatives?

8. In the cartoon series, what was the name of the Flintstones' yapping prehistoric pet dinosaur?

9. Who was the first person to win Pulitzer Prizes in both fiction and poetry categories, and in 1986 was made the first American Poet Laureate?

10. Which 'Line' became widely known as the symbolic divider between the Northern and Southern states during America's Civil War?

The Animal Kingdom

1 What kind of creatures are the mountain-dwelling marmots?

2 Which acute viral infection transmitted by animals is alternatively known as hydrophobia?

3 What sort of creature is an agouti?

4 What sort of creature is a rorqual?

5 What sort of creature is a douroucouli?

6 What sort of creature is a takahe?

7 What sort of creature is a white-eye?

8 How many legs does a lobster have?

9 Which word is used to describe thick-skinned animals such as the elephant or rhinoceros?

10 The black-eared flying fox is a species of which creature?

The Answer's a Number

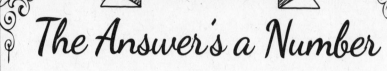

1 What is the smallest whole number which, when written as a word contains eight letters?

2 In the binary system of numbers, which number is written as 1111?

3 When said aloud, how many states of the U.S.A. have one syllable?

4 In which year did Alaska become the 49th state of the U.S.A.?

5 Including the zero, how many compartments (into which the ball may come to rest) appear on a single zero roulette wheel?

6 What is the total number of pips (spots or dots) on all the tiles in a standard set of 28 dominoes?

7 In the NATO phonetic alphabet (aka the international radiotelephony spelling alphabet), how many of the 26 words end with a vowel (a, e, i, o, u)?

8 What is the smallest whole number which, when written as a word contains both the letter X and the letter Y?

9 How many edges has a cube?

10 In the game of American football, how many points are awarded for a touchdown?

Literature

1 Which novel by Jerzy Kosinski was made into a 1979 movie starring Peter Sellers and Shirley MacLaine?

2 Which crime-novel author also writes under the name Barbara Vine?

3 With what sort of books is the German publisher, Karl Baedeker, associated?

4 What was the pen name of authors Frederic Dannay and Manfred B. Lee?

5 In which story by Nathaniel Hawthorne is Hester Prynne the main character?

6 Which U.S. novelist wrote 'The Man with the Golden Arm' and 'A Walk on the Wild Side'?

7 Which U.S. dramatist won the 1955 Pulitzer Prize for Drama with 'Cat on a Hot Tin Roof'?

8 Which sociologist, historian and economist co-wrote 'The Communist Manifesto' with Friedrich Engels?

9 Which English author wrote 'Love in a Cold Climate'?

10 Which science fiction author wrote the novel, 'Hothouse', and the 'Helliconia' trilogy?

Entertainment

1 Which American comedy duo performed the routine 'Who's On First'?

2 Which star of 'The X Files' played Lily Bart in the movie 'The House of Mirth'?

3 Which much-married former child star was born Joe Yule?

4 Which American actor starred in 'The Third Man' and 'Under Capricorn'?

5 What was the title of Robert Flaherty's 1922 documentary movie about Eskimos?

6 Which Canadian-born actress and dancer married Al Jolson in 1928?

7 Which French entertainer starred in the movies 'Love in the Afternoon' and 'Gigi'?

8 Which movie received 12 nominations for the 2001 Oscars?

9 Which American actress was the elder sister of Joan Fontaine?

10 Which American media mogul founded CNN?

General Knowledge

1 Which Royal Navy ship, that between 1872 and 1876 sailed 70,000 miles around the world on an oceanographic survey, gives its name to a deep-sea trench in the Pacific and to a NASA space shuttle?

2 What is the more familiar name of the sea creature, the 'orca'?

3 Which class of animals can live in, as well as out, of water?

4 Which common material is the chief source of silicon dioxide, the main constituent of glass?

5 'The Man of a Thousand Faces' was the nickname of which silent-film actor?

6 What nationality was the 19th century operatic soprano, Jenny Lind, known as 'The ___ Nightingale'?

7 In which U.S. state is the city and port of Mobile?

8 In 1967, The Beatles released a double A-side record: 'Penny Lane' was on one side, what was on the other?

9 The airport for which European city has the three-letter code ZRH?

10 What are the two principal divisions of the Islamic faith?

Sport

1 What is Tiger Woods' real first name?

2 The Modern Pentathlon involves riding, running, fencing, swimming and which other event?

3 What term is used for a time period in the game of polo?

4 The first international soccer match was played in 1883; between England and which other country?

5 Which continent is the only one not to have a national rugby team?

6 The then future King Constantine of Greece won a gold medal at the 1960 Olympic Games; in which event?

7 The 1936 Winter Olympics were held in which German town?

8 The 'Long Count Fight', in 1927 Chicago, was a boxing match between the reigning heavyweight champ and the man he'd taken the title from just a year earlier. Who were the two opponents?

9 The Winter Olympics have been staged in the same U.S. place twice: where?

10 Shergar, the horse that won the 1981 Epsom Derby, set a record by winning the race by how many lengths?

World Heritage Sites

1. On which Chilean island in the south Pacific are the Moai stone statues to be found?

2. 'The Rose Red City' is a name for which World Heritage Site located in Jordan?

3. Cave dwellings of the Pueblo people can be seen in Mesa Verde National Park; in which U.S. state?

4. The World Heritage Sites of the Palmarel of Elche and the Vizcaya Bridge are in which European country?

5. Together with its sister-site at Avebury, which Heritage pre-historic site stands in the English county of Wiltshire?

6. The ancient city of Chichen Itza stands in which country?

7. The Vredevort Dome is a mound in the centre of a crater created by a meteorite strike around two billion years ago. In which African country is this World Heritage Site?

8. Which New York landmark is designated a World Heritage Site?

9. In which country are the Red Fort Complex and Mahabodhi Temple Complex sites?

10. Xanadu, Inner Mongolia, designated a World Heritage Site in 2012, was founded by which Mongol leader in around 1270?

Language

1. What is the French equivalent of 'Miss', referring to an unmarried female?

_____

2. What is the French equivalent of Mister?

_____

3. What name is given to a fear of closed or confined spaces?

_____

4. What name is given to the two dots placed above a vowel in German?

_____

5. Mandarin and Cantonese are dialects of which language?

_____

6. What is the official language of Argentina?

_____

7. What is the official language of the Republic of San Marino?

_____

8. What is the singular of graffiti?

_____

9. Which supposedly magical word was used by Gnostics in the 2nd century?

_____

10. What was the name of the tower where, according to the biblical story, God made the builders all speak different languages?

Movies

1. Who starred as Daisy Miller in the 1974 movie version of Henry Miller's novel of the same name?

2. In the 1950 movie 'Born Yesterday', which actress won an Oscar for her role as Broderick Crawford's mistress?

3. What was the name of the character played by Malcolm McDowell in 'A Clockwork Orange'?

4. What was the title of the Mel Gibson 1990 movie about C.I.A. pilots playing fast and loose over and in Laos?

5. Who starred in the 1998 movie about an asteroid threatening the Earth, 'Armageddon'?

6. What was the title of the 2000 movie in which Tom Hanks is marooned on a desert island?

7. Who wrote, directed and starred in the 1975 movie 'The Adventures of Sherlock Holmes's Smarter Brother'?

8. Who were the male and female leads in the classic comedy thriller released in 1934 'The Thin Man'?

9. What was the name of the character played by Daniel Day Lewis in the movie 'Last of the Mohicans'?

10. Which U.S. comedy writer, actor, and moviemaker directed 'Young Frankenstein'?

General Knowledge

1. In which London park can one find Speakers' Corner and the Serpentine boating lake?

2. What is the name for the middle value of a set of numbers arranged in order of magnitude?

3. What sort of creature is a mallard?

4. Which constellation of the zodiac means 'scales' in Latin?

5. What is the capital of Tibet?

6. Which term describes an industry in which the market is supplied by one supplier?

7. What are incisors, canines and molars examples of?

8. Which Jewish philosopher and physician wrote 'The Guide of the Perplexed'?

9. On which date of the year does the feast day of St. Valentine occur?

10. In which series of movies did the maniac Michael Myers appear?

Politics

1 Angela Merkel became German chancellor in 2005, and became leader of which political party in the year 2000?

2 Of which country did Helen Clark become the first-ever woman prime minister in 1999?

3 Fulgencio Batista was the dictator of which country before he was overthrown by another dictator in 1959?

4 Which European country was led by Konrad Adenauer from 1949 to 1963?

5 In the U.S.A. the 'right to keep and bear arms' is embedded in which Amendment to the Constitution?

6 Which Argentine dictator was removed from power shortly after his country was defeated by Britain in the Falklands War in 1982?

7 Robert Menzies was the prime minister of which country from 1939 to 1941 and from 1949 to 1966?

8 In 1999, who succeeded Nelson Mandela as the president of South Africa?

9 Who was sworn in as the U.S.A.'s first female secretary of state in January 1997?

10 Who was the prime minister of Italy from 1963 to 1968 and from 1974 to 1976?

Mythology

1. The 'Kalevela' is an epic poem which describes events from the mythology of which Nordic country?

2. Which character in Greek mythology is also known as Ulysses in Roman mythology?

3. In Greek mythology, which race of creatures were part horse and part man?

4. Which Egyptian goddess was the sister and wife of Osiris?

5. Who was the Greek goddess of the Moon?

6. After which Roman god is January named?

7. Which Germanic god of war gave his name to Tuesday?

8. Who was the Greek god of war, identified by the Romans with Mars?

9. The Colossus of Rhodes was a statue of which god?

10. In medieval legends of the Trojan War, who was the daughter of Calchas, a priest? She was faithless to her lover Troilus, a son of Priam.

Art

1   Which Belgian artist painted 'Golconda', in which bowler-hatted men fall like rain?

2   Which Spanish artist painted the 'Rokeby Venus'?

3   Which ancient Greek sculptures were sold to the British Museum in 1816 for £35,000?

4   Don McLean's song which begins with 'Starry, starry night' was a tribute to which artist?

5   George Stubbs is best known for his paintings of which kind of animals?

6   Which Swiss sculptor and painter created an abstract construction entitled 'The Palace at 4 a.m.'?

7   Which British sculptor is known for his Peter Pan in Kensington Gardens and the Edith Cavell memorial?

8   In which Italian city is the Uffizi art gallery situated?

9   What nationality was the painter Hieronymus Bosch?

10 Which French movie director, whose works include 'La Grande Illusion', was the son of an impressionist painter?

Pop Music

1 'Love Will Tear Us Apart' was whose message on the 1979 hit single?

2 Who first sang 'Stand By Me'?

3 Who was the 'Dedicated Follower of Fashion'?

4 Who claimed that 'Girls Just Want to Have Fun'?

5 Who was the top pop artist who had hits like 'Peggy Sue' and 'That'll Be The Day'?

6 Which group specialized in hit singles like 'California Dreamin' and 'Dedicated to the One I Love'?

7 Who first sang 'And I Love You So'?

8 With what hit single did Kylie Minogue break upon the scene in 1987?

9 Which British group had a big hit with 'You Can't Hurry Love'?

10 'See You Later Alligator' was one of whose big hits?

General Knowledge

1. Pancho Villa (1878-1923) was a revolutionary in which country?

2. Where in the human body are the intercostal muscles?

3. The passerine order of avians denotes birds that can do what?

4. Which 18th-19th century Spanish artist created the 82 prints known collectively as 'The Disasters of War'?

5. At the Battle of Dettingen in 1743, which British monarch was the last to personally lead his troops into battle?

6. The name of which Mexican volcano translates as 'smoking mountain'?

7. The bone-deforming childhood disease, rickets, is caused mainly by a deficiency of which vitamin?

8. In the human body, what is the more common name for the clavicle?

9. Entomology is the scientific study of which kinds of creatures?

10. The gestation period of an elephant lasts approximately how many days?

Geography

1. Which strait separates the mainland of South America from Tierra del Fuego?

2. Victoria Falls is situated on the border of which two African countries?

3. Of which state of the U.S.A. is Baton Rouge the capital?

4. Which reef off the coast of north-east Australia is the largest coral reef in the world?

5. Andalusia is a region of which European country?

6. In which continent can the Kalahari Desert be found?

7. Which Slovakian city was the capital of Hungary until 1784?

8. What is the capital of the Australian state of New South Wales?

9. In which U.S. state is the city of Fairbanks?

10. In which European country is the city of Winterthur?

Religion

1. In Christianity and Judaism, what are the highest order of angels called?

2. Which religion was established by Mohammed?

3. What name is given to the national religious folk cult of Haiti?

4. Which religion, based on the Four Noble Truths, has more than 500 million followers?

5. Which palace in Lhasa, Tibet was the residence of that country's religious leader, the Dalai Lama, until 1959?

6. John Wesley started which religious movement in the eighteenth century?

7. Sufism is a branch of which major religion?

8. Inti, Kon and Apu were deities within the religion of which South American people?

9. Masjid al-Haram, the world's largest mosque is located in which Middle Eastern city?

10. In which country did Jainism originate?

Science

1   Which metal can be made pure by the puddling process?

2   What is the boiling point of water in degrees Celsius?

3   Which type of medically useful electromagnetic radiation was originally called Roentgen rays?

4   Haematite is the principal ore of which metal?

5   Which colourless liquid is found in all living matter?

6   What is an ammeter used to measure?

7   A speed of approximately how many miles per second must a space vehicle achieve in order to escape Earth's gravity?

8   How is the explosive trinitrotoluene much more commonly known?

9   Alabaster is a form of which mineral?

10 What is the common name for pyrite or iron pyrites?

General Knowledge

1 The dance, the Rumba originated on which Caribbean island?

2 What does the Latin phrase 'Vox populi' mean in English?

3 What was the full name of the Dutch artist known as Rembrandt?

4 Which Royal Navy cruiser, that took part in the sinking of the German battleship 'Scharnhorst' on Boxing Day 1943, is today moored near London's Tower Bridge?

5 Which Christian festival is named after an Anglo-Saxon goddess of the dawn, and possibly also of the spring equinox?

6 Author of the novels 'The Stranger' and 'The Plague', which French philosopher died, aged 46, in a car crash in 1960?

7 The Cathedral of the Intercession of the Blessed Virgin on the Moat: how is this famous Russian religious building better known?

8 Of which U.S. state is Little Rock the capital?

9 What nationality is the film actor, Rutger Hauer?

10 Of which state of the U.S.A. is Richmond the capital?

Classical Music

1 In which year did Gustav Mahler die?

_____

2 By what name is Mozart's Symphony No 38 in D major, (K. 504) known?

_____

3 Haydn's symphony No 94 in G major Opus 80, is also known as ___?

_____

4 By what name is Beethoven's 6th Symphony in F, Opus 68, known?

_____

5 By what name is Tchaikovsky's 6th Symphony in B minor, Opus 74, known?

_____

6 Who composed a choral symphony entitled 'The Bells'?

_____

7 Who composed the symphonic poems 'En Saga' and 'Finlandia'?

_____

8 What is the unusual element in Saint-Saens Symphony No 3 in C minor, Opus 78, which gives the work its popular title?

_____

9 Who composed the piano suite 'Pictures at an Exhibition'?

_____

10 Who composed three nocturnes for piano and orchestra called 'Nights in the Gardens of Spain'?

Sport

1 What is basketball player Magic Johnson's real first name?

2 What is the minimum number of points needed to win a tie-break in tennis?

3 Who was the first heavyweight boxer to win the world title four times?

4 In which country is the Interlagos motor racing circuit situated?

5 In the high jump, what is the maximum number of attempts each competitor is allowed at each height?

6 Davo Karničar was the first man to ski non-stop down which mountain?

7 Which Austrian motor-racing driver was Formula One world champion in 1975, 1977, and 1984?

8 What nationality is tennis player Gustavo Kuerten?

9 Which Texas city has an American football team called the Cowboys?

10 Which is the oldest of the three classic races that constitute the American Triple Crown?

Poetry

1 Which Greek poet is said to have introduced actors into dramatic performances?

2 Which French-born poet wrote 'Cautionary Tales'?

3 In verse, which metrical foot consists of an unstressed syllable followed by a stressed syllable?

4 Which Italian poet won the 1959 Nobel Prize for Literature?

5 The 'Epic of Gilgamesh' is possibly the earliest surviving poem. It belonged to which ancient Asian civilisation?

6 Dante's epic 'Divine Comedy' is in three sections. The first two are 'Inferno' and 'Purgatorio'; what is the third?

7 Noted mainly as a poet, which German also wrote several novels, including 'The Sorrows of Young Werther'?

8 Having the same name as a fairground steam-powered musical organ, which daughter of Zeus was the muse of epic poetry?

9 Which American-born poet was imprisoned for treason for his support for Hitler and Mussolini, spent time in a U.S. psychiatric hospital and died in Venice in 1972?

10 What were the first names of Anglo-Irish poet W.B. Yeats?

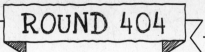

Asia

1. What is both Pakistan's largest city by population and its chief seaport?

2. The 'Deccan', an upland plateau of fertile soils sited between the Eastern and Western Ghats mountain ranges, is in which country?

3. Which part of the Indian Ocean is the largest bay in the world?

4. Which Asian river's name translates from Sanskrit as 'Son of Brahma'?

5. Vientiane is the capital city of which Asian country?

6. Taken from the Persian language; what does the suffix 'stan' mean in the names of countries such as Afghanistan, Pakistan etc.?

7. Which Turkish sea-strait forms a boundary between Europe and Asia?

8. The Asian continent's easternmost and northernmost points are in which country?

9. Which country is at the eastern end of the ancient Silk Road?

10. The Kuril Islands chain stretches south from Russia's Kamchatka peninsula to the northern reaches of which country?

General Knowledge

1   Enver Hoxha was the communist leader of which country from 1944 until his death in 1985?

2   From which country did Iceland gain independence in May 1944, the mother country at that time being under the heel of German occupation?

3   Which gas is produced by the Haber-Bosch process?

4   The Beagle Channel is a channel connecting which two oceans?

5   According to the Book of Deuteronomy, how old was Moses when he died?

6   Wadi in Arabic and arroyo in Spanish both refer to which kind of geographical feature?

7   In 1960, who did John F Kennedy defeat to become U. S. president?

8   The adjective 'Jovian' refers to which planet of the solar system?

9   The Allegheny, Blue Ridge and Catskill mountain ranges in the eastern U.S.A. are part of which greater range?

10   Cesar Romero, Jack Nicholson and Heath Ledger have all played TV or film roles of which of Batman's enemies?

Movies

1 What was the title of the 1971 Woody Allen movie about an angst-ridden New Yorker who accidentally becomes a South American revolutionary hero?

2 Who played the lead in the 1999 movie 'Being John Malkovich'?

3 Who played the part of Axel Foley in the series of movies between 1984 and 1994 about a 'Beverley Hills Cop'?

4 Who played the lead male role in the 1990 movie 'Betsy's Wedding'?

5 Who played the lead role in the 1980 movie 'Private Benjamin'?

6 What was the title of the 1996 movie in which a wronged wife and her family drive from Long Island to confront her husband in Manhattan?

7 Who played the lead in the 1982 movie 'Dead Men Don't Wear Plaid'?

8 Who played the part of the Scottish hairdresser in Los Angeles in the 1999 movie 'The Big Tease'?

9 Which sex symbol made her screen debut with a one-line speaking part in the 1948 movie 'Scudda-Hoo, Scudda-Hay'?

10 Who played Joan of Arc in the 1948 movie of that name?

Entertainment

1. By what name was American lyricist Samuel Cohen known?

2. Which actor appeared in 'Superman' and 'Apocalypse Now'?

3. Which Canadian comedian starred in the movies 'Planes, Trains and Automobiles' and 'Cool Runnings'?

4. Which rank did 'Six Million Dollar Man' Steve Austin hold?

5. Which resort on the French Riviera is famous for its annual movie festival?

6. By which acronym is the International Association of Poets, Playwrights, Editors, Essayists, and Novelists known?

7. Which Canadian actor starred in the movie 'East of Eden' and the TV series 'Dr. Kildare'?

8. By what name was American comedian Louis Francis Cristillo known?

9. How was French cabaret and music-hall singer Edith Giovanna Gassion better known?

10. Robbie Coltrane and Whoopi Goldberg have both appeared in movies where their characters disguised themselves as what?

General Knowledge

1 How many points does a Star of David have?

2 What is the currency unit of Australia?

3 What nationality was chemist and Nobel Prize founder Alfred Nobel?

4 Which two countries are linked by the Brenner Pass?

5 What is the square root of 121?

6 By what name were supporters of the Youth International Party known?

7 Which American city is known as the 'City of Brotherly Love'?

8 In which sea can the vast sandbank Dogger Bank be found?

9 Which Italian islet in the Tyrrhenian Sea features in the title of a novel by Alexandre Dumas?

10 How is 'acquired immune deficiency syndrome' better known?

History

1   To which English monarch was Catherine Parr married?

2   In which present day country are the remains of the ancient city of Locri?

3   What was the name for the Nazi secret police formed in 1933 under Göring?

4   What was the tallest building in the world before the Chrysler Building in New York was completed in 1930?

5   Which former country was also known as the G.D.R.?

6   Which ancient unit of length is based on the distance from the elbow to the tip of the middle finger?

7   Which Roman general and statesman did Marcus Junius Brutus help to assassinate?

8   Which animal was called camelopardalis or spotted camel by the Romans?

9   Who was the first woman to make a solo flight across the Atlantic Ocean?

10   Who was the French signatory to the Munich Agreement of 1938?

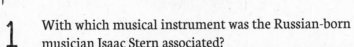

Music

1 With which musical instrument was the Russian-born musician Isaac Stern associated?

2 With which musical instrument was Paul Tortelier associated?

3 What name is given to three or more notes sounded together?

4 With which musical instrument is Fritz Kreisler associated?

5 Which musical composition takes its name from the French for 'study'?

6 What name is given to a musical composition for six instruments?

7 What name is given to a musical composition for five instruments?

8 Which musical term literally means 'beautiful singing' in Italian?

9 With which musical instrument is Ravi Shankar primarily associated?

10 Which U.S. pianist and bandleader wrote 'Artistry in Rhythm'?

General Knowledge

1. Mount Rainier is the highest mountain of the Cascade range, a mountain chain that lies within which two countries?

2. The quotation "A classic is something that everybody wants to have read but nobody wants to read", is a classic in itself! Which American author said it?

3. The Aoraki/Mount Cook National park is located in which country?

4. In which Middle East country is the wide, arid valley of Wadi Rum?

5. The acronym LED (tiny low-energy lights, often red - e.g. a TV standby indicator) stands for what?

6. The 53rd Academy Awards (Oscars) event of 31st March 1981 was delayed by one day due to the attempted murder of which public figure on the 30th?

7. In which country is the Rub' al Khali (meaning 'empty quarter') desert?

8. The word 'thug' (an aggressive criminal) comes from 'thugee' a member of a gang of thieves/killers active in which country during the 14th to the 19th centuries?

9. On which date is St Nicholas' Day?

10. Possibly the world's largest cathedral, the Cathedral of St John the Divine stands in which U.S. city?

World Cities

1 Although La Paz, Bolivia's de facto capital is higher, which South American city is the world's highest-altitude official capital?

2 Which African city is one of only two capital cities that straddle the Equator?

3 Graz and Linz are the second and third cities of which European country?

4 Olympia is the capital, and Portland the largest city of which U.S. state?

5 Located at the eastern end of the Trans-Siberian Railway, which is Russia's largest port on that country's Pacific coast?

6 Which Spanish city, at the foot of the Sierra Nevada mountains, is famous for its Alhambra palace?

7 Which is the world's most southerly capital city?

8 Espoo is the second-largest city of which European country?

9 Which city is located at the confluence of the Mississippi and Missouri rivers?

10 Which is England's easternmost city?

Literature

1. Which Danish author of fairy tales wrote 'The Little Mermaid'?

2. Which American novelist wrote 'The Wonderful Wizard of Oz'?

3. The fearsome and wily dragon, Smaug, appears in which popular children's novel?

4. Which American novelist wrote the adventure story 'Moby Dick'?

5. Which American novelist, who died aged 37 in a car accident in 1940, wrote 'The Day of the Locust'?

6. Which Spanish novelist wrote 'The Three-Cornered Hat'?

7. Which British novelist wrote 'Voyage in the Dark' and 'Good Morning, Midnight'?

8. Which title by Cornelius Ryan relates the events of D-Day during World War II?

9. Which American author wrote the novels 'Show Boat' and 'Giant'?

10. Which Canadian author, a critic of corporate globalization, wrote the exposés 'No Logo' and 'Shock Doctrine'?

Pop Music

1   Who first insisted that 'It's a Man's Man's Man's World'?

_____

2   Who was 'Leavin' On A Jet Plane' in 1970?

_____

3   Who told us that 'The Times They Are A'-Changin'' in 1963?

_____

4   In 1964, 'The House of the Rising Sun' and 'We've Gotta Get Out Of This Place' were hits by ___?

_____

5   Who took us on a trip down the 'Tunnel of Love' in 1980?

_____

6   Who is the American soloist with a whole list of hits to his name, like 'Georgia', 'Hit the Road Jack', and many more?

_____

7   What was the name of the group, one of the earliest, who had many hits, including 'Mrs Brown You've Got A Lovely Daughter'?

_____

8   Which group had an early smash hit with 'Stop! In The Name of Love'?

_____

9   Who had a hit with 'This Old Heart Of Mine'?

_____

10   Whose 1986 big hit single was 'When I Think Of You'?

General Knowledge

1   Which English king was executed in January 1649?

2   The common phrase 'the real McCoy' is thought to have come from the Scots phrase 'real McKay'. What is McKay?

3   Which of these Nordic capital cities is furthest north: Oslo, Copenhagen, Stockholm or Helsinki?

4   In 1969, a gang led by Charles Manson murdered which film actress and four others at her house in Los Angeles?

5   Which Kentucky military base is the site of the U.S. Depository, which contains U.S. gold reserves?

6   Before South Sudan gained independence in 2011, Sudan was the largest country in Africa. What is the largest country in Africa in 2014?

7   From which European country did Madagascar gain independence in 1960?

8   What is the better-known name of Saloth Sar who caused a genocide in Cambodia from 1975 to 1979?

9   Someone suffering from hippophobia has a fear of which kinds of animal?

10 Which Russian physiologist is famous for his experiments on the reflexes of animals, especially dogs?

Food and Drink

1 How is an eggplant otherwise known?

---

2 Which round yellow Dutch cheese has a red outer coating?

---

3 What is added to vodka to make a screwdriver?

---

4 Which alcoholic drink takes its name from the Spanish city of Jerez de la Frontera?

---

5 What kind of fruit comes from the tree Prunus domestica?

---

6 What name is given to the fruits of plants of the genus Ficus?

---

7 Which carbohydrate found in fruit is an essential ingredient for the gelling of jam?

---

8 Which two vegetables are used in the making of the traditional Irish dish called colcannon?

---

9 Gyoza is a dumpling, usually stuffed with minced meat and vegetables, and is a dish originating in which country?

---

10 A grasshopper is a cocktail made from crème de cacao, cream, and which other spirit, the colour of which gives this cocktail its name?

Sport

1. Which golfer, then age 22, was the youngest ever to win the British Open Golf tournament on his victory in 1979?

2. Who won the 2013 Wimbledon Men's Singles title; the first British man to do so in 77 years?

3. Miguel Indurain is best-known as the five times winner of which event?

4. Built in 1907, which British motor-racing circuit was the first purpose-built circuit in the world?

5. Which Australian became the first woman to swim 100 metres in under a minute when she won a gold medal at the 1964 Olympics?

6. How many gold medals did swimmer Mark Spitz amass at the 1972 Olympics?

7. Who took the British Heavyweight boxing title from Henry Cooper in March 1971?

8. Which former American football player appeared as Detective Nordberg in the 'Naked Gun' films?

9. In football, how far is the penalty spot from the goal-line?

10. Colin McRae, Hannu Mikkola and Tommi Makinen are all former winners of which competition?

Movies

1. What was the title of the 1951 movie in which a chimpanzee is brought up as a human baby? It starred a future U.S. president.

2. What was the title of the 2000 movie set in a dog show in Philadelphia?

3. Who played the male and female leads in the 1993 movie 'Dave' in which a Baltimore businessman is invited to the White House to impersonate the president?

4. Who wrote and directed the 1973 French comedy 'La Nuit Americaine'?

5. Who played the two female leads in the 1992 movie 'Death Becomes Her'?

6. What was the title of Woody Allen's 1997 movie about a writer who goes to a ceremony in his honour at his old school?

7. Who played the male and female leads in the 1999 movie 'Galaxy Quest'?

8. Who took the male and female leads in the 1985 movie 'Prizzi's Honor'?

9. In which city was the movie 'Bullitt' set?

10. Which actor, whose movies included 'The Sting' and 'Jaws', wrote 'The Man in the Glass Booth'?

General Knowledge

1. Henry John Deutschendorf, Jr. died in October 1997 in a plane crash in California. By what name is this singer better remembered?

2. To the nearest two days, what is the gestation period of the common brown rat (Rattus norvegicus)?

3. Which company sponsored the 1928 Olympic Games in Amsterdam, and has supported every Olympic Games since?

4. The Republic of Yemen is bordered by Saudi Arabia and which other country?

5. Phytopathology is the branch of science that deals with the diseases of what?

6. In Hinduism, who is the benevolent goddess, a wife of Shiva, mother of Ganesha and Skanda, often identified in her malevolent aspect with Durga and Kali?

7. The 'one-child policy', officially 'the family planning policy', mandated nationwide in 1979, is the population control policy of which country?

8. What is the capital of Greenland?

9. In which Australasian game are two coins tossed in the air, with bets being made on both falling heads or tails?

10. Which disease is caused by a deficiency of vitamin C, characterized by spongy and bleeding gums followed by subcutaneous bleeding and pain in the limbs?

Geography

1. Which European country has a lake district called the Salzkammergut?

2. In which American state is the tourist centre, Orlando?

3. What is the capital of the Republic of Ireland?

4. On which river does the city of Rome stand?

5. What is the largest city in the U.S. state of Washington?

6. Running through Warsaw, which is Poland's longest river?

7. Köln is the native name of which German city?

8. Bulgaria, Romania, Russia, Turkey and Ukraine all have coastlines on which sea?

9. What is the capital of Azerbaijan?

10. Of which East European country is Brno the second largest city?

ROUND 421

The End

1. The 1992 film 'Howards End' earned 'best actress' Oscar for which cast member?

2. Appearing on an album in 1967, 'The End' was a song written by Jim Morrison and performed by which band?

3. 'The End' a black comedy film of 1978, starred Dom DeLuise, Sally Field, and which other actor in the role of a terminally-ill man who botches several suicide attempts?

4. 'That's All Folks!' appeared at the end of which series of Warner Bros. cartoon films?

5. On which date in 1945 did Adolf Hitler commit suicide?

6. What kind of star will our Sun become when it expands and engulfs the Earth in several billion year's time?

7. 'The Last Man', a science fiction novel published in 1826, was written by which authoress, who had produced a much more famous novel eight years earlier?

8. Covered by many other artists since the song first appeared in 1962, which American female singer was the first to have a big hit with the song 'The End of the World'?

9. "This is the way the world ends, not with a bang but a whimper" is the end of 'The Hollow Men', a poem by which American-born British poet?

10. Where is the westernmost point of mainland England?

ANSWERS

Round 1 1 Thomas Jefferson, 2 1837, 3 Spain, 4 Australia, 5 1789, 6 The American Revolutionary War , 7 Ireland, 8 Big Bertha, 9 1990, 10 Jamestown.

Round 2 1 New Zealand, 2 Blue whale, 3 Hibernation, 4 International Fund for Animal Welfare, 5 A rodent, 6 A dog, 7 Lioness and tiger, 8 Chow chow, 9 Wolves, 10 A snake.

Round 3 1 Saturn, 2 Persephone, 3 Echo, 4 Siegfried, 5 Prometheus, 6 A swan, 7 Poseidon, 8 Atlas, 9 Ivanhoe, 10 Lethe.

Round 4 1 Henry James, 2 Le Corbusier, 3 Colonel Jacob Schick, 4 Dutch elm disease, 5 Phobia, 6 Evergreen, 7 Athlete's foot, 8 Broken, 9 Albatross, 10 Yen.

Round 5 1 'Wives and Daughters', 2 Ray Bradbury, 3 Canadian, 4 Germaine Greer, 5 Sigmund Freud, 6 The Black Narcissus, 7 The Beat Movement, 8 Colombian, 9 Charles Darwin, 10 His shadow.

Round 6 1 Caldera, 2 La Scala, 3 New England, 4 Yellowstone National Park, 5 Bay of Fundy, 6 Buenos Aires, 7 Berlin, 8 Norway, 9 Hydrology, 10 Earthquakes.

Round 7 1 Norway, 2 The decathlon, 3 Carl Lewis, 4 Vince Lombardi Trophy, 5 Motorcycle speedway, 6 Skeleton sled, 7 St. Andrews, 8 Red Rum, 9 Sao Paulo , 10 Brussels.

Round 8 1 Medical profession, 2 The Ritz, 3 Thumb, 4 Parkinson's disease, 5 Geriatrics, 6 Prague, 7 Beryl, 8 Chicago, 9 Rudyard Kipling, 10 Mark Twain.

Round 9 1 Iago, 2 Celine Dion, 3 'The Emperor's New Groove', 4 'The Fox And The Hound', 5 William Hurt, 6 'Leprechaun', 7 Francois Truffaut, 8 Cuba Gooding Jr., 9 'Blow Dry', 19 'The Trial'.

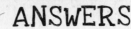

ANSWERS

Round 10 1 1999, 2 Ronald Reagan, 3 Mikhail, 4 Paraguay, 5 Thomas Jefferson, 6 Duma, 7 Archbishop Makarios, 8 Winfield Scott, 9 Washing DC, 10 Carl Gustav Mannerheim.

Round 11 1 Thermodynamics, 2 The speed of light, 3 Pinchbeck, 4 Geiger counter, 5 Tantalum, 6 Coulomb, 7 Salicylic, 8 Plutonium, 9 Tellurium, 10 Pressure.

Round 12 1 Point, 2 Halley's Comet, 3 Hypnosis, 4 Norway, 5 Thomas Telford, 6 Wind speed, 7 Venezuela, 8 Washington DC, 9 Acid rain, 10 Bear.

Round 13 1 St Mary (of the Immaculate Conception), 2 Mount Carmel, 3 St. Francis of Assisi , 4 The 19th (1826), 5 The 13th, 6 Urban II, 7 Druidism, 8 Aztecs, 9 Shinto, 10 Saladin.

Round 14 1 Take That, 2 'Could It Be Magic?', 3 'Boom! Shake the Room', 4 All Saints, 5 Hanson, 6 Edwyn Collins, 7 Blur, 8 Ricky Martin, 9 'This Is My Moment', 10 The Temptations.

Round 15 1 Igneous, 2 Mantle, 3 Rocks, 4 65-66 million years, 5 Aquifer, 6 A gas or steam-emitting hole or vent, 7 Brown coal, 8 Undersea earthquake, 9 Sinkhole, 10 Sedimentary.

Round 16 1 The Prague Spring, 2 Kent State, 3 Charles de Gaulle, 4 The Matterhorn, 5 1969, 6 The Vietnam War, 7 World War I, 8 Algeria, 9 Trans-Siberian, 10 John Hunt.

Round 17 1 Biosphere, 2 The Beatles, 3 Saudi Arabia, 4 Ocelot, 5 Penguin, 6 Astronomy, 7 China clay, 8 Aluminium, 9 Bears, 10 Saturn.

Round 18 1 Paul Gauguin, 2 Madrid, 3 Pablo Picasso, 4 A Christmas card, 5 Ikebana, 6 Salvador Dali, 7 Turner Prize, 8 Andy Warhol, 9 France, 10 Raphael.

ANSWERS

Round 19 1 Coors, 2 Schlitz, 3 India, 4 Onion, 5 Beef Stroganoff, 6 Basil, 7 Thousand Island, 8 Potato, 9 Aubergine/eggplant, 10 Chicken.

Round 20 1 German measles, 2 Allergy, 3 A horse, 4 The ear, 5 The brain, 6 Nicotinic acid, 7 Squint, 8 The spine, 9 The lower leg, 10 Frostbite.

Round 21 1 Jake La Motta, 2 Macavity, 3 King Lear, 4 Amilcare Ponchielli, 5 Rita Hayworth, 6 German, 7 Amelia Bloomer, 8 Scheherazade, 9 The Brothers Grimm, 10 Anthony Quinn.

Round 22 1 Euclid, 2 Ontario, 3 Carat, 4 Wool, 5 Electro-convulsive therapy, 6 Ross, 7 Sixty, 8 Australia, 9 9 (nine), 10 Ernest Hemingway.

Round 23 1 Martinique, 2 Chesapeake Bay, 3 Ecuador, 4 Dominican Republic, 5 Quebec, 6 Kentucky, 7 Cornwall, 8 Ecuador, 9 South America, 10 Chile.

Round 24 1 Josef Stalin, 2 Aldo Moro, 3 George Bush Sr, 4 King Idris I, 5 General Galtieri, 6 Leonid Brezhnev, 7 The KGB, 8 Dan Quayle, 9 Gerhard Schröder, 10 1994.

Round 25 1 Dentistry, 2 George, 3 Carson City, 4 Jedediah Smith, 5 Montana, 6 James Bowie, 7 Davy Crockett, 8 Tombstone, 9 Sitting Bull, 10 Annie Oakley.

Round 26 1 'Around the World in Eighty Days', 2 'Nicholas Nickleby', 3 Eminem, 4 James M. Cain, 5 Richard Scarry, 6 James Joyce, 7 James Bond, 8 'The Brothers Karamazov', 9 Mark Twain, 10 Buck.

Round 27 1 New York Times, 2 Malaysia Airlines, 3 Mickey Rooney, 4 'Abide with Me', 5 New Zealand, 6 Boeing B-29 Superfortress, 7 'Annie Get Your Gun', 8 Arthur Wellesley, Duke of Wellington, 9 The Dominicans, 10 Josef Mengele.

Round 28 1 Enrico Caruso, 2 Beniamino Gigli, 3 Mikhail Glinka, 4 Christoph Gluck, 5 At Glyndebourne, Sussex, 6 Charles Gounod, 7 'Xerxes' (or 'Serse'), 8 Engelbert Humperdinck, 9 'Spades', 10 'Tosca'.

Round 29 1 Seven, 2 Paris, 3 Austin, 4 Kurt Browning, 5 Manchester United, 6 Skiing, 7 Graham and Damon Hill, 8 Tennis, 9 China (231), 10 Louisville.

Round 30 1 Virgo, 2 Parsec, 3 Mars, 4 Eros, 5 Sirius, 6 Jupiter, 7 Saturn, 8 1965, 9 Television and Infra-red Observation Satellite, 10 Mars.

Round 31 1 The seven hills of Rome, 2 Ralph Waldo Emerson, 3 Walter Gropius, 4 Rikki Tikki Tavi, 5 Voltaire, 6 Frank Lloyd Wright, 7 Oliver Wendell Holmes, 8 Benedict Arnold, 9 Darling, 10 A fairy drops down dead.

Round 32 1 France, 2 Liechtenstein, 3 Portugal, 4 Malta, 5 Belgium, 6 Mongolia, 7 Turkey, 8 Kyrgyzstan, 9 New Zealand, 10 The Netherlands (or Holland).

Round 33 1 France, 2 Philip Henry Sheridan, 3 Emile Zola, 4 Jean Jacques Rousseau, 5 Gestapo, 6 Portugal, 7 Photograph, 8 Israel, 9 A hospital, 10 Canada.

Round 34 1 'The Count of Monte Cristo', 2 'Nineteen Eighty-Four', 3 'Death in Venice', 4 'Moby-Dick', 5 George Smiley, 6 'Of Mice and Men', 7 Billy Pilgrim, 8 Terry Pratchett's 'Discworld' novels, 9 'Martin Chuzzlewit', 10 'Lolita'.

Round 35 1 Joseph Lister, 2 Ten per cent, 3 Two, Hawaii and Alaska, 4 Robert Peel, 5 5,280, 6 Zip fasteners, 7 George Orwell, 8 January, 9 James Brown, 10 Mutual Assured Destruction.

Round 36 1 Mae West, 2 'The Carpetbaggers', 3 'The World is Full of Married Men', 4 'Showboat', 5 'Kiss Me Kate', 6 Macbeth, 7 Bullfighting, 8 Maria Schneider, 9 'Alien', 10 "Rhett, Rhett, Rhett, if you go, where shall I go, what shall I do?".

Round 37 1 Jacob and Esau, 2 Absalom, 3 A whirlwind, 4 Barabbas, 5 Salome, 6 Golgotha, 7 Nebuchadnezzar, 8 The two stone tablets bearing the Ten Commandments, 9 Elizabeth, 10 An angel.

Round 38 1 Atoll, 2 Holly, 3 Hot, dry desert winds, 4 Eucalyptus, 5 Robin, 6 Fronds, 7 Migration, 8 Corolla, 9 Eagle, 10 Magpie.

Round 39 1 The arm, 2 Prime number, 3 The Cheshire Cat, 4 Kruger, 5 Homburg, 6 Papillon, 7 Basenji, 8 Dome shaped, 9 American, 10 Three-stringed musical instrument.

Round 40 1 Ferdinand and Isabella, 2 Battle of New Orleans, 3 Russia, 4 India, 5 Genghis Khan, 6 Colin Powell, 7 Joachim Murat, 8 Catherine the Great, 9 George Washington, 10 Chester Nimitz.

Round 41 1 Denmark, 2 Ankara, 3 Pennsylvania, 4 Istanbul, 5 The Pacific, 6 Norway, 7 Sweden, 8 Mexico, 9 Valencia, 10 Mexico City.

Round 42 1 Luther Vandross, 2 Tina Turner, 3 Cat Stevens, 4 Neil Sedaka, 5 Chris De Burgh, 6 Guns 'n Roses, 7 Blondie, 8 Abba, 9 The Jam, 10 The Stranglers.

Round 43 1 Nickel, 2 Hydrocarbons, 3 Pascal, 4 Radium, 5 Lathe, 6 Slide rule, 7 Carbon, 8 Iron, 9 Cupronickel, 10 Geometry.

Round 44 1 Magna Carta, 2 Mr. Burns (Montgomery Burns), 3 17th, 4 Rodin, 5 Puccini, 6 Raymond Chandler, 7 Moldova, 8 Madrid, 9 1994, 10 Tennyson.

Round 45 1 Dean Koontz, 2 Agatha Christie, 3 Benjamin Franklin, 4 J.K. Rowling, 5 Isaac Asimov, 6 Stephen King, 7 Sylvia Plath, 8 Tove Jansson, 9 Mark Twain, 10 Ruth Rendell.

Round 46 1 2000, 2 Stephen Hendry, 3 Arthur Ashe, 4 London 2012, 5 Floyd Patterson, 6 Jai alai, 7 Marathon, 8 Brazil, 9 Swimming, 10 Badminton.

Round 47 1 1666, 2 1000 A.D., 3 Henry V, 4 Denmark, Norway and Sweden, 5 Dag Hammarskjöld, 6 Cro-magnon, 7 Switzerland, 8 1923, 9 Leningrad, 10 1905.

Round 48 1 'Johnny Spielt Auf' ('Johnny Strikes Up'), 2 Ruggiero Leoncavallo, 3 'Leonora' or 'Conjugal Bliss', 4 'Let's Make An Opera', 5 'Falstaff' and 'Macbeth', 6 Cho-Cho-San, 7 'The Magic Flute', 8 'The Marriage of Figaro', 9 'Giselle', 10 A small, light opera.

Round 49 1 Kuala Lumpur, 2 Thebes, 3 Buffalo, 4 1969, 5 1984, 6 Jogging, 7 H.G. Wells, 8 Alabama, 9 Taiwan, 10 Madrid and Barcelona.

Round 50 1 Britain, 2 Australia, 3 Melanesia, 4 Sicily, 5 Hawaii, 6 South America, 7 Ecuador, 8 Corsica, 9 U.S.A., 10 Manila.

Round 51 1 Shorthand, 2 The Romans, 3 Thomas Edison, 4 Barbie, 5 Cartoons, 6 Steel, 7 Air-conditioning, 8 Phosphorus, 9 He invented the first one-piece W.C. china pan, 10 The chain-driven bicycle.

Round 52 1 Jehovah's Witnesses, 2 1096, 3 Cistercians, 4 The Dead Sea Scrolls, 5 Istanbul, 6 Lhasa, 7 St. Agnes, 8 St. Anne, 9 Kali, 10 Archangels.

Round 53 1 David Lean, 2 Rio de Janeiro, 3 Lewis Carroll, 4 Jimmy Carter, 5 Fabergé, 6 Rubens, 7 Petra, 8 Jenson Button, 9 Neil Armstrong, 10 Nell Gwyn.

Round 54   1 Faye Dunaway, 2 Gary, 3 Bagatelle, 4 'Washington Post', 5 Roger Vadim, 6 He showed up for an inspection stark naked, 7 George Gershwin, 8 R.L. Stine, 9 Newfoundland, 10 Afghan Hound.

Round 55   1 Douglas MacArthur, 2 American Civil War, 3 Schutzstaffel, 4 The Seventeenth Parallel, 5 Utah, 6 George Patton, 7 Spain, 8 Agent Orange, 9 Spanish Civil War, 10 Sitting Bull.

Round 56   1 Joel Chandler Harris, 2 'Pequod', 3 Zane Grey, 4 William Faulkner, 5 H. Rider Haggard, 6 F. Scott Fitzgerald, 7 Oliver Goldsmith, 8 Miguel, 9 'The Cherry Orchard', 10 Simone De Beauvoir.

Round 57   1 Eugenics, 2 Sievert, 3 Quartz, 4 Carbon, 5 Hydrochloric acid, 6 Max Planck, 7 Acceleration, 8 Germanium, 9 Ammonia, 10 Green Monkey disease.

Round 58   1 Iowa, 2 Stockholm, 3 The shilling, 4 Jack the Ripper, 5 Botswana, 6 Venus, 7 Portugal, 8 Orson Welles, 9 Burkina Faso, 10 Wagons.

Round 59   1 South China Sea, 2 Bangladesh, 3 Libya, 4 Somalia, 5 Northern Territory, 6 Florida, 7 Zimbabwe, 8 Turkey, 9 Mull, 10 Brunei.

Round 60   1 The Be Sharps, 2 Kirk and Luann, 3 Comic Book Guy, 4 Costington's, 5 King Toots, 6 Fudd, 7 The Frying Dutchman, 8 Springfield Retirement Castle, 9 Ringo Starr, 10 Michael Jackson.

Round 61   1 Baron Joseph Lister, 2 China, 3 Pocahontas, 4 Ebola, 5 Seattle, 6 The plough, 7 Johnny Appleseed, 8 Hungary, 9 Tiberius, 10 Farouk.

Round 62   1 2005, 2 U.S. Masters, 3 The Netherlands (or Holland), 4 Scotland, 5 3,000 metres, 6 Maserati, 7 Daley Thompson, 8 Six, 9 Seattle Seahawks and Denver Broncos, 10 Max Schmeling.

Round 63   1 Oxygen, 2 Australia, 3 Blood pressure, 4 Five, 5 Kuwait, 6 Pacific, 7 Nero, 8 Lead, 9 League of Nations, 10 The Eiger.

Round 64   1 Daniel Day-Lewis, 2 Oscar Hammerstein II, 3 Venice, 4 Soliloquy, 5 Blues, 6 Enid Blyton, 7 Sophocles, 8 Choreography, 9 The Brontës, 10 Wolfman Jack.

Round 65   1 Edmund Halley, 2 Mercury, 3 Yuri Gagarin, 4 1959, 5 Magnitude, 6 Crux or Southern Cross, 7 Cape Canaveral, 8 Edwin 'Buzz' Aldrin, 9 Johannes Kepler, 10 Mars.

Round 66   1 Dolly Parton, 2 Linda Blair, 3 Obi-Wan Kenobi, 4 'South Pacific', 5 'Calamity Jane', 6 Marlon Brando, 7 Dracula, 8 It was being eaten by an advancing vast army of red ants, 9 Trini Lopez, 10 'Road To Utopia'.

Round 67   1 Metric ton (tonne), 2 Covent Garden, 3 Oil, 4 1982, 5 Sigmund Freud, 6 Metre, 7 A cactus, 8 Mexico, 9 Sidewinder, 10 Compact Disc - Read Only Memory.

Round 68   1 Colombia, 2 Nellie Bly, 3 Cabral, 4 1973, 5 Bathyscaphe, 6 Torque, 7 Volkswagen Beetle, 8 'The Mayflower', 9 Paris, 10 Three.

Round 69   1 The Boston Tea Party, 2 Spain, 3 Lisbon, 4 Elba, 5 1899, 6 Aztec, 7 New York, 8 The Northwest Passage, 9 Sweden, 10 The Wars of the Roses.

Round 70   1 Martha, 2 The Synoptic Gospels, 3 Daniel, 4 Mary Magdalene, 5 Armageddon, 6 Abraham, 7 St. Mark, 8 Moses, 9 Ur, 10 St. Paul.

Round 71   1 Syllabub, 2 Pepper (traditionally black peppercorns, crushed), 3 Norway, 4 Orange, 5 1900, 6 Spain, 7 Italy, 8 Squid, 9 Gazpacho, 10 Chartreuse.

Round 72   1 Ghana, 2 B, 3 24, 4 Deuteronomy, 5 Saturn, 6 One and a half, 7 Geneva Convention, 8 Almonds, 9 Colorado, 10 A cannibal.

Round 73   1 Adolphe Charles Adam, 2 Giacomo Meyerbeer, 3 'Lucia', 4 Richard Strauss, 5 Nicolai Rimsky-Korsakov, 6 'Prince Igor', 7 Pietro Mascagni, 8 Leo Delibes, 9 Johann Sebastian, 10 Nikolai Rimsky-Korsakov.

Round 74   1 Mae West, 2 Henry Kissinger, 3 Lana Turner, 4 Bob Hope, 5 Woody Allen, 6 Mark Twain, 7 W.C. Fields, 8 Agatha Christie, 9 Groucho Marx, 10 Winston Churchill.

Round 75   1 Jack Russell terrier, 2 Bee hummingbird, 3 Cheetah, 4 A dog, 5 Ostrich, 6 Ungulate, 7 A vulture, 8 A fish, 9 A lemur, 10 A bird.

Round 76   1 Bullfrogs, 2 Canada, 3 One (A), 4 Spiders, 5 Marie Antoinette, 6 Helen of Troy, 7 Red, 8 12, 9 Andrew Jackson, 10 The sixth.

Round 77   1 Hungary, 2 Rhine, 3 Alaska, 4 Lake Ontario, 5 St. Petersburg, 6 Newfoundland, 7 Lake Huron, 8 Fjord (or fiord), 9 A volcano, 10 Cape Town.

Round 78   1 Pancho Villa, 2 Herbert Hoover, 3 Bolivia, 4 Sir Winston Churchill, 5 Mikhail Gorbachev, 6 Pierre Trudeau, 7 Ross Perot, 8 Hitler and Mussolini, 9 Slobodan Milosevic, 10 Indira Gandhi.

Round 79   1 Ricky Nelson, 2 Tomaso Albinoni, 3 Emmanuel Chabrier, 4 Ronnie Wood, 5 Edelweiss, 6 'Look At Me', 7 Copacabana, 8 Calypso, 9 Angela Bassett, 10 Mozart.

Round 80   1 Basketball, 2 2003, 3 Leon and Michael, 4 Pete Sampras, 5 1984, 6 Michael Jackson, 7 Kevin Moran, 8 Denver, 9 Chris Froome, 10 Motorcycle racing.

ANSWERS

Round 81   1 Dances, 2 Edwin Landseer, 3 John Brown, 4 Ohio, 5 Zambia, 6 The vacuum flask, 7 Einstein's, 8 Tomato, 9 Whitney Houston, 10 Paraguay.

Round 82   1 Osteoporosis, 2 Vagus nerve, 3 Pancreas, 4 Athlete's foot, 5 Grinding your teeth, 6 Poliomyelitis, 7 Measles, 8 Croup, 9 The hand, 10 Pupil or iris.

Round 83   1 A.E. Housman, 2 Lorenzo da Ponte, 3 'A Visit from St. Nicholas', 4 Ezra Pound, 5 Tony Harrison, 6 'The Hunting of the Snark', 7 Albatross, 8 W.H. Auden, 9 Dante Alighieri, 10 G.K. Chesterton.

Round 84   1 Herman Melville, 2 Jean-Paul Sartre, 3 Charlie Chaplin, 4 John Updike, 5 A car salesman, 6 Marlon Brando, 7 Nero Wolfe, 8 Wallace and Gromit, 9 'New York Tribune', 10 Hillary Clinton.

Round 85   1 John Cabot, 2 Hyperion, 3 Primrose, 4 The brain, 5 Sir Joseph Thomson, 6 The equator, 7 Megaton, 8 The Little Mermaid statue, 9 La Mancha, 10 John De Lorean.

Round 86   1 Brazil, 2 Italy, 3 Canada, 4 River Lena, 5 Delaware, 6 Rio Grande, 7 Los Angeles, 8 Mount McKinley, 9 River Po, 10 The Alps.

Round 87   1 1978, 2 Suttee, 3 Dalai Lama, 4 Excommunication, 5 Passover, 6 Passion plays, 7 Red, 8 Jainism, 9 Stigmata, 10 Rastafarianism.

Round 88   1 Lorelei, 2 Pigs, 3 Hephaestus, 4 Atlas, 5 Cow, 6 Manitou, 7 Osiris, 8 Brunhild, 9 Loki, 10 Golem.

Round 89   1 Potato, cabbage and onion, 2 Gordon Brown, 3 Violet (or purple), 4 Douwe Egberts, 5 Iceland, 6 Beetroot, 7 Belgium, 8 Brazil nuts, 9 Pasta, 10 Peach Melba.

Round 90   1 The ace of spades, 2 Brazilian, 3 Salt, 4 Four, 5 Hobart, 6 Donatello, 7 Wolves, 8 Pinocchio, 9 12, 10 Jordan.

Round 91 1 'Jezebel', 2 'Far and Away', 3 'Dr. Strangelove', 4 'The Poseidon Adventure', 5 Angie Dickinson, 6 Jane Fonda, 7 Pig, 8 Samuel L. Jackson, 9 Robert Altman, 10 'X-Men'.

Round 92 1 Aerobics, 2 Wrinkled, 3 Empty, 4 For example, 5 Left-handed, 6 Martyr, 7 Hispanic, 8 A war dance, 9 Market quarter, 10 Tulle.

Round 93 1 Capacitor, 2 Halogens, 3 Jethro Tull, 4 Platinum, 5 Galileo Galilei, 6 Marie Curie, 7 Water, 8 James Hargreaves, 9 Acetic acid, 10 Infinity.

Round 94 1 Paul Robeson, 2 Thorstein Veblen, 3 Napoleon, 4 J Edgar Hoover, 5 Aristotle, 6 Praetorian Guard, 7 Porphyria, 8 General John Sedgwick, U.S. Army, 1813-1864, 9 Bikini, 10 1973.

Round 95 1 500, 2 Russia, 3 293, 4 1977, 5 Metronome, 6 Morocco, 7 Nitrogen, 8 Australia, 9 Millefiori, 10 Narcissus.

Round 96 1 Australia, 2 Iran, Afghanistan, China and India, 3 Kazakhstan, 4 The Amur River, 5 The Kara Sea, 6 Japan, 7 Quito (Ecuador), 8 Somalia, 9 Rio de Janeiro, 10 Poland.

Round 97 1 Aretha Franklin, 2 Dinah Washington, 3 Johnny Green, 4 Euday L. Bowman, 5 W.C. Handy, 6 Gertrude Rainey, 7 Bessie Smith, 8 Dinah Washington, 9 Courtney Pine, 10 John McLaughlin.

Round 98 1 Aristophanes, 2 Gabriele D'Annunzio, 3 Anton Chekhov, 4 John Le Carré, 5 George Eliot, 6 Daphne Du Maurier, 7 Count Leo Tolstoy, 8 Doris Lessing, 9 Herman Melville, 10 Matthew Kneale.

Round 99 1 Ten, 2 Pinball, 3 Atlantic City, 4 Yo-yo, 5 Grand National, 6 Pelota, 7 Austrian, 8 Eagle, 9 Whist, 10 Dummy.

Round 100   1 Westminster Abbey, 2 Libra (scales), 3 Chlorophyll, 4 The Nike 'Swoosh', 5 Cloud Cuckoo Land, 6 Fukushima Daiichi, 7 Pierce Brosnan, 8 Tumble dry, 9 Jakarta, 10 Casablanca.

Round 101   1 Palaeozoic, 2 Hannibal, 3 Crimean War, 4 Poland, 5 Black Hand, 6 Vasco da Gama, 7 Italy, 8 Ezra Pound, 9 Marco Polo, 10 Pliny the Elder.

Round 102   1 Jules Verne, 2 'The Time Machine' by H.G. Wells, 3 Isaac Asimov, 4 'The Thing', 5 '2001: A Space Odyssey', 6 'The Man Who Fell to Earth', 7 Robert Heinlein, 8 Edgar Rice Burroughs, 9 Ray Bradbury, 10 Margaret Atwood.

Round 103   1 Greece, 2 Greece, 3 St. Lucia, 4 The Cook Islands, 5 Tenerife, 6 Hawaii, 7 Sable Island, 8 The Pacific Ocean, 9 Sicily, 10 Indonesia.

Round 104   1 The Pretenders, 2 'Don't You Forget About Me', 3 Tears For Fears, 4 Womack and Womack, 5 New Kids On The Block, 6 'Ebony and Ivory', 7 Crowded House, 8 Adam and the Ants, 9 The Specials, 10 Lil Wayne.

Round 105   1 The Adriatic, 2 Nebraska, 3 Pompeii, 4 A wine store, 5 Mail order, 6 The Empire State Building, 7 90, 8 Sphere, 9 Zero, 10 Henry Harley.

Round 106   1 Iron, 2 A tree, 3 A barometer, 4 Friends of the Earth, 5 A fish (a type of cod), 6 Five, 7 A bird, 8 Botany, 9 Black Widow, 10 Chlorophyll.

Round 107   1 Assisi, 2 Sun Myung Moon, 3 Tarsus, 4 Mother Teresa, 5 St. Christopher, 6 St. Eustace, 7 March 17, 8 Christadelphians, 9 Panchen Lama, 10 Shamrock.

Round 108   1 Parker and Barrow, 2 In flagrante delicto, 3 Subpoena, 4 Counterfeiting, 5 Arson, 6 Bugsy, 7 Libyan, 8 Harold Shipman, 9 Jack the Ripper, 10 Habeas corpus.

Round 109 1 A Lockheed U2 high-altitude spy plane, 2 Valentina Tereshkova, 3 Cyprus, 4 Theodore Roosevelt (1901), 5 'Lusitania', 6 Austria, 7 Martin Luther, 8 Amerigo Vespucci, 9 Cairo, 10 1865.

Round 110 1 'The Crucible', 2 'The Cruel Sea', 3 Lime, 4 Kenya, 5 Conifers, 6 Milan, 7 Samuel Johnson, 8 Switzerland, 9 Birds, 10 Jefferson.

Round 111 1 Five (four still exist), 2 Jules Massenet, 3 'The Mastersingers', 4 'Meditation', 5 Emil Nikolaus von Reznicek, 6 Franz von Suppe, 7 Johann Strauss the Younger, 8 Franz Lehar, 9 Beethoven, 10 Tchaikovsky.

Round 112 1 Nova Scotia, 2 Lake Ladoga, 3 KwaZulu/Natal, 4 North Island, 5 Pakistan and Afghanistan, 6 The Alps, 7 Tiber, 8 Alberta, 9 U.S. Virgin Islands, 10 Reykjavik.

Round 113 1 Henry James, 2 Beatrix Potter, 3 Thomas Mann, 4 Edgar Allan Poe, 5 Iris Murdoch, 6 Jean Racine, 7 Michael Ondaatje, 8 Leon Uris, 9 Anthony Powell, 10 Wilbur Smith.

Round 114 1 Dan, 2 Strike, 3 The Thames, 4 Kung Fu, 5 Dressage, 6 Alan Bond, 7 Birdie, 8 Bogey, 9 Michael Schumacher, 10 Weightlifting.

Round 115 1 Moscow, 2 New York, 3 Prague, 4 1951, 5 Swan, 6 Helium, 7 Xerography, 8 Confucius, 9 U.N.I.C.E.F., 10 Gracie Allen.

Round 116 1 Binary, 2 Worm, 3 Read only memory, 4 Hard copy, 5 Surfing, 6 Hypertext Transfer Protocol, 7 Pentium, 8 Server, 9 Mouse, 10 Chip.

Round 117 1 'Before the Rain', 2 'Waterworld', 3 'Species', 4 'Pocahontas', 5 Gene Hackman, 6 Dennis Hopper, 7 'Country Life', 8 Robert Mitchum, 9 'Reversal of Fortune', 10 Ann Miller.

Round 118
1 Philip II, 2 Pat Garrett, 3 Harvard, 4 The Korean War, 5 Leif Erikson, 6 Douglas MacArthur, 7 Benito Mussolini, 8 Iran and Iraq, 9 Klondyke, 10 Cook.

Round 119
1 65000 (Pennsylvania 6-5000), 2 18, 3 94, 4 21, 5 52, 6 16, 7 4, 8 42, 9 13, 10 30.

Round 120
1 Cooper, 2 Japan, 3 Alaska, 4 Chicago, 5 Hermann Rorschach, 6 Geneva, 7 Austrian, 8 Quetzal, 9 Micro, 10 Beaufort Scale.

Round 121
1 Lake Superior, 2 Austria, Germany and Switzerland, 3 The Dead Sea, 4 St. Petersburg, 5 Caspian Sea, 6 Australia, 7 Turkey, 8 Lake Nasser, 9 Lake Baikal, 10 Canada.

Round 122
1 Hieronymous Bosch, 2 M.C. Escher, 3 Rembrandt, 4 Amsterdam, 5 Tintoretto, 6 Brueghel, 7 Botticelli, 8 El Greco, 9 Frank Lloyd Wright, 10 The Louvre.

Round 123
1 Orwell, 2 'Tosca', 3 Pam Dawber, 4 Michael Douglas, 5 Trampas, 6 Smith, 7 Bat, 8 Mean Machine, 9 Carl Sagan, 10 John Goodman.

Round 124
1 Saluki, 2 A cat, 3 Manitoba, 4 Whippoorwill, 5 Ostrich, 6 Kiwi, 7 An antelope, 8 Marsupials, 9 Falcon, 10 Great Dane.

Round 125
1 1950-1953, 2 Codes, 3 Zucchini, 4 Yarmulke or Kippah, 5 Lust, 6 Condor, 7 'Apocalypse Now', 8 Caledonian Canal, 9 Rice, 10 Le Corbusier.

Round 126
1 Battle of Jutland, 2 'Dreadnought', 3 'Big Bertha', 4 Sea-launched cruise missile, 5 The Battle of Trafalgar, 6 World War I, 7 D-Day, 8 The Third Reich, 9 The Red Baron, 10 Omar Bradley.

Round 127
1 Tandoori, 2 Louisiana, 3 Switzerland, 4 Saffron crocus, 5 Africa, 6 Barding, 7 Kedgeree, 8 Waldorf salad, 9 Paella, 10 Chestnut.

Round 128 1 Pandora, 2 Delphi, 3 Lohengrin, 4 Demeter, 5 Amazons, 6 Europa, 7 Abominable snowman, 8 Thor, 9 Monday, 10 Pegasus.

Round 129 1 Blondie, 2 Mickey Mouse, 3 Microphone, 4 Broadway, 5 General Tom Thumb, 6 Lionel Barrymore, 7 George Gershwin, 8 Jimi Hendrix, 9 Bill Haley, 10 Drew Barrymore.

Round 130 1 Adriatic, 2 Michael Caine, 3 Black Sea, 4 Brian Epstein, 5 Laputa, 6 Washington, 7 Burma, 8 Pyrometer, 9 Richard II, 10 Sappho.

Round 131 1 The Great Bear Lake, 2 Martha's Vineyard, 3 Tierra del Fuego, 4 Texas, 5 Lake Ontario, 6 Maelstrom, 7 The Faeroe Islands, 8 Tel Aviv-Jaffa, 9 Florida, 10 Nunavut.

Round 132 1 Anita Loos, 2 Mars, 3 'The Mayor of Casterbridge', 4 Uriah Heep, 5 Mark Twain, 6 Ray Bradbury, 7 Elsa, 8 Desmond Morris, 9 Yukio Mishima, 10 Ray Bradbury.

Round 133 1 American (U.S.), 2 Montezuma, 3 Britain and France, 4 R.101, 5 1929, 6 Ghana, 7 Crossword puzzle, 8 The first to reach the North Pole, 9 Maria Theresa, 10 Spanish Civil War.

Round 134 1 Ecuador, 2 Samovar, 3 Three-stringed guitar or lute, 4 A musician, 5 Jupiter, 6 Marengo, 7 Sherry, 8 Staffa, 9 Washington DC, 10 Wadi.

Round 135 1 The Black Eyed Peas, 2 Bon Jovi, 3 'With or Without You', 4 George Michael, 5 The Human League, 6 The Police, 7 Frankie Goes To Hollywood, 8 Band Aid, 9 Culture Club, 10 'Mull of Kintyre'.

Round 136 1 U.S.A., 2 Russia, 3 An eagle, 4 Tour of Britain, 5 60, 6 Foil, 7 Jack and Brian, 8 Ben Johnson, 9 Stanley Matthews, 10 U.S.A. and Europe.

Round 137   1 Igor Sikorsky, 2 Coffee, 3 Hans Lippershey, 4 Alfred Nobel,
             5 Shrapnel, 6 Gabriel Fahrenheit, 7 Polaroid, 8 Belgian,
             9 Montgolfier, 10 Isaac Newton.

Round 138   1 Spain, 2 Hugo Chavez, 3 The Marshall Plan, 4 Cyrus Vance,
             5 Canada, 6 Eamon de Valera, 7 Republican Party, 7 COMECON,
             9 Liberia, 10 Theodore Roosevelt.

Round 139   1 Edward Gibbon, 2 Babylonian, 3 A hundred, 4 'The Prisoner',
             5 Leonardo da Vinci, 6 Keratin, 7 'Your tiny hand is frozen',
             8 Mandrake, 9 The Spanish Inquisition, 10 Austerlitz.

Round 140   1 London, 2 Karl Benz, 3 Gyroscope, 4 'Ra', 5 Casey Jones,
             6 U.S.S. 'Nautilus', 7 Chuck Yeager, 8 Troika, 9 Two, 10 Amtrak.

Round 141   1 'The Prince Of Tides', 2 'Bugsy', 3 'Goodfellas', 4 'Missing',
             5 Rita Hayworth, 6 'Annie Hall', 7 Tom Jones, 8 Cameron Diaz,
             9 'The Lady And The Tramp', 10 'Robin Hood: Prince Of Thieves'.

Round 142   1 Jules Maigret, 2 Jim Rockford, 3 Sam Spade, 4 Edgar Allan
             Poe, 5 Frank Drebin, 6 Dr. Watson, 7 Ellery Queen, 8 'Dragnet',
             9 Raymond Chandler, 10 Hercule Poirot.

Round 143   1 The Reformation, 2 Rastafarianism, 3 The Ka'aba, 4 Jordan,
             5 Hindu, 6 Jainism, 7 St. Peter, 8 Czech Republic (then Bohemia),
             9 Turkey, 10 Ganesha.

Round 144   1 Greece, 2 Gross Domestic Product, 3 Marlon Brando, 4 Brasilia,
             5 Ink blots, 6 Sociology, 7 Michael Flatley, 8 Pisa, 9 Trespass,
             10 Canada.

Round 145   1 Sand, 2 Carbon, 3 Amplitude Modulation, 4 Heavenly bodies,
             5 Silver, 6 Gun-metal, 7 Lewis Waterman, 8 Sonar, 9 Acoustics,
             10 The neutron.

Round 146   1 Italy, 2 Ireland, 3 Jay Sebring, 4 Amelia Earhart, 5 Josef Mengele, 6 Sewing machine, 7 1973, 8 Vitus Bering, 9 Ceylon, 10 Võ Nguyên Giáp.

Round 147   1 'Dallas', 2 Jock Ewing, 3 'Dynasty', 4 'Falcon Crest', 5 A plane crash, 6 General Hospital, 7 Southfork, 8 Denver, 9 'Neighbours', 10 'The Colbys'.

Round 148   1 Kalahari, 2 Yellowstone Park, 3 Sea of Galilee, 4 Hondo, 5 Mekong, 6 California, 7 Berkeley, 8 South America, 9 Angel Falls, 10 Prague.

Round 149   1 Czechoslovakia, 2 A dog (Bob), 3 Twelve, 4 Mars, 5 'Treasure Island', 6 Oil of wormwood, 7 Lakshmi, 8 Scaly anteater, 9 Miss Havisham, 10 Beijing.

Round 150   1 Jochen Rindt, 2 200, 3 Melbourne, 4 John Austin, 5 South African, 6 Le Mans 24-hour Race, 7 1872, 8 Boris Becker, 9 Paavo Nurmi, 10 Jack Dempsey.

Round 151   1 Rosa Parks, 2 Sri Lanka, 3 Venus, 4 Burma, 5 Condoleezza Rice, 6 Mother Teresa, 7 Anne Frank, 8 Caroline Herschel, 9 Lucrezia Borgia, 10 Catherine the Great.

Round 152   1 Anastasia, 2 Atahualpa, 3 Ibn Saud, 4 Pepin the Short, 5 Henry II, 6 Versailles, 7 Spain, 8 Pierre Trudeau, 9 Winston Churchill, 10 Atatürk.

Round 153   1 James Cook, 2 Alexei Kosygin, 3 T.E. Lawrence, aka Lawrence of Arabia, 4 Taoism, 5 Foxes, 6 The Chrysler Building, 7 Poland, 8 China, 9 Edward VIII, 10 Prehensile.

Round 154   1 Johnny Mercer, 2 The sixth symphony ('Pastoral'), 3 The Ronettes, 4 James Galway, 5 Cremona, 6 Bizet, 7 Noel Coward, 8 'A Little Night Music', 9 Schumann, 10 Vienna Philharmonic.

Round 155 1 Scrimshaw, 2 'Mona Lisa', 3 Nimbus, 4 Der Blaue Reiter
(or The Blue Rider), 5 Paris, 6 Barbara Hepworth, 7 Augustus John,
8 William Hogarth, 9 Pietro Annigoni, 10 Gertrude Stein.

Round 156 1 Neptune, 2 Nicolaus Copernicus, 3 Earth, 4 Pluto, 5 Sirius,
6 Percival Lowell, 7 Taurus, 8 Uranus, 9 Jupiter, 10 Hypergiant.

Round 157 1 China, 2 Italy, 3 Austria, 4 France, 5 Spain, 6 Venezuela,
7 Argentina, 8 Greece, 9 Tanzania, 10 Nepal.

Round 158 1 Silver, 2 Mel Gibson, 3 Irrigation, 4 Internet service provider,
5 Metropolitan Opera, 6 Austrian, 7 Parchment, 8 Igloo, 9 Aries,
10 Orson Welles.

Round 159 1 Mount Everest, 2 Fridtjof Nansen, 3 Orville and Wilbur,
4 American Civil War, 5 Bob Dole, 6 Mikhail Gorbachev,
7 Quisling, 8 France and Britain, 9 Apartheid, 10 Konrad Adenauer.

Round 160 1 'Snow White And The Seven Dwarfs', 2 Alfred Hitchcock, 3 Tim
Burton, 4 'A Clockwork Orange', 5 Jacques, 6 Claire Trevor, 7 Andy,
8 Hopalong Cassidy, 9 'The Silence Of The Lambs', 10 'Bambi'.

Round 161 1 Tiramisu, 2 Beer, 3 Pâté de Foie Gras, 4 Doner kebab, 5 Paella,
6 Nan, 7 Jambalaya, 8 Béchamel, 9 Coleslaw, 10 Curaçao.

Round 162 1 The brain, 2 O, 3 32, 4 The id, 5 12, 6 William Harvey, 7 Achilles
tendon, in the ankle, 8 Dialysis, 9 Rhinitis, 10 Serum.

Round 163 1 30th April, 2 Colombia, 3 Gustav Holst, 4 Mt. Rushmore, 5 Raven,
6 Cruise missile, 7 Atmospheric humidity, 8 Betamax, 9 Kew,
10 Cyprus.

Round 164 1 Ian Fleming, 2 H.P. Lovecraft, 3 Vikram Seth, 4 Catherine
Cookson, 5 Claudius, 6 Jean Genet, 7 Aladdin, 8 Umberto Eco,
9 Herman Wouk, 10 Wilbur Smith.

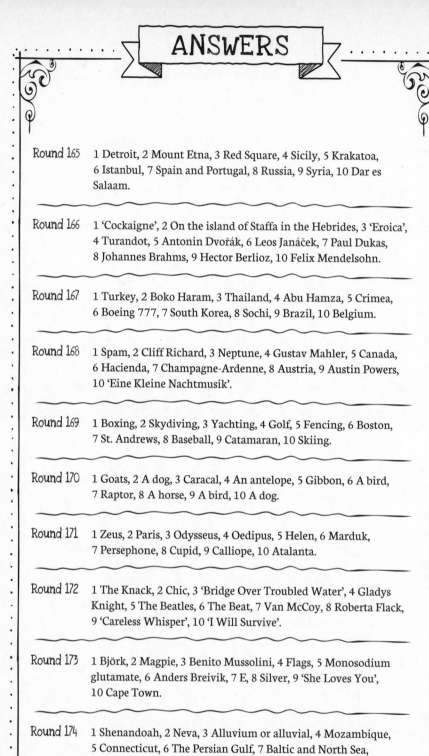

Round 165 1 Detroit, 2 Mount Etna, 3 Red Square, 4 Sicily, 5 Krakatoa, 6 Istanbul, 7 Spain and Portugal, 8 Russia, 9 Syria, 10 Dar es Salaam.

Round 166 1 'Cockaigne', 2 On the island of Staffa in the Hebrides, 3 'Eroica', 4 Turandot, 5 Antonin Dvořák, 6 Leos Janáček, 7 Paul Dukas, 8 Johannes Brahms, 9 Hector Berlioz, 10 Felix Mendelsohn.

Round 167 1 Turkey, 2 Boko Haram, 3 Thailand, 4 Abu Hamza, 5 Crimea, 6 Boeing 777, 7 South Korea, 8 Sochi, 9 Brazil, 10 Belgium.

Round 168 1 Spam, 2 Cliff Richard, 3 Neptune, 4 Gustav Mahler, 5 Canada, 6 Hacienda, 7 Champagne-Ardenne, 8 Austria, 9 Austin Powers, 10 'Eine Kleine Nachtmusik'.

Round 169 1 Boxing, 2 Skydiving, 3 Yachting, 4 Golf, 5 Fencing, 6 Boston, 7 St. Andrews, 8 Baseball, 9 Catamaran, 10 Skiing.

Round 170 1 Goats, 2 A dog, 3 Caracal, 4 An antelope, 5 Gibbon, 6 A bird, 7 Raptor, 8 A horse, 9 A bird, 10 A dog.

Round 171 1 Zeus, 2 Paris, 3 Odysseus, 4 Oedipus, 5 Helen, 6 Marduk, 7 Persephone, 8 Cupid, 9 Calliope, 10 Atalanta.

Round 172 1 The Knack, 2 Chic, 3 'Bridge Over Troubled Water', 4 Gladys Knight, 5 The Beatles, 6 The Beat, 7 Van McCoy, 8 Roberta Flack, 9 'Careless Whisper', 10 'I Will Survive'.

Round 173 1 Björk, 2 Magpie, 3 Benito Mussolini, 4 Flags, 5 Monosodium glutamate, 6 Anders Breivik, 7 E, 8 Silver, 9 'She Loves You', 10 Cape Town.

Round 174 1 Shenandoah, 2 Neva, 3 Alluvium or alluvial, 4 Mozambique, 5 Connecticut, 6 The Persian Gulf, 7 Baltic and North Sea, 8 The Dead Sea, 9 Francisco de Orellana, 10 Atlantic Ocean.

Round 175   1 'West Side Story', 2 'Othello', 3 'Hamlet', 4 'Macbeth', 5 'The Merchant of Venice', 6 Stratford-upon-Avon, 7 The Globe, 8 Susanna, 9 1616, 10 'Twelfth Night'.

Round 176   1 The Belgian Franc, 2 Jacques Cartier, 3 1947, 4 General MacArthur, 5 Louis Bleriot, 6 Canada, 7 The Salvation Army, 8 1943, 9 White Star Line, 10 Captain Bligh.

Round 177   1 Judy Garland, 2 Al Jolson, 3 David Niven, 4 Jacqueline Susann, 5 Elliot, 6 Dolly Parton, 7 Ogden Nash, 8 'Colonel' Tom Parker, 9 Gypsy Rose Lee, 10 'Time'.

Round 178   1 Mint, 2 Swiss cheese plant, 3 René Descartes, 4 The Pentagon, 5 The mistral, 6 Keratin, 7 Damages, 8 90, 9 Vacuum, 10 Goldwyn.

Round 179   1 Sir Isaac Newton, 2 Erg, 3 Aspirin, 4 Supercooling, 5 Thomas Edison, 6 Aluminium, 7 Cyanide, 8 Angel dust, 9 Bazooka, 10 Hydrochloric acid.

Round 180   1 Luke, 2 Samson, 3 Elisha, 4 Abraham, 5 'The Voice', 6 John the Baptist, 7 Herodias, 8 Solomon, 9 Frankincense, 10 Belshazzar.

Round 181   1 Nadia Comaneci, 2 'Cy' Young (Denton True Young), 3 Larry Bird, 4 Nathan Deakes, 5 Stanislas Wawrinka, 6 Marion Bartoli, 7 Great Britain, 8 Tokyo, 9 Arnold Schwarzenegger, 10 Muhammad Ali.

Round 182   1 Bilbao, 2 The White House, 3 The Empire State Building, New York, 4 Sydney Opera House, 5 Dale Carnegie, 6 The Shard, 7 The Crystal Palace, 8 The Pentagon, 9 Ulm Minster, 10 Pyongyang, North Korea.

Round 183   1 Donovan, 2 Wanderer, 3 Willow, 4 Sequoia, 5 Methuselah, 6 The ear, 7 Winnipeg, 8 Sweden, 9 Hugh Hefner, 10 Jamaica.

Round 184 1 Kevin Kline, 2 Gwyneth Paltrow, 3 'Neptune's Daughter', 4 Rossano Brazzi, 5 Sophie Tucker, 6 'Duel', 7 Alfred Hitchcock, 8 Devil's Tower, 9 'Atlantic City', 10 'Midnight Express'.

Round 185 1 The Aleutian Islands, 2 1991, 3 President Somoza, 4 Hawaii, 5 Japan, 6 1917, 7 Appian Way, 8 U.S.S. 'Vincennes', 9 Montgomery, 10 65 million years.

Round 186 1 Ben Jonson, 2 Henrik Ibsen, 3 Norman Mailer, 4 Arthur Schopenhauer, 5 Sir Walter Scott, 6 Frank Yerby, 7 Margaret Atwood, 8 Snowy, 9 Stephen Crane, 10 Winston Churchill.

Round 187 1 An ape, 2 Pituitary gland, 3 Porcupine, 4 A wild sheep, 5 Hinny, 6 A dog, 7 A pride, 8 An antelope, 9 A camel, 10 A cat.

Round 188 1 Boeing 747, 2 De Havilland Comet, 3 Tupolev Tu-144, 4 Dakota, 5 Lockheed, 6 Vickers, 7 Pan American, 8 All have/had the same configuration of three engines at the rear of the fuselage and a high tail-plane, 9 Dreamliner, 10 Air France and British Airways.

Round 189 1 Suttee, or sati, 2 Jazz, 3 Richard Nixon, 4 Norway, 5 Jet streams, 6 St Peter, 7 London Heathrow, 8 Plum, 9 James Gandolfini, 10 Svalbard.

Round 190 1 Dusty Springfield, 2 Janis Joplin, 3 Joni Mitchell, 4 Cyndi Lauper, 5 Adele, 6 Dinah Washington, 7 Christina Aguilera, 8 Kathryn Dawn, 9 'Good Girl Gone Bad', 10 Anni-Frid Lyngstad and Agnetha Feltskog.

Round 191 1 Vienna, 2 Huron, 3 Germany, 4 Zambezi, 5 Colorado, 6 Severn, 7 Murmansk, 8 Morocco, 9 The Mediterranean, 10 Piraeus.

Round 192 1 Watergate, 2 'Black is beautiful', 3 Saddam Hussein, 4 Chicago, 5 New York, 6 Mahatma, 7 Bonn, 8 Haiti, 9 Daniel Webster, 10 Walter Mondale.

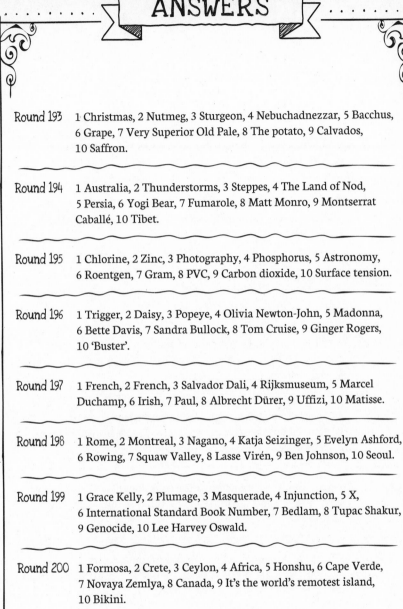

ANSWERS

Round 193 1 Christmas, 2 Nutmeg, 3 Sturgeon, 4 Nebuchadnezzar, 5 Bacchus, 6 Grape, 7 Very Superior Old Pale, 8 The potato, 9 Calvados, 10 Saffron.

Round 194 1 Australia, 2 Thunderstorms, 3 Steppes, 4 The Land of Nod, 5 Persia, 6 Yogi Bear, 7 Fumarole, 8 Matt Monro, 9 Montserrat Caballé, 10 Tibet.

Round 195 1 Chlorine, 2 Zinc, 3 Photography, 4 Phosphorus, 5 Astronomy, 6 Roentgen, 7 Gram, 8 PVC, 9 Carbon dioxide, 10 Surface tension.

Round 196 1 Trigger, 2 Daisy, 3 Popeye, 4 Olivia Newton-John, 5 Madonna, 6 Bette Davis, 7 Sandra Bullock, 8 Tom Cruise, 9 Ginger Rogers, 10 'Buster'.

Round 197 1 French, 2 French, 3 Salvador Dali, 4 Rijksmuseum, 5 Marcel Duchamp, 6 Irish, 7 Paul, 8 Albrecht Dürer, 9 Uffizi, 10 Matisse.

Round 198 1 Rome, 2 Montreal, 3 Nagano, 4 Katja Seizinger, 5 Evelyn Ashford, 6 Rowing, 7 Squaw Valley, 8 Lasse Virén, 9 Ben Johnson, 10 Seoul.

Round 199 1 Grace Kelly, 2 Plumage, 3 Masquerade, 4 Injunction, 5 X, 6 International Standard Book Number, 7 Bedlam, 8 Tupac Shakur, 9 Genocide, 10 Lee Harvey Oswald.

Round 200 1 Formosa, 2 Crete, 3 Ceylon, 4 Africa, 5 Honshu, 6 Cape Verde, 7 Novaya Zemlya, 8 Canada, 9 It's the world's remotest island, 10 Bikini.

Round 201 1 Borodino, 2 'Challenger', 3 1990, 4 Slavery, 5 Suez Canal, 6 Austrian, 7 Potato, 8 New Netherland, 9 The Moors, 10 The Knights Templar.

ANSWERS

Round 202 1 'The Absent Minded Professor', 2 Rudolph Valentino, 3 D.W. Griffith, 4 Warren Beatty, 5 Brigitte Bardot, 6 'I Confess', 7 Michaelangelo, 8 Robert Redford, 9 A St. Bernard, 10 Dean Martin.

Round 203 1 Jugular veins, 2 Elbow, 3 Multiple sclerosis, 4 Duodenum, 5 Swallowing, 6 Whooping cough, 7 Collar bone, 8 Tuberculosis, 9 The aorta, 10 The gums.

Round 204 1 Kursk, 2 Horse, 3 Mickey Dolenz, 4 Sleep and/or dreams, 5 Montevideo, 6 Jean-Paul Sartre, 7 Wyoming, 8 Athos, Porthus and Aremis, 9 Tin, 10 Oscar Wilde.

Round 205 1 The Jinn (or Djinn), 2 Mary, Queen of Scots, 3 The Valkyries, 4 Beowulf, 5 Dido, 6 Arachne, 7 Perseus, 8 Cassandra, 9 The Inuit (or Eskimo), 10 Australian Aborigines.

Round 206 1 Charlie Chaplin, 2 Mae West, 3 Richard Nixon, 4 Audrey Hepburn, 5 Margaret Thatcher, 6 Pierre Trudeau, 7 Peter Ustinov, 8 Victor Hugo, 9 Dan Quayle, 10 Stephen Hawking.

Round 207 1 A.J.P. Taylor, 2 Nuremberg, 3 Dutch, 4 Waterloo, 5 1941, 6 Kurt Vonnegut, 7 'Enola Gay', 8 1914, 9 The International Red Cross, 10 Korean War.

Round 208 1 The Sound, 2 Benin, 3 Venezuela, 4 Arizona, 5 Africa, 6 California, 7 North Korea, 8 Chile, 9 Bay of Pigs, 10 South Africa.

Round 209 1 Mars, 2 Eddie Izzard, 3 Intelligence quotient, 4 Rudolf Nureyev, 5 Euclid, 6 Hippocratic oath, 7 M. People, 8 Aquarius, 9 Chalcedony, 10 French.

Round 210 1 Carole King, 2 Elvis Presley, 3 Chubby Checker, 4 The Beach Boys, 5 'She Loves You', 6 The Righteous Brothers, 7 Tom Jones, 8 Roger Miller, 9 Sonny and Cher, 10 Nigeria.

Round 211 1 Eli Whitney, 2 Sir Frank Whittle, 3 Sir Barnes Wallis, 4 Fahrenheit, 5 Alexander Graham Bell, 6 John Napier, 7 The clockwork radio, 8 Charles Macintosh, 9 Samuel Pierpoint Langley, 10 The power loom.

Round 212 1 El Niño, 2 Affidavit, 3 Sub judice, 4 Non compos mentis, 5 Faux pas, 6 Chinook, 7 Shanghai, 8 Fait accompli, 9 Gringo, 10 Touché.

Round 213 1 Jacky Ickx, 2 Discus, 3 Max Schmeling, 4 Six metres, 5 Iran, 6 Larry Holmes, 7 Baseball, 8 Cambridge, 9 The Walker Cup, 10 Britain and the U.S.A.

Round 214 1 Prometheus, 2 R.M.S. 'Lusitania', 3 Soccer, 4 Kiwi, 5 'The Catcher in the Rye', 6 'the life in my men', 7 Carrara 8 Mark Twain, 9 Juniper, 10 First to transit, submerged, the north polar icecap.

Round 215 1 'Humoresques', 2 Paul Hindemith, 3 Brahms, 4 Liszt, 5 Albeniz, 6 J.S. Bach, 7 Icelandic, 8 Eileen Joyce, 9 'La Marseillaise', 10 Ravel.

Round 216 1 Forum, 2 Saratoga, 3 1975, 4 The Battle of the Bulge, 5 1963, 6 Bastille Day, 7 Anno Domini, 8 Yugoslavia, 9 Bangladesh, 10 The Spanish Armada.

Round 217 1 Baltimore, 2 Montana, 3 Newport, 4 Sierra Nevada, 5 Yellowstone, 6 Lake Michigan, 7 Galveston, 8 Appalachians, 9 Santa Fe, New Mexico, 10 Arizona.

Round 218 1 The Globe, 2 Bertolt Brecht, 3 Ruritania, 4 'Pequod', 5 James M. Cain, 6 Henry James, 7 Beatrix Potter, 8 Nathaniel Hawthorne, 9 J.D. Salinger, 10 Alexandre Dumas.

Round 219 1 His first wife, 2 Norway, 3 Heart, or cardiovascular disease, 4 Mary Kingsley, 5 Rwanda, 6 Oscar Pistorius, 7 Good intentions, 8 Maserati, 9 York, 10 Telly Savalas.

Round 220 1 Enrico Caruso, 2 A, 3 Björk, 4 Norwegian, 5 Lorenz Hart, 6 Frank Sinatra, 7 Julian and Sean Lennon, 8 George Harrison, 9 'Symphony of a Thousand', 10 Cello.

Round 221 1 Gemini, 2 Supernova, 3 Sir William Herschel, 4 Steady State Theory, 5 Earth, 6 Salyut, 7 Venus, 8 Black hole, 9 Canopus, or Alpha Carinae, 10 Viking 1 and Viking 2.

Round 222 1 Medina, 2 The Annunciation, 3 Reincarnation, 4 Calvary, 5 Yom Kippur, 6 Karma, 7 Chalice, 8 Charles V, 9 Lilith, 10 Sodom and Gomorrah.

Round 223 1 Thyroid cartilage, 2 Daniel Craig, 3 Francis Bacon, 4 Porsche Spyder, 5 Libya, 6 John Lennon, 7 Carbon dioxide (CO_2), 8 Eisenhower, 9 Peeping Tom, 10 Pancreas.

Round 224 1 Lavrenti Beria, 2 Richard Cheney, 3 The Un-American Activities Committee, 4 Gerrymandering, 5 Downing Street, 6 Israel, 7 Palestine Liberation Organization, 8 Khmer Rouge, 9 Jan Smuts, 10 Austria.

Round 225 1 Seoul, 2 Warsaw, 3 Illinois, 4 Yukon, 5 Lake Superior, 6 France, 7 Cape Agulhas, 8 Hawaii, 9 Kazakhstan, 10 Bangkok.

Round 226 1 Sherlock Holmes, 2 Mel Blanc, 3 'Jaws', 4 Popeye, 5 'Bambi', 6 Devil's Island, 7 Peter Finch, 8 John Wayne, 9 George Cukor, 10 'U-57'.

Round 227 1 Yemen, 2 Lactose, 3 Pasteurization, 4 Enchilada, 5 Gnocchi, 6 Cocaine, 7 Switzerland, 8 Granny Smith, 9 Italy, 10 Biscuit.

Round 228 1 Gargoyle, 2 Cavalry, 3 Court-martial, 4 The Purple Heart, 5 Vaudeville, 6 Dr. Dolittle, 7 Leo, 8 17th, 9 Pisces, 10 Coven.

ANSWERS

Round 229   1 John Keats, 2 Percy Shelley, 3 Catullus, 4 Arthur Rimbaud, 5 Chinese, 6 T.S. Eliot, 7 Hart Crane, 8 Torquato Tasso, 9 Samuel Taylor Coleridge, 10 Chilean.

Round 230   1 Le Mans 24-hour Race, 2 Joe Louis, 3 Canada, 4 Ice hockey, 5 Pierre de Coubertin, 6 Augusta, 7 Scotland, 8 The Golden Boot, 9 The Goodwill Games, 10 Stockholm.

Round 231   1 The Thirty Years War, 2 Turkey, 3 The Black Death/Great Plague, 4 The Mongols, 5 Spartacus, 6 Wales, 7 Tunisia, 8 The Spanish Inquisition, 9 'Kon-Tiki ', 10 Troy.

Round 232   1 Cleo Laine, 2 Ella Fitzgerald, 3 Marion Montgomery, 4 Tom Delaney, 5 Fats Waller and Harry Brooks, 6 Nat 'King' Cole, 7 John Lee Hooker, 8 Harold Arlen, 9 Trumpet, 10 John Lewis.

Round 233   1 'Curiosity', 2 Horus, 3 Felix Wankel, 4 Hectopascal, 5 Georges Pompidou, 6 Björk, 7 The Gherkin, 8 New Zealand, 9 Freezing rain, 10 Pixie and Dixie.

Round 234   1 Spain, 2 Canada, 3 Switzerland, 4 Germany, 5 The Netherlands (or Holland), 6 Italy, 7 Georgia, 8 South Korea, 9 Namibia, 10 Jamaica.

Round 235   1 Yew, 2 Clouds, 3 North America, 4 Lassa fever, 5 Guano, 6 Brown coal, 7 Itch mite, 8 Soil, 9 Centipede, 10 Plane trees.

Round 236   1 Imelda Marcos, 2 Jelly Roll Morton, 3 George, 4 Nicholas II, 5 Florence Nightingale, 6 Katherine of Aragon, 7 Cleopatra, 8 Argentina, 9 Henry Kissinger, 10 Roald Amundsen.

Round 237   1 Neptune, 2 Vega, 3 The distance from Earth to the Sun, 4 Orion, 5 Mercury, 6 A binary, or double star, 7 Fred Hoyle, 8 Taurus, 9 Corona Borealis , 10 William Herschel.

Round 238 1 12, 2 Beethoven, 3 St. Brendan, 4 Hallé Orchestra, 5 Scotland, 6 1905, 7 Hudson Bay, 8 'God Save the Queen', 9 T.E. Lawrence, 10 Finland.

Round 239 1 'The Thomas Crown Affair', 2 George Murphy and Ronald Reagan, 3 Loretta Swit (Hotlips in 'M*A*S*H'), 4 Christopher Reeve, 5 'Singing in the Rain', 6 'Grease', 7 'Waterworld', 8 Dr. Seuss, 9 Richard Burton and Elizabeth Taylor, 10 Tallulah Bankhead.

Round 240 1 Abraham Lincoln, 2 James K. Polk, 3 John F. Kennedy, 4 Theodore Roosevelt, 5 Andrew Jackson, 6 Franklin D. Roosevelt, 7 Woodrow Wilson, 8 Gutzon Borglum, 9 1969, 10 Calvin Coolidge.

Round 241 1 Edgar Allan Poe, 2 Arthur Miller, 3 Erich Maria Remarque, 4 Edward Elgar, 5 Robert Ludlum, 6 Stieg Larsson, 7 Ian Fleming, 8 Washington Irving, 9 Anne McCaffrey, 10 Beethoven.

Round 242 1 Morocco, 2 South America, 3 Peru, 4 Romania, 5 The Netherlands, 6 Armenia, 7 Laos, 8 Burkina Faso, 9 Argentina, 10 Chicago.

Round 243 1 Zimbabwe, 2 Cairo, 3 Japan, 4 Denier, 5 Sigmund Freud, 6 Mule, 7 A musical instrument, 8 Estonia, 9 1,000, 10 Horsepower.

Round 244 1 The electric vacuum cleaner, 2 The safety match, 3 Jet engine, 4 Bakelite, 5 China, 6 Thomas Newcomen, 7 Magnifying glass, 8 The three-point safety belt, 9 The Gestetner document copier, 10 Hungarian.

Round 245 1 Franz Liszt, 2 Jean-Baptiste Lully, 3 His 'hot cakes', 4 Mendelssohn, 5 'The Months', 6 'Moonlight Sonata', 7 Gerald Moore, 8 'Preludes', 9 It is for the left-hand only, 10 Richard Strauss.

Round 246 1 Persia, 2 Titans, 3 The Oceanides, 4 Cerberus, 5 Kali, 6 Neptune, 7 Aeolian harp, 8 Atlas, 9 Antigone, 10 Charon.

Round 247　1 Charlton Heston, 2 Pinniped, 3 Zebra, 4 B2, 5 The Moluccas, 6 Michael Schumacher, 7 Venus, 8 Frank Lloyd Wright, 9 Honda, 10 Piano.

Round 248　1 Austria and Germany, 2 13, 3 Kristallnacht, 4 Istanbul, 5 1914, 6 Dark Ages, 7 Dauphin, 8 Nostradamus, 9 Britain and China, 10 Star Wars.

Round 249　1 Don Budge, 2 Motor racing, 3 Emil Zatopek, 4 Monica Seles, 5 The Triple Crown, 6 Ice skating, 7 High jump, 8 Jennifer Capriati, 9 Hank, 10 Kendo.

Round 250　1 Anchor, 2 Submarine, 3 Afterburner, 4 Greyhound, 5 The Netherlands, 6 Republic of Ireland, 7 Fiat, 8 A ship, 9 Bicycle, 10 First aircraft to break the sound-barrier.

Round 251　1 Simon and Garfunkel, 2 The Monkees, 3 The Doors, 4 Frank and Nancy Sinatra, 5 Chuck Berry, 6 Mary Hopkin, 7 'Hey Jude', 8 'Eleanor Rigby', 9 'I Get Around', 10 Dusty Springfield.

Round 252　1 A warship, 2 Black Forest, 3 Le Corbusier, 4 Germany, 5 Bhopal, 6 Larynx, 7 Already seen, 8 Manfred von Richthofen (aka the Red Baron), 9 Nero, 10 Switzerland.

Round 253　1 Graphical user interface, 2 Database management system, 3 Optical character recognition, 4 Lara Croft, 5 The binary system, 6 Computer programming languages, 7 Paul Allen, 8 UNIX, 9 Digital Network Service, 10 Eight.

Round 254　1 'The Time Machine' by H.G. Wells, 2 Edmund Clerihew Bentley, 3 I Ching, 4 Molière, 5 Iceland, 6 Len Deighton, 7 Alex Haley, 8 Aslan, 9 Molly Keane, 10 'The English Patient'.

Round 255　1 Heinrich Himmler, 2 David Dinkins, 3 Germany and Poland, 4 Watergate, 5 Lech Walesa, 6 Adlai E. Stevenson, 7 George Gallup, 8 Nigerian, 9 Poland, 10 Turkey.

Round 256   1 Samuel Plimsoll (the Plimsoll line), 2 Harvey Milk, 3 Aleksey Leonov, 4 Houston, 5 Denmark, 6 Seahorse, 7 John Dankworth, 8 Ivan the Terrible, 9 Sumatra, 10 Red Cross.

Round 257   1 'High Noon', 2 Sean Connery, 3 'Cabaret', 4 'Last Chance Saloon', 5 'Call Me Madam', 6 'In Dreams', 7 'The Trail of the Lonesome Pine', 8 Mel Gibson, 9 Fritz Lang, 10 'Flying Down to Rio'.

Round 258   1 Messerschmitt Me262, 2 Republic Shooting Star, 3 Stuka, 4 Warthog, 5 MIG 15, 6 McDonnel Douglas, 7 Boeing B-52, 8 Mustang, 9 Typhoon, 10 SAAB.

Round 259   1 James Bay, 2 Nepal, 3 Laos, 4 Birmingham, 5 New Zealand, 6 Mozambique, 7 Mexico, 8 Israel, 9 Zimbabwe, 10 Croatia.

Round 260   1 The Dead Sea Scrolls, 2 Garden of Gethsemane, 3 Damascus, 4 Sea of Galilee, 5 Mount Sinai, 6 Mount Ararat, 7 Mount Nebo, 8 Gabriel, 9 Lazarus, 10 Peter.

Round 261   1 1984, 2 Zürich, 3 Pakistan, 4 The Scarlet Pimpernel, 5 They are the mutual equivalents in Greek and Roman mythology, 6 Iran, 7 William Calley, 8 World War II, 9 Prince Rainier III of Monaco, 10 Loki.

Round 262   1 Paul Whiteman, 2 Bass tuba, 3 A large gong, 4 Dissonance, 5 Reggae, 6 Violin, 7 Jimi Hendrix, 8 Harmonica, 9 An ancient Greek harp, 10 Violin.

Round 263   1 The hare, 2 One, 3 The Komodo dragon, 4 A hinny, 5 Habitat, 6 Mollusc shells, 7 Rubber plant, 8 The tsetse fly, 9 The capybara, 10 Quinine.

Round 264   1 1946, 2 The Colossus of Rhodes, 3 Silhouette, 4 Caravaggio, 5 Sir Joshua Reynolds, 6 Sculpture, 7 David Hockney, 8 Pablo Picasso, 9 Rubens, 10 Salvador Dali.

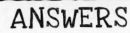

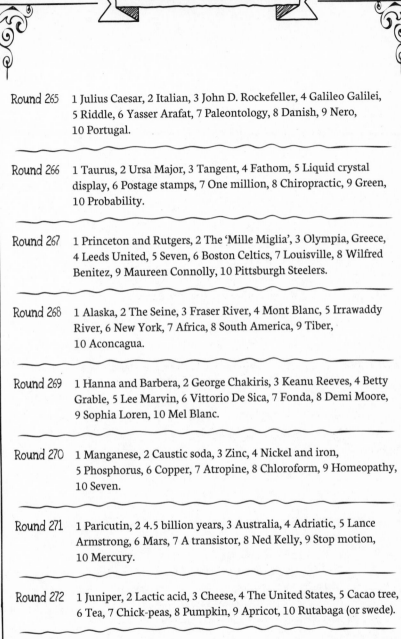

Round 265 1 Julius Caesar, 2 Italian, 3 John D. Rockefeller, 4 Galileo Galilei,
5 Riddle, 6 Yasser Arafat, 7 Paleontology, 8 Danish, 9 Nero,
10 Portugal.

Round 266 1 Taurus, 2 Ursa Major, 3 Tangent, 4 Fathom, 5 Liquid crystal
display, 6 Postage stamps, 7 One million, 8 Chiropractic, 9 Green,
10 Probability.

Round 267 1 Princeton and Rutgers, 2 The 'Mille Miglia', 3 Olympia, Greece,
4 Leeds United, 5 Seven, 6 Boston Celtics, 7 Louisville, 8 Wilfred
Benitez, 9 Maureen Connolly, 10 Pittsburgh Steelers.

Round 268 1 Alaska, 2 The Seine, 3 Fraser River, 4 Mont Blanc, 5 Irrawaddy
River, 6 New York, 7 Africa, 8 South America, 9 Tiber,
10 Aconcagua.

Round 269 1 Hanna and Barbera, 2 George Chakiris, 3 Keanu Reeves, 4 Betty
Grable, 5 Lee Marvin, 6 Vittorio De Sica, 7 Fonda, 8 Demi Moore,
9 Sophia Loren, 10 Mel Blanc.

Round 270 1 Manganese, 2 Caustic soda, 3 Zinc, 4 Nickel and iron,
5 Phosphorus, 6 Copper, 7 Atropine, 8 Chloroform, 9 Homeopathy,
10 Seven.

Round 271 1 Paricutin, 2 4.5 billion years, 3 Australia, 4 Adriatic, 5 Lance
Armstrong, 6 Mars, 7 A transistor, 8 Ned Kelly, 9 Stop motion,
10 Mercury.

Round 272 1 Juniper, 2 Lactic acid, 3 Cheese, 4 The United States, 5 Cacao tree,
6 Tea, 7 Chick-peas, 8 Pumpkin, 9 Apricot, 10 Rutabaga (or swede).

Round 273 1 Missing Link, 2 Elizabeth I, 3 Richard I, 4 William Tell, 5 Shirley
Temple (Black), 6 Brazil, 7 1941, 8 France, 9 Alcoholic drinks,
10 Greenpeace.

Round 274   1 24, 2 16, 3 35, 4 40, 5 66, 6 27, 7 45, 8 11, 9 28, 10 12.

Round 275   1 Al Jolson, 2 Dinosaur, 3 Robert Walker, 4 Swedish, 5 After Earth, 6 Nero, 7 'As Time Goes By', 8 'King Kong', 9 Roman Polanski, 10 Mae West.

Round 276   1 Wilhelm II, 2 New Amsterdam, 3 The Sheriff of Nottingham , 4 1947, 5 New Mexico, 6 Thule, 7 Royal Canadian Mounted Police (Mounties), 8 Ludwig Wittgenstein, 9 Zimbabwe, 10 Computer-generated imagery.

Round 277   1 Cartography, 2 Slovenia, 3 New Zealand, 4 Coromandel Coast, 5 India, 6 Colombo, 7 Louisiana, 8 Genoa, 9 Salt Lake City, 10 Pakistan.

Round 278   1 Colin Forbes, 2 Bill Bryson, 3 Hermann Hesse, 4 Aleksandr Solzhenitsyn, 5 Henning Mankell, 6 Sheridan Le Fanu, 7 Horatio Hornblower, 8 'The Day of the Jackal', 9 Watergate, 10 Arthur C. Clarke.

Round 279   1 A bird, 2 Ladybirds (or ladybugs), 3 A bird, 4 A dog, 5 Goat, 6 A marsupial, 7 A fish, 8 A salamander, 9 North America, 10 A dog.

Round 280   1 Each musician leaves as he finishes his part, 2 The 'London Symphonies', 3 He introduced the four-movement symphony, 4 'The Italian Symphony', 5 'Jupiter', 6 Vaughan Williams, 7 Sibelius, 8 Because Beethoven, Bruckner, Dvorak and Schubert had all died after completing their ninth symphonies, 9 'Papillons' (Butterflies), 10 'Rhapsody on a Theme of Paganini'.

Round 281   1 Jogging, 2 Pierre Cardin, 3 Imprinting, 4 Illiteracy, 5 Totem poles, 6 An antelope, 7 S, 8 Interest, 9 Bob Hope, 10 Smog.

Round 282 1 Maria Theresa, 2 Khedive, 3 Kublai Khan, 4 Ivan the Terrible, 5 Turkey, 6 Elizabeth, 7 Shogun, 8 Bonaparte, 9 The Huns, 10 Russia.

Round 283 1 Tiger Woods, 2 Volleyball, 3 Basketball, 4 Venus Williams, 5 Dressage, 6 0 (The U.S. boycotted the Games), 6 3, 8 Racing toboggan, 9 Buster Crabbe, 10 Carl Fogarty.

Round 284 1 Madagascar, 2 Japan, 3 Sweden, 4 Timor, 5 The Pacific Ocean, 6 France, 7 Cyprus, 8 Vanuatu, 9 Caribbean Sea, 10 Puerto Rico.

Round 285 1 Wole Soyinka, 2 'Arabian Nights', 3 Pearl S. Buck, 4 William Burroughs, 5 John Fowles, 6 Nikos Kazantzakis, 7 Simone de Beauvoir, 8 John, 9 Arundhati Roy, 10 Edmond Rostand.

Round 286 1 The Koran, 2 Larry Sanders, 3 Cranium, 4 Infinity, 5 Pils or Pilsner (from Pilsen), 6 Red, 7 Suriname, 8 Prague, 9 U.S.A., 10 Hyper Text Markup Language.

Round 287 1 Jacques Cousteau, 2 Doris Day, 3 Jim Carrey, 4 Popeye Doyle, 5 Brigitte Bardot, 6 'Slumdog Millionaire', 7 Jean Arthur, 8 Gloria Swanson, 9 Robert Altman, 10 Otto Preminger.

Round 288 1 Strontium, 2 Half-life, 3 Ivan Pavlov, 4 Joule, 5 Louis Pasteur, 6 CO, 7 Vector, 8 Nitric acid and hydrochloric acid, 9 Copper, 10 Guglielmo Marconi.

Round 289 1 Artemis, 2 Calchas, 3 Venus, 4 Medea, 5 Atlas, 6 Vulcan, 7 Minotaur, 8 Eurydice, 9 Damocles, 10 Andromeda.

Round 290 1 A hard wood, 2 'Bismarck', 3 OPEC, 4 39, 5 Siegfried, 6 Petra, 7 English and French, 8 7th December 1941, the Japanese attack on Pearl Harbor, 9 Yin and yang, 10 Sri Lanka.

Round 291   1 U.S. Civil War, 2 Norwegian, 3 Charles Lindbergh, 4 Grant, 5 Albania, 6 Egypt, 7 Red Square, Moscow, 8 Ottoman Empire, 9 Slave trade, 10 Louis the Sixteenth.

Round 292   1 Roy Orbison, 2 Gene Pitney, 3 Elvis Presley, 4 Public Image Ltd, 5 Johnnie Ray, 6 Lou Reed, 7 The Rolling Stones, 8 The Shangri-Las, 9 John Denver, 10 Neil Diamond.

Round 293   1 Antarctica, 2 Ohio, 3 France, 4 Strait of Gibraltar, 5 Giant's Causeway, 6 Sears Tower, 7 Egypt, 8 Somalia, 9 Chemnitz, 10 Australia.

Round 294   1 Niki Lauda, 2 Italy, 3 Blue, black, red, yellow and green, 4 William Empson, 5 Charlie Wax, 6 Mexico, 7 Bats, 8 Mars, 9 Indian Ocean, 10 Australia.

Round 295   1 The kidney, 2 Femur, 3 Endorphins, 4 Dandruff, 5 The eye, 6 The placenta, 7 The eyes, 8 The skin, 9 Alzheimer's disease, 10 Cramp.

Round 296   1 Samuel, 2 St. Nicholas, 3 The Sistine Chapel, 4 Hanukkah, 5 Hinduism, 6 Tomas de Torquemada, 7 Poland, 8 Shinto, 9 Carthusians, 10 Islam.

Round 297   1 The Phantom, 2 Gene Hackman, 3 Spiderman, 4 Wonder Woman, 5 The Riddler, 6 The Flash, 7 Green Lantern, 8 Margot Kidder, 9 The Fantastic Four, 10 Catwoman.

Round 298   1 J. Wellington Wimpy, 2 'Peter and the Wolf', 3 Woody Allen, 4 Mickey Rooney, 5 Harry Belafonte, 6 John Wayne, 7 'Shanghai Noon', 8 Harry Potter, 9 Stephen Sondheim, 10 Matt Damon and Ben Affleck.

Round 299   1 Humidity, 2 U.N.I.C.E.F., 3 Paris, 4 Bunsen burner, 5 Halley's Comet, 6 Cochineal, 7 Napalm, 8 Mock orange, 9 Woodcock, 10 Tommy Lee Jones.

Round 300   1 Nicaragua, 2 The Philippines, 3 Fulgencio Batista, 4 Austria, 5 Edmund Barton, 6 18th, 7 2014, 8 James (Jim) Callaghan, 9 James (Jimmy) Carter, 10 Knesset.

Round 301   1 1994, 2 Thailand, 3 France and Italy, 4 Honshu, 5 Tower Bridge, London, 6 Tay Bridge, 7 Golden Gate Bridge, 8 Norway, 9 Spain and Morocco, 10 St. Lawrence River.

Round 302   1 Laura Davies, 2 Real Madrid, 3 Dressage, 4 Los Angeles Galaxy, 5 1987, 6 Speed skating, 7 Olga Korbut, 8 Water polo, 9 Gary Player, 10 George Foreman.

Round 303   1 Tannin, 2 Parma, 3 Whisky, 4 Carbon dioxide, 5 Rice, 6 Vodka, 7 Cabbage, 8 Greece, 9 Caffeine, 10 Tandoori.

Round 304   1 Four, 2 Krakatoa, 3 Croatia, 4 Morocco, 5 Malaysia Airlines, 6 Boadicea (or Boudicca), 7 Ethiopian, 8 Libya, 9 Neptune, 10 Yamuna.

Round 305   1 The Flying V , 2 Harmonica, 3 The Theramin, 4 Cello, piano and violin, 5 Trumpet , 6 Violins, violas, and cellos , 7 Guitar, 8 Sousaphone, 9 Oboe, 10 Zither.

Round 306   1 Apollo 13, 2 1969, 3 Galileo, 4 17 percent (about one-sixth), 5 Canis Major, 6 None, all have at least two, 7 Voyager 1, 8 Mir, 9 Binary star, 10 Saturn.

Round 307   1 Debonair (De bon aire), 2 Lunar, 3 Terracotta, 4 Kulak, 5 A sluggish creek flowing through swampy terrain, 6 Synonym, 7 Sweden, 8 Z, 9 Peso, 10 I think, therefore I am.

Round 308   1 Vesuvius, 2 Portuguese, 3 1960s, 4 Portugal and Spain, 5 'Limelight', 6 Buffalo Bill, 7 Christiaan Barnard, 8 Cheops, 9 Hippocrates, 10 Germany and Italy.

Round 309 1 Biltong, 2 William Shakespeare, 3 Norman Schwarzkopf, 4 Hong Kong, 5 Mexico, 6 The Ottoman, or Turkish, Empire, 7 New Zealand, 8 Jerusalem, 9 Mexico, 10 Key West, on the Florida Keys.

Round 310 1 Italy, 2 Andorra, 3 The Gulf of Guinea, 4 The Cascade Mountains, 5 Hungary, 6 The Bay of Biscay, 7 Maine, 8 Albania, 9 The Waikato River, 10 The Appalachian Trail.

Round 311 1 Sally Field, 2 John Schlesinger, 3 Bela Lugosi, 4 George Clooney, 5 Tom Hanks, 6 Lena Horne, 7 Billy Wilder, 8 A wookie, 9 Elliott Gould, 10 'A Few Good Men'.

Round 312 1 Hercule Poirot, 2 Captain Nemo, 3 Louisa May Alcott, 4 A.N. Whitehead, 5 August Strindberg, 6 Lew Wallace, 7 Vicente Blasco Ibanez, 8 Richard Hannay, 9 'The Moon's a Balloon', 10 Peter Pan.

Round 313 1 Boris Spassky, 2 Boris Yeltsin, 3 Andrei Sakharov, 4 Lenin, 5 In a military plane crash, 6 Vladimir Putin, 7 Nikita Khrushchev, 8 Leon Trotsky, 9 Valentina Tereshkova, 10 Igor Sikorsky.

Round 314 1 Aluminium (aluminum), 2 Hobart, 3 Malaysia, 4 7 (B, E, J, Q, X, Y and Z), 5 Nipper, 6 Vanessa-Mae, 7 Argentina, 8 Long-sightedness, 9 Celine Dion, 10 1924.

Round 315 1 Leopard seal, 2 A snake, 3 A mollusc, 4 Sperm whales, 5 A rodent, 6 Chameleon, 7 A caterpillar, 8 Jaguar, 9 Crab, 10 Termites.

Round 316 1 Boris Becker, 2 Five, 3 1962, 4 The Olympic Games, 5 Eric Liddell, 6 Kendo, 7 Marat Safin, 8 South African, 9 Boxing, 10 Jack Nicklaus.

Round 317 1 Carly Simon, 2 Kate Bush, 3 'How Deep Is Your Love?', 4 Little Jimmy Osmond, 5 Al Green, 6 The Sex Pistols, 7 Queen, 8 The Bee Gees, 9 The Commodores, 10 Bob Marley.

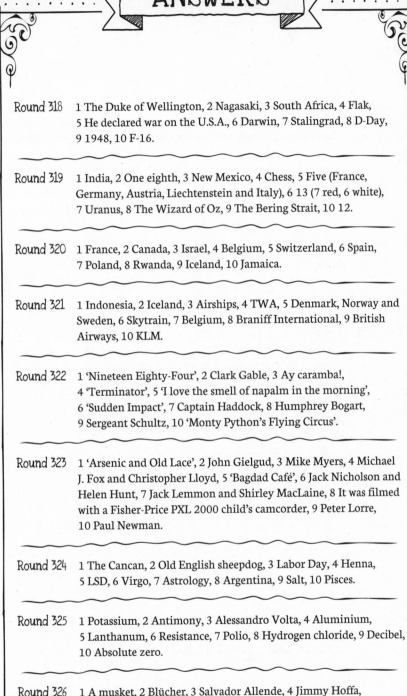

ANSWERS

Round 318 1 The Duke of Wellington, 2 Nagasaki, 3 South Africa, 4 Flak, 5 He declared war on the U.S.A., 6 Darwin, 7 Stalingrad, 8 D-Day, 9 1948, 10 F-16.

Round 319 1 India, 2 One eighth, 3 New Mexico, 4 Chess, 5 Five (France, Germany, Austria, Liechtenstein and Italy), 6 13 (7 red, 6 white), 7 Uranus, 8 The Wizard of Oz, 9 The Bering Strait, 10 12.

Round 320 1 France, 2 Canada, 3 Israel, 4 Belgium, 5 Switzerland, 6 Spain, 7 Poland, 8 Rwanda, 9 Iceland, 10 Jamaica.

Round 321 1 Indonesia, 2 Iceland, 3 Airships, 4 TWA, 5 Denmark, Norway and Sweden, 6 Skytrain, 7 Belgium, 8 Braniff International, 9 British Airways, 10 KLM.

Round 322 1 'Nineteen Eighty-Four', 2 Clark Gable, 3 Ay caramba!, 4 'Terminator', 5 'I love the smell of napalm in the morning', 6 'Sudden Impact', 7 Captain Haddock, 8 Humphrey Bogart, 9 Sergeant Schultz, 10 'Monty Python's Flying Circus'.

Round 323 1 'Arsenic and Old Lace', 2 John Gielgud, 3 Mike Myers, 4 Michael J. Fox and Christopher Lloyd, 5 'Bagdad Café', 6 Jack Nicholson and Helen Hunt, 7 Jack Lemmon and Shirley MacLaine, 8 It was filmed with a Fisher-Price PXL 2000 child's camcorder, 9 Peter Lorre, 10 Paul Newman.

Round 324 1 The Cancan, 2 Old English sheepdog, 3 Labor Day, 4 Henna, 5 LSD, 6 Virgo, 7 Astrology, 8 Argentina, 9 Salt, 10 Pisces.

Round 325 1 Potassium, 2 Antimony, 3 Alessandro Volta, 4 Aluminium, 5 Lanthanum, 6 Resistance, 7 Polio, 8 Hydrogen chloride, 9 Decibel, 10 Absolute zero.

Round 326 1 A musket, 2 Blücher, 3 Salvador Allende, 4 Jimmy Hoffa, 5 Richard I, 6 Rob Roy, 7 Quebec, 8 F.D. Roosevelt, 9 1933, 10 Australia.

Round 327 1 Roger Moore and Tony Curtis, 2 Fred Astaire and Ginger Rogers, 3 The Everly Brothers, 4 Robin Williams, 5 Jerry Lewis, 6 Bud and Lou, 7 Pierre and Marie, 8 Gilbert and Sullivan, 9 Laurel and Hardy, 10 Dorothy Lamour.

Round 328 1 Phoebe's, 2 Helen Baxendale, 3 'Days of Our Lives', 4 Carol, 5 Jennifer Aniston, 6 Phoebe, 7 No. 10, 8 Emma, 9 Ross and Monica, 10 Tom Selleck.

Round 329 1 Universal Serial Bus, 2 Hungary, 3 Minus 40 degrees, 4 Phi, 5 Jeremiah, 6 Green, 7 The Andes, 8 France, 9 Three, 10 Anakin Skywalker.

Round 330 1 Tallahassee, 2 Auckland, 3 The Atlantic, 4 The Pacific Ocean, 5 The Netherlands (or Holland), 6 Portugal and Spain, 7 Saudi Arabia, 8 South Carolina, 9 Montana, 10 Angola.

Round 331 1 Windpipe, 2 A mole, 3 The kidney, 4 Amnesia, 5 Insulin, 6 Oesophagus, 7 Paediatrics, 8 Prickly heat, 9 The heart, 10 The skin.

Round 332 1 'The Seed and the Sower', 2 Edna O'Brien, 3 Raymond Chandler, 4 Joan Crawford, 5 Philip Roth, 6 Mungo Park, 7 Scott Turow, 8 Joseph Conrad, 9 Sir Thomas Malory, 10 'Barnaby Rudge'.

Round 333 1 Squash, 2 German, 3 The Melbourne Cup, 4 Judo, 5 Diving, 6 Chris Froome, 7 Jonathan Edwards, 8 Tennis (real tennis), 9 David Weir, 10 Faster, Higher, Stronger.

Round 334 1 John Ireland, 2 Tchaikovsky, 3 Rossini, 4 Sir William Walton, 5 Ermanno Wolf-Ferrari, 6 Anton Bruckner, 7 Carl Maria von Weber, 8 Ludwig van Beethoven, 9 Hoagy Carmichael, 10 Jean Sibelius.

Round 335 1 1988, 2 1989, 3 1948, 4 2003, 5 1978, 6 1960, 7 1977, 8 1995, 9 1945, 10 1997.

Round 336 1 Belgium, 2 Crawl and breaststroke, 3 Johnny Weissmuller, 4 Golf, 5 Skating, 6 Joe DiMaggio, 7 Sugar Ray Robinson, 8 Rodney Marsh, 9 Ethiopia, 10 Canada.

Round 337 1 Fish, 2 Seaweed, 3 Cheese, 4 Hummus (houmous), 5 Apples, walnuts, celery and mayonnaise, 6 Soya beans (mashed), 7 Avocado, 8 Almonds, 9 Tequila, 10 Roquefort.

Round 338 1 Java, 2 1978, 3 Morocco, 4 Hannibal, 5 Two, 6 Turkey, 7 Lidice, 8 Daisy Duck, 9 Tchaikovsky, 10 Dublin.

Round 339 1 U.S.S. 'Triton', 2 Britain and France, 3 'Endeavour', 4 Jeep, 5 Sailing vessel, 6 Denmark, 7 Pan American, 8 Milan, 9 Fridtjof Nansen, 10 Japan.

Round 340 1 John Malkovich and Glenn Close, 2 'Prince of Foxes', 3 Dean Martin and Jacqueline Bisset, 4 Karen Black, 5 Robert Redford and Dustin Hoffman, 6 Richard Gere, 7 Yul Brynner and Ingrid Bergman, 8 Tom Hanks, 9 'Random Harvest', 10 'Peyton Place'.

Round 341 1 Methane, 2 DDT, 3 Edward Jenner, 4 Francium, 5 Fahrenheit, 6 Formic acid, 7 Electric current, 8 Carbon, 9 Ultrasonics, 10 Kiloton.

Round 342 1 Amnesty International, 2 Desmond Tutu, 3 The Berlin Wall, 4 Alfred Nobel, 5 Yugoslavia, 6 Montgolfier, 7 Grenada, 8 Coventry, 9 Suriname, 10 Simón Bolívar.

Round 343 1 Lauren Bacall, 2 United States, 3 Jodie Foster, 4 Nicotine, 5 Kaolin, 6 Lira, 7 Clairvoyance, 8 Technicolor, 9 Kilogram, 10 A musical instrument.

Round 344 1 Art Deco, 2 Andy Warhol, 3 William Blake, 4 Pieter Breughel the Elder, 5 Anthony van Dyck, 6 Tempera, 7 The Rijksmuseum, Amsterdam, 8 Diego Velazquez, 9 Titian, 10 Gustav Klimt.

Round 345   1 'Turandot', 2 Counterpoint, 3 B*Witched, 4 Cello, 5 Frank Zappa, 6 Roy Orbison, 7 Saturn, 8 St. Cecilia, 9 Andrew Lloyd Webber, 10 Chicago Symphony Orchestra.

Round 346   1 Psalms, 2 John, 3 A rainbow, 4 His heel, 5 Bethel, 6 A burning bush, 7 Psalm 23, 8 Seven, 9 Cattle, silver and gold, 10 An altar.

Round 347   1 A lion, 2 Russia, 3 The Egyptian deity Serapis and the Greek god Poseidon, 4 Menelaus, 5 Cyclops, 6 Icarus, 7 Ajax, 8 His heel, 9 Hera, 10 Echo.

Round 348   1 Sheep, 2 Green, yellow, red, blue, white and black, 3 The Monaco Grand Prix, 4 Ecuador, 5 American football, 6 Dopey, 7 The Salvation Army, 8 Joseph, 9 Chicken (it is chicken stew), 10 Mercury and Venus.

Round 349   1 The Canary Islands, 2 Yosemite, 3 Uzbekistan, 4 Denmark, 5 Copenhagen, 6 Jordan, 7 San Francisco, 8 Rhône, 9 Great Rift Valley, 10 Norway, Sweden and Finland.

Round 350   1 Warren Christopher, 2 Watergate, 3 Winnie, 4 Yuri Andropov, 5 François Mitterrand, 6 Republic of the Congo (today known as Democratic Republic of the Congo), 7 Romania, 8 James Hertzog, 9 Engels, 10 Israel.

Round 351   1 Wet Wet Wet, 2 Sheryl Crow, 3 D:Ream, 4 Prodigy, 5 'Wannabe', 6 Bryan Adams, 7 Whitney Houston, 8 Billy Ray Cyrus, 9 No Doubt, 10 Elton John.

Round 352   1 Discworld, 2 Buffy the Vampire Slayer, 3 Amity, 4 'To Kill a Mockingbird', 5 The Emerald City, 6 'The Prisoner of Zenda', 7 Colorado, 8 Shelbyville, 9 Rocky and Bullwinkle, 10 J.R.R. Tolkien.

Round 353 1 The speed of light, 2 212 degrees, 3 Istanbul, 4 'The Daily Planet', 5 The Ostmark, 6 Rotterdam, 7 White, 8 France, 9 Hardness and Blackness, 10 Potassium.

Round 354 1 116 years, 2 Augustus (Gaius Octavius), 3 Woomera, 4 Lake Ontario and Lake Erie, 5 Helen of Troy, 6 Harrison Ford, 7 Maxim Gorky, 8 Wednesday (after Woden), 9 Hockey (ice hockey), 10 Gibraltar.

Round 355 1 Diamond, 2 Hibernation, 3 Mount St Helen's, 4 Kookaburra, 5 Loris, 6 Pearl, 7 Strychnine, 8 Tadpole, 9 The North Pole, 10 Rubber.

Round 356 1 John, 2 Bad Attitude, 3 Jennifer Aniston, 4 Baker and Ponch, 5 Hanna and Barbera, 6 Stavros, 7 Oprah Winfrey, 8 'The Flintstones', 9 Lucille Ball, 10 Boston.

Round 357 1 Indonesia, 2 Easter Island, 3 Barbados, 4 Baffin Island, 5 Britain, 6 Greenland, 7 Iceland, 8 Zanzibar, 9 Bikini, 10 Tonga.

Round 358 1 Hypotenuse, 2 Aldi, 3 Google, 4 An odometer, 5 Julian Assange, 6 Pepé Le Pew, 7 Jennifer Lopez, 8 Sancho Panza, 9 Pinocchio, 10 Bellerophon.

Round 359 1 India, 2 Captain James Cook, 3 Rouen, 4 Sir Henry Morton Stanley, 5 Neanderthals, 6 George C. Marshall, 7 Carthage, 8 Blackshirts, 9 Germany and Japan, 10 4th July 1776.

Round 360 1 Insolvency, 2 Aardvark, 3 Lignum vitae, 4 Thiamine, 5 Mnemonic, 6 Spanish, 7 Hindi, 8 Vienna, 9 Cyrillic alphabet, 10 Catalan.

Round 361 1 1980s, 2 Mary (Nichols and Kelly) , 3 A sword, 4 Lizzie Borden, 5 1983, 6 John Christie, 7 Butch Cassidy and the Sundance Kid, 8 The Yorkshire Ripper, 9 Timothy McVeigh, 10 Nick Leeson.

Round 362 1 'Crying', 2 Cancer, 3 Liver, 4 1986, 5 Portugal, 6 Standard Oil, 7 Organization of the Oil Exporting Countries, 8 New Zealand, 9 "... as equals", 10 Reykjavik, Iceland.

Round 363 1 'X-Men', 2 Mae West, 3 Jean-Claude Van Damme, 4 Jon Voight, 5 Harry Connick Jnr., 6 Tony Curtis, 7 Liv Ullmann, 8 Charles Bronson, 9 'Rules of Engagement', 10 'Dogfight'.

Round 364 1 Aldous Huxley, 2 Harold Robbins, 3 'The Borrowers', 4 Angus Wilson, 5 Singapore, 6 Monologue, 7 Robertson Davies, 8 Jessica Mitford, 9 J.P. Donleavy, 10 Margaret Drabble.

Round 365 1 Tasman Sea, 2 Bering Sea, 3 Black Sea, 4 Bay of Bengal, 5 Ionian Sea, 6 Antarctica, 7 Gulf of Mexico, 8 The so-called Bermuda Triangle, 9 Spain, 10 Sea of Okhotsk.

Round 366 1 Radar, 2 Transuranic, 3 Dynamite, 4 Nitrogen, 5 Solder, 6 Perspex or Lucite, 7 Dounreay, 8 Opium, 9 B12, 10 Teflon.

Round 367 1 Bogota, 2 Sergei Diaghilev, 3 Fallopian tubes, 4 France, 5 St. Nicholas, 6 Seven, 7 Coco, 8 Lace, 9 U.S.A., 10 Dogs.

Round 368 1 Dvorak, 2 Johann Sebastian Bach, 3 Bela Bartok, 4 'The Emperor', 5 The 'Pathetique', 6 The 'Revolutionary', 7 'Clair de Lune', 8 Muzio Clementi, 9 Richard Strauss, 10 'The Flying Dutchman'.

Round 369 1 Argentina, 2 The Philippines, 3 Alexander the Great (Alexandria), 4 Iran, 5 Haiti, 6 South Africa, 7 Eva Braun, 8 Mao Zedong (Mao Tse Tung), 9 Woodrow Wilson, 10 Gordon Brown.

Round 370 1 Michael Phelps, 2 Nike (Greek goddess of victory), 3 Copper, 4 A car (Audi), 5 Alicia Coutts, 6 China, 7 Lizzy Yarnold, 8 Austria, 9 Tyler Clary, 10 Ashton Eaton.

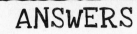

Round 371 1 Wasabi, 2 Veal, 3 Cabbage, 4 Peaches, 5 Holland (The Netherlands), 6 Profiteroles, 7 Spinach, 8 White, 9 Apples, 10 Horse meat.

Round 372 1 Kangchenjunga, 2 Pomegranate, 3 Dolphin, 4 Odysseus, 5 Horn of plenty, 6 World War II, 7 Buck's fizz, 8 Egypt, 9 Finland, 10 Eiger (film: 'The Eiger Sanction').

Round 373 1 The Atlantic Ocean, 2 The Mediterranean Sea, 3 The Pacific Ocean, 4 Washington, 5 Lisbon, 6 Pakistan, 7 Missouri, 8 Florida, 9 Portugal, 10 Doldrums.

Round 374 1 742, 2 Fox, 3 Oregon, 4 Bouvier, 5 7G, 6 Jub-Jub, 7 Todd, 8 Julius, 9 Yeardley Smith, 10 David Silverman.

Round 375 1 Twenty, 2 Rapunzel, 3 Thumbelina, 4 'The Emperor's New Clothes', 5 'Hansel and Gretel', 6 The fox, 7 France, 8 Chicken Licken (Little), 9 Turn straw into gold on her spinning wheel, 10 The Little Red Hen.

Round 376 1 Poland and Lithuania, 2 Six, 3 Archimedes, 4 Hillary Clinton, 5 Chewing gum, 6 Los Alamos, 7 M16 rifle, 8 Bertrand Russell, 9 1961, 10 Escudo.

Round 377 1 R, 2 The Mackenzie River, 3 Elizabeth, 4 Menorah, 5 White, 6 Endocrine, 7 Lance Armstrong, 8 Magnificat, 9 Mensa, 10 Albany.

Round 378 1 Bristol Britannia, 2 BAC 111, 3 Fokker, 4 Airbus A320, 5 Caravelle, 6 Mc Donnell Douglas DC-10, 7 Boeing 747, 8 De Havilland Canada, 9 Convair, 10 Canadair CL-44.

Round 379 1 Martial Solal, 2 Oscar Peterson, 3 Billie Holiday, 4 Ethel Waters, 5 Frank Sinatra, 6 'Fats' Waller, 7 Jack Pettis and Elmer Schoebel, 8 Sarah Vaughan, 9 B.B. King, 10 John Coltrane.

Round 380   1 Iowa, Ohio and Utah, 2 Salem, 3 California, 4 Wyoming, 5 Alaska, 6 California, 7 Tennessee, 8 Kansas, 9 Oregon, 10 Maryland.

Round 381   1 Captain Jean-Luc Picard, 2 Isadora Duncan, 3 Jimmy (James) Carter, 4 Mr. T, 5 Istanbul, 6 Buddha, 7 Quahog, 8 Dino, 9 Robert Penn Warren, 10 The Mason-Dixon Line.

Round 382   1 Rodents, similar to groundhogs, 2 Rabies, 3 A rodent, 4 A whale, 5 A monkey, 6 A bird, 7 A bird, 8 Ten, 9 Pachyderm, 10 A bat.

Round 383   1 13, 2 15, 3 One (Maine), 4 1959, 5 37, 6 168, 7 15, 8 26, 9 12, 10 6.

Round 384   1 'Being There', 2 Ruth Rendell, 3 Travel guidebooks, 4 Ellery Queen, 5 'The Scarlet Letter', 6 Nelson Algren, 7 Tennessee Williams, 8 Karl Marx, 9 Nancy Mitford, 10 Brian Aldiss.

Round 385   1 Abbott and Costello, 2 Gillian Anderson, 3 Mickey Rooney, 4 Joseph Cotten, 5 'Nanook of the North', 6 Ruby Keeler, 7 Maurice Chevalier, 8 'Gladiator', 9 Olivia de Havilland, 10 Ted Turner.

Round 386   1 H.M.S. 'Challenger' , 2 Killer whale, 3 Amphibians, 4 Sand, 5 Lon Chaney Sr, 6 Swedish, 7 Alabama, 8 'Strawberry Fields', 9 Zürich, 10 Shia and Sunni.

Round 387   1 Eldrick, 2 Pistol shooting, 3 Chukka, 4 Scotland, 5 Antarctica, 6 Yachting, 7 Garmisch-Partenkirchen, 8 Jack Dempsey and Gene Tunney, 9 Lake Placid, 10 Ten.

Round 388   1 Easter Island, 2 Petra, 3 Colorado, 4 Spain, 5 Stonehenge, 6 Mexico, 7 South Africa, 8 The Statue of Liberty, 9 India, 10 Kublai Khan.

Round 389   1 Mademoiselle, 2 Monsieur, 3 Claustrophobia, 4 Umlaut, 5 Chinese, 6 Spanish, 7 Italian, 8 Graffito, 9 Abracadabra, 10 Babel.

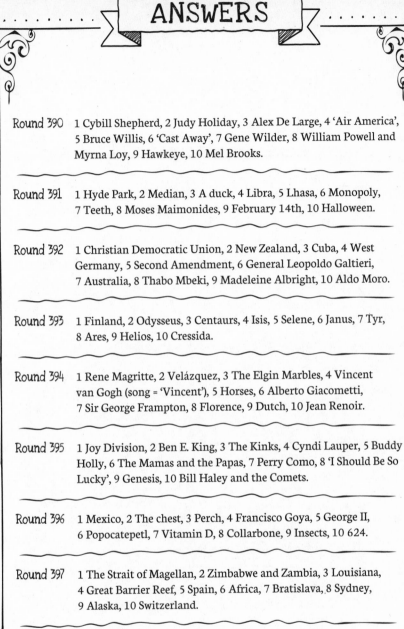

Round 390   1 Cybill Shepherd, 2 Judy Holiday, 3 Alex De Large, 4 'Air America', 5 Bruce Willis, 6 'Cast Away', 7 Gene Wilder, 8 William Powell and Myrna Loy, 9 Hawkeye, 10 Mel Brooks.

Round 391   1 Hyde Park, 2 Median, 3 A duck, 4 Libra, 5 Lhasa, 6 Monopoly, 7 Teeth, 8 Moses Maimonides, 9 February 14th, 10 Halloween.

Round 392   1 Christian Democratic Union, 2 New Zealand, 3 Cuba, 4 West Germany, 5 Second Amendment, 6 General Leopoldo Galtieri, 7 Australia, 8 Thabo Mbeki, 9 Madeleine Albright, 10 Aldo Moro.

Round 393   1 Finland, 2 Odysseus, 3 Centaurs, 4 Isis, 5 Selene, 6 Janus, 7 Tyr, 8 Ares, 9 Helios, 10 Cressida.

Round 394   1 Rene Magritte, 2 Velázquez, 3 The Elgin Marbles, 4 Vincent van Gogh (song = 'Vincent'), 5 Horses, 6 Alberto Giacometti, 7 Sir George Frampton, 8 Florence, 9 Dutch, 10 Jean Renoir.

Round 395   1 Joy Division, 2 Ben E. King, 3 The Kinks, 4 Cyndi Lauper, 5 Buddy Holly, 6 The Mamas and the Papas, 7 Perry Como, 8 'I Should Be So Lucky', 9 Genesis, 10 Bill Haley and the Comets.

Round 396   1 Mexico, 2 The chest, 3 Perch, 4 Francisco Goya, 5 George II, 6 Popocatepetl, 7 Vitamin D, 8 Collarbone, 9 Insects, 10 624.

Round 397   1 The Strait of Magellan, 2 Zimbabwe and Zambia, 3 Louisiana, 4 Great Barrier Reef, 5 Spain, 6 Africa, 7 Bratislava, 8 Sydney, 9 Alaska, 10 Switzerland.

Round 398   1 Seraphim, 2 Islam, 3 Voodoo, 4 Buddhism, 5 Potala Palace, 6 Methodist, 7 Islam, 8 Inca, 9 Mecca, 10 India.

Round 399   1 Iron, 2 100 degrees, 3 X-rays, 4 Iron, 5 Water, 6 Electric current, 7 Seven miles a second, 8 T.N.T., 9 Gypsum, 10 Fool's gold.

Round 400 1 Cuba, 2 Voice of the people, 3 Rembrandt (Harmenszoon) van Rijn, 4 H.M.S. 'Belfast', 5 Easter (Ēostre), 6 Albert Camus, 7 St Basil's Cathedral, Moscow, 8 Arkansas, 9 Dutch, 10 Virginia.

Round 401 1 1911, 2 'Prague', 3 The 'Surprise', 4 'Pastoral Symphony', 5 'Pathetique', 6 Sergei Rachmaninov, 7 Sibelius, 8 It contains a major part for an organ, 9 Mussorgsky, 10 De Falla.

Round 402 1 Earvin, 2 Seven, 3 Muhammad Ali, 4 Brazil, 5 Three, 6 Mount Everest, 7 Niki Lauda, 8 Brazilian, 9 Dallas, 10 Belmont Stakes.

Round 403 1 Thespis, 2 Hilaire Belloc, 3 Iamb, 4 Salvatore Quasimodo, 5 Sumerian, 6 Paradiso, 7 Goethe, 8 Calliope, 9 Ezra Pound, 10 William Butler.

Round 404 1 Karachi, 2 India, 3 Bay of Bengal, 4 Brahmaputra, 5 Laos, 6 Land of/place of, 7 Bosphorus, 8 Russia, 9 China, 10 Japan.

Round 405 1 Albania, 2 Denmark, 3 Ammonia, 4 Atlantic and Pacific, 5 120 years, 6 A dry river-bed, 7 Richard Nixon, 8 Jupiter, 9 Appalachian, 10 The Joker.

Round 406 1 'Bananas', 2 John Cusack, 3 Eddie Murphy, 4 Alan Alda, 5 Goldie Hawn, 6 'The Daytrippers', 7 Steve Martin, 8 Craig Ferguson, 9 Marilyn Monroe, 10 Ingrid Bergman.

Round 407 1 Sammy Cahn, 2 Marlon Brando, 3 John Candy, 4 Colonel, 5 Cannes, 6 PEN, 7 Raymond Massey, 8 Lou Costello, 9 Edith Piaf, 10 Nuns.

Round 408 1 Six, 2 Australian dollar, 3 Swedish, 4 Austria and Italy, 5 Eleven, 6 Yippies, 7 Philadelphia, 8 The North Sea, 9 Monte Cristo, 10 AIDS.

Round 409   1 Henry VIII, 2 Italy, 3 The Gestapo, 4 Eiffel Tower, 5 East Germany, 6 Cubit, 7 Julius Caesar, 8 Giraffe, 9 Amelia Earhart, 10 Edouard Daladier.

Round 410   1 The violin, 2 The cello, 3 A chord, 4 The violin, 5 Étude, 6 Sextet, 7 Quintet, 8 Bel canto, 9 The sitar, 10 Stan Kenton.

Round 411   1 Canada and U.S.A., 2 Mark Twain, 3 New Zealand, 4 Jordan, 5 Light-emitting diode, 6 Ronald Reagan, 7 Saudi Arabia, 8 India, 9 6th December, 10 New York.

Round 412   1 Quito, Ecuador, 2 Kampala, Uganda, 3 Austria, 4 Washington State, 5 Vladivostok, 6 Granada, 7 Wellington, New Zealand, 8 Finland, 9 St. Louis, 10 Norwich.

Round 413   1 Hans Christian Andersen, 2 L. Frank Baum, 3 'The Hobbit' by J.R.R. Tolkien, 4 Herman Melville, 5 Nathanael West, 6 Pedro Antonio de Alarcón, 7 Jean Rhys, 8 'The Longest Day', 9 Edna Ferber, 10 Naomi Klein.

Round 414   1 James Brown, 2 Peter, Paul and Mary, 3 Bob Dylan, 4 The Animals, 5 Dire Straits, 6 Ray Charles, 7 Herman's Hermits, 8 The Supremes, 9 The Isley Brothers, 10 Janet Jackson.

Round 415   1 Charles I, 2 Whisky, 3 Helsinki, 4 Sharon Tate, 5 Fort Knox, 6 Algeria, 7 France, 8 Pol Pot, 9 Horses, 10 Ivan Pavlov.

Round 416   1 Aubergine, 2 Edam, 3 Orange juice, 4 Sherry, 5 Plum, 6 Figs, 7 Pectin, 8 Cabbage and potatoes, 9 Japan, 10 Crème de menthe.

Round 417   1 Seve Ballesteros, 2 Andy Murray, 3 Tour de France, 4 Brooklands, 5 Dawn Fraser, 6 Seven, 7 Joe Bugner, 8 O.J. Simpson, 9 36 feet, 10 World Rally Championship.

Round 418 1 'Bedtime for Bonzo', 2 'Best in Show', 3 Kevin Kline and Sigourney Weaver, 4 Francois Truffaut, 5 Meryl Streep and Goldie Hawn, 6 'Deconstructing Harry', 7 Tim Allen and Sigourney Weaver, 8 Jack Nicholson and Kathleen Turner, 9 San Francisco, 10 Robert Shaw.

Round 419 1 John Denver, 2 22 days, 3 Coca-Cola, 4 Oman, 5 Plants, 6 Parvati, 7 The People's Republic of China, 8 Nuuk, 9 Two-up, 10 Scurvy.

Round 420 1 Austria, 2 Florida, 3 Dublin, 4 The Tiber, 5 Seattle, 6 The Vistula, 7 Cologne, 8 The Black Sea, 9 Baku, 10 Czech Republic.

Round 421 1 Emma Thompson, 2 The Doors, 3 Burt Reynolds, 4 Loony Tunes, 5 30th of April, 6 Red giant, 7 Mary Shelley, 8 Skeeter Davis, 9 T.S. Eliot, 10 Land's End.